Decision-Making under Uncertainty

Decision-Making under Uncertainty

AN APPLIED STATISTICS APPROACH

George K. Chacko

91433

PRAEGER

New York
Westport, Connecticut
London

Library of Congress Cataloging-in-Publication Data

Chacko, George Kuttickal, 1930–
    Decision-making under uncertainty :   an applied statistics approach
    George K. Chacko.
        p.   cm.
    Includes bibliographical references.
    ISBN 0–275–93569–8 (alk. paper)
    1.   Statistical decision.   I.   Title.
QA279.4.C452   1991
658.4′03—dc20   89–78157

Library of Congress Catalog Card Number: 89–78157
ISBN: 0–275–93569–8

First published in 1991

Praeger Publishers, One Madison Avenue, New York, NY 10010
An imprint of Greenwood Publishing Group, Inc.

Printed in the United States of America

The paper used in this book complies with the Permanent
Paper Standard issued by the National Information Standards
Organization (Z39.48–1984).

10   9   8   7   6   5   4   3   2   1

Copyright Acknowledgments

The author and publisher are grateful to the Literary Executor of the Late Sir Ronald A. Fisher, F.R.S., to Dr. Frank Yates, F.R.S., and the Longman Group Ltd, London for permission to reprint Tables III and IV from their book *Statistical Tables for Biological, Agricultural and Medical Research* (6th Edition 1974).

Grateful acknowledgment is also made to the following:

Table from *A Million Random Digits with 100,000 Normal Deviates* by the RAND Corporation (New York: The Free Press, 1955). Copyright 1955, and 1983 by the RAND Corporation.

Table from *Biometrika Tables for Statisticians*, Vol. 1, edited by E. S. Pearson and H. O. Hartley. Used with the kind permission of E. S. Pearson and the trustees of *Biometrika*.

Table from *Introduction to Statistical Decision Theory*, by Pratt, Raiffa, and Schlaifer (New York: McGraw-Hill, 1965). Used with permission.

Excerpts from *Thirteen Days: A Memoir of the Cuban Missile Crisis*, by Robert F. Kennedy, by permission of W. W. Norton & Company, Inc. Copyright © 1971, 1969 by W. W. Norton & Company, Inc. Copyright © 1968 by McCall Corporation.

Dedicated affectionately to
Our new daughter,
KAREN,
Who communicates with
Computers and consumers on
Statistical analysis and software

Contents

Tables and Figures   ix

Preface   xiii

**Part I. Single-Variable Decision-Making with Very Few
            Data Points**   1

  1. Irrevocable Commitment with Incomplete Data   3

  2. Decision-Making with Very Few Data Points   17

**Part II. Single-Variable Decision-Making with Very Many
             Data Points**   33

  3. Decision-Making with Very Many Data Points   35

  4. Null Hypothesis Foundations of Standard Statistical Tables   55

**Part III. Multiple-Variable Decision-Making with Very Many
              Data Points**   77

  5. Pairwise and Groupwise Togetherness   79

  6. Dynamic Replication of Reality   103

**Part IV. Single- and Multiple-Variable Decision-Making with
             Very Few Data Points—Single Decision-Makers**   123

  7. Improving the Initial Guess with New Data   125

  8. Firm Decisions on Fuzzy Foundations   143

Part V. Single- and Multiple-Variable Decision-Making with Very Few Data Points—Multiple Decision-Makers 153

  9. Attitude Toward Outcomes—Single and Multiple Decision-Makers 155

  10. Aggregate Action-Outcome Anticipations of Multiple Decision-Makers 177

Part VI. Answers to Questions 201

  11. Development and Discussion of Process and Products 203

  Appendix: Standard Statistical Tables 237

  Bibliography 247

  Index 251

Tables and Figures

TABLES

1.1	Western Jurisprudence: Hypothesis of Innocence	7
1.2	"Wild West" Jurisprudence: Hypothesis of Guilt	7
1.3	Strategic Missile Launching: Hypothesis of Soviet Innocence	9
1.4	Strategic Missile Launching: Hypothesis of Soviet Guilt	10
2.1	U.S. Presidents Elected to Office in Years Ending in Zero, 1840–1960	19
2.2	Children Learn What They Live	25
3.1	Heart Attack Contingency Table: Condition	39
3.2	Heart Attack Contingency Table: Condition and Effect	40
3.3	Convergence Illustration	42
3.4	Heart Attack Contingency Table: Joint and Marginal Probabilities	43
3.5	Heart Attack: Observed and Expected Frequencies	46
3.6	Binomial Distribution Fit to Coin Toss Data	48
3.7	Pearsonian, Normal, and Binomial Fits to Coin Toss Data	50
4.1	Heart Attack Contingency Table Data: Normal Approximation to Chi-Squared	60
4.2	Per Capita Personal Income in Constant (1972) Dollars	65
4.3	Test of Significance of Difference between 1973 Per Capita Income: New England Region and the U.S.	65

4.4	Test of Significance of Difference between Per Capita Income in 1973 and 2000: New England Region	67
4.5	Time for Blood to Coagulate of 24 Animals Randomly Allocated to Four Different Diets	69
4.6	Per Capita Personal Income in Constant (1972) Dollars and Projections	72
5.1	Age and Height Data of Upper-Division Statistics Students: Section 1	83
5.2	Age and Height Data of Upper-Division Statistics Students: Section 2	86
5.3	Multiple Regression: Illustrative Numerical Data	92
5.4	Multiple Regression of Commission Earned by State and Advertising Outlay on Bookings	94
5.5	Multiple Regression of Retail Volume and Effective Buying Income on Bookings by State	99
5.6	Observed Bookings and Expected Bookings	100
6.1	Sample Data on Performance Characteristics: Demand	109
6.2	Sample Data on Performance Characteristics: Supply	110
6.3	Table of Correspondence for Service Station Data	111
6.4	First Six Elements of Demand and Supply for Service Station Simulation	112
6.5	Monte Carlo Simulation of 20 Customers at a Service Station	113
7.1	Introduction of a New Product: Hypothesis of Adequate Break-Even Market Share	132
7.2	Introduction of a New Product: Hypothesis of Inadequate Break-Even Market Share	133
7.3	Conditional Opportunity Table: Prior	136
7.4	Calculation of Posterior Probabilities: New Product	137
7.5	Prior and Posterior Probabilities	138
7.6	Conditional Opportunity Table: Posterior	139
8.1	Combining Conflicting Evidence	146
9.1	Monetary Payoffs	157
9.2	Utility Function of Money	160
9.3	Utility of Monetary Payoffs	161
9.4	Expected Payoffs: Monetary vs. Utility	161

9.5	Nonlinear Vertical Weights of PFN	172
10.1	General Strategies of Bluffs of Initiation and Threats of Resolution	190
10.2	Bluffs–Threats Matrix: Bluffs of Initiation and Threats of Resolution	192
10.3	U.S. Transition Matrix: Illustrative	196
10.4	USSR Transition Matrix: Illustrative	197
11.1	High School Taxes: Condition (Sex)	212
11.2	Tax Increase Contingency Table: Joint and Marginal Probabilities	212
11.3	Tax Increase: Observed and Expected Frequencies	213
11.4	Mean and Standard Deviations of Per Capita Income, 1973 (in 1972 Dollars) and 2000: East South Central Region	217
11.5	Computational Table: Age, Height of Female Students, Section 1	222
11.6	Computational Table: Age, Height of Matching Male Students, Section 1	223
11.7	Calculation of Posterior Probabilities: Batch Product I	228
11.8	Calculation of Posterior Probabilities: Batch Product II	228
11.9	Calculation of Posterior Probabilities: Batch Product III	229
11.10	Calculation of Posterior Probabilities: New Product I	229
11.11	Calculation of Posterior Probabilities: New Product II	230
A.1	Chi-Squared Table	238
A.2	Partial *t* Table	239
A.3	Areas of the Standardized Normal Probability Distribution	240
A.4	F Values: 95%, 99%	242
A.5	Partial Binomial Table	244
A.6	Random Numbers	246

FIGURES

P.1	Applied Statistics Applications to Missions and Markets	xiv
4.1	Pearsonian, Binomial, and Normal Distribution Fits to Coin Toss Data	58
9.1	Utility Function of Money	162

9.2	Objectives Hierarchy: WPPSS	168
9.3	Action-Level Items of WPPSS Objectives Hierarchy	169
9.4	PFN Scores and Weights of WPPSS Objectives Hierarchy	172
10.1	Overview of Escalation of Encounter Variables	194
10.2	Illustrative Interactive Sequence	195

Preface

This work focuses on the use of incomplete data for irrevocable commitment of resources in business, social and political, physical and biological, and military environments. The 24 real-life and real-to-life applications motivate the selection of appropriate concepts and computations to solve problems and make decisions. The applications are grouped by area: market (9), social and political (7), physical and biological (5), and military (3), as shown in Figure P.1.

The schematic at the beginning of each part of the book shows "Decision-making" in tier 1, leading to the combination of Decision-Makers (single, multiple) and Decision-Variables (single, multiple) in tier 2. The three elements critical to decision-making—(1) Outcome, (2) Probability, and (3) Attitude—appear in tier 3.

Part I discusses several one-of-a-kind decision situations. The schematic presents "Single Decision-Maker (DM), Single Variable" as the primary theme. Chapter 1 opens with the bone-chilling choices faced by the North American Air Defense Command (NORAD) when the computers flashed (for real, not as an exercise): "It is 99.9 percent certain that you are under attack!" In that never-before-faced situation, the decision had to be based on the "worse" of the two consequences: annihilate the Soviet Union, or be annihilated. In preparation for handling that one-of-a-kind situation, a less awesome, but extremely grave, decision situation that is repeatedly faced, is discussed: Hanging an innocent man. Central to both is the development of a *Null Hypothesis* (NH) based on the "worse" of the consequences: Hanging an innocent man, or letting a first-degree murderer go free.

Chapter 2 discusses one-of-a-kind and few-of-a-kind situations that use *logical* and *subjective* probabilities. Given that six out of six U.S. presidents elected to office in a year ending in zero died in office, what logical relationship can be

Figure P.1
Applied Statistics Applications to Missions and Markets

Chapter 1

1. Military Mission APP 1: "It is 99.9 percent certain that you are under ICBM Attack!"
2. Social Mission APP 1: Upholding justice in first-degree murder trials

Chapter 2

3. Political Mission APP 1: "The future will have to necessarily answer . . . both as to my aspirations and my fate should I have the privilege of occupying the White House."
4. Social Mission APP 2: Choosing one's spouse for the first time
5. Military Mission APP 2: "This would mean war."

Chapter 3

6. Social Mission APP 3: An aspirin every other day keeps the heart attack away.
7. Physical APP 1: 100 tosses of 10 coins

Chapter 4

8. Heavenly Mission APP 1: "Irregularities will bear no proportion to the recurrency of that order which naturally results from original design."
9. Social Mission APP 4: Normal curve analysis of heart attack study
10. Market APP 1: Per capita personal income in 1973, 1983, 2000
11. Biological Mission APP 1: The time for blood coagulation with four different diets

Chapter 5

12. Social Mission APP 5: "Regression toward mediocrity in hereditary stature"
13. Social Mission APP 6: Simple regression of height on age of upper division students
14. Market APP 2: Effect of sales commission and advertising outlay on sales (bookings)

Chapter 6

15. Market APP 3: Must I install an additional gas pump?
16. Market APP 4: Justifying 25% increase in personnel in my section

Chapter 7

17. Heavenly Mission APP 2: "Recurrency or order. . . is derived from stable causes or regularities in nature, and not from irregularities of chance."
18. Physical Mission APP 2: Posterior probabilities of a physical constant
19. Market APP 5: Introduction of a new product a priori
20. Market APP 6: Introduction of a new product a posteriori

Figure P.1—Continued

Chapter 9

21. Market APP 7: Utility function of stock market investor
22. Market APP 8: Multi-attribute utility function for nuclear power plant site selection
23. Market APP 9: Penalty for nonfulfillment (PFN) for nuclear power plant site selection

Chapter 10

24. Military Mission APP 3: The odds that the Soviets would go all the way to war [John F. Kennedy] later said, seemed to him then "somewhere between one out of three and even."

deduced by Candidate John F. Kennedy, and how does he override the obvious inference? Not only candidates in political life, but also spouses-to-be in every-day personal life override logical probability when the latter marry despite high logical probability of failure of their marriage.

Part II presents several many-of-a-kind situations with "Multiple Decision-Makers, Single Variable" as the primary theme of the schematic. Chapter 3 focuses on decision situations with many data points, as in the case of 22,071 male physicians aged 40 to 84, half of whom took aspirin for more than five years and the other half, placebo. Could the results of the heart attack study on these men have occurred by chance? We define the *relative frequency concept of probability* and compare the observed number of heart attacks with the expected number under the NH of the Chi-Squared Table that the condition (aspirin) had zero relation to the effect (no heart attacks).

Chapter 4 develops NH underlying other standard statistical tables: Normal distribution, t-distribution, and F-distribution. Several data sets are evaluated to decide if the NH relating to them can be accepted or rejected with specified levels of confidence.

Part III discusses *noninteracting variables* determining the outcome (simple/multiple regression), and *interacting variables* (simulation). The schematic highlights "Single Decision-Maker, Multiple Variables." Chapter 5 changes the focus from single variables to multiple variables. Simple regression asks: Given a value of X, what is the corresponding value of Y? Multiple regression asks: Given the value of two or more variables, what is the corresponding value of Z?

Chapter 6 considers two or more *interacting variables* that determine the outcome of an entity, unlike simple and multiple regression, in which the variables do not interact. The individual values of the variables are chosen randomly according to the frequency of their observed occurrence, and their interaction develops the profile of the entity's performance.

Part IV develops the *Bayesian* approach to decision-making in business and scientific inference. The schematic shows "Single Decision-Maker, Single Variable" as the primary theme. Chapter 7 computes the a posteriori revision of a businessman's a priori value of market share with the results of a market survey, and the a posteriori revision of a scientist's a priori value of a physical constant with the results of a laboratory experiment.

Chapter 8 explores situations in which the outcome is a qualitative characteristic(s), whose values are not assumed precisely, to handle which fuzzy sets offer the possibility distribution.

Part V relates outcomes and attitudes in decision-making. The schematic accents "Multiple Decision-Makers, Multiple Variables." Chapter 9 presents the impact of the decision-maker's attitude toward outcome. Although net return is a readily understood single outcome, multiple outcomes such as radiation hazard, loss of salmon, additional cost of nuclear plant construction with respect to nuclear plant locations, and so on require the construction of a utility function.

Penalty for Nonfulfillment (PFN) develops an approach different from that of the utility function. Instead of finding the decision-maker's indifference between alternatives, PFN requires "greater than" relationships between alternatives. The degradation of the system mission owing to nonperformance at the subsystem or lower levels determines the allocation of resources.

Chapter 10 examines the applicability of (a) subjective probability, (b) Bayes' Theorem, (c) construction of probability argument, and (d) fuzzy sets to the single nuclear brink experienced in human history, the Cuban Missile Crisis. A *Bluffs-Threats Matrix* is developed to choose from different alternatives the course of action that best fulfills the decision-maker's objectives on the basis of aggregate action-outcome.

This work is designed for those who manage resources and their advisers who have to use incomplete data for irrevocable commitment of resources in the short or long run. The self-contained treatment of the book and its 24 real-life and real-to-life applications will make it useful to students from several disciplines in schools of business, systems, management, and behavioral sciences.

To make the work suitable for the practitioner and the student, each chapter contains *questions* which total 210. Our focus is problem-solving, not number-crunching. Therefore, we divide the reinforcement of the text material into six categories: (1) Concepts: Foundational, (2) Concepts: Formulational, (3) Computations, (4) Conclusions, (5) [Resource] Commitments, and (6) Caveats. *Answers to questions* accents the development and discussion of the process and products, so that the practitioner and the student may know why he(she) is choosing the given approach to the specific problem and what the limitations are in committing resources based on the approach.

Ideal for the practitioner, this work is suitable for a one- or two-semester graduate or advanced undergraduate course. It also offers an integrated approach to decision-making in many important fields of personal, business, and national life.

Part I Single-Variable Decision-Making with Very Few Data Points

Part I
Single-Variable Decision-Making with Very Few Data Points

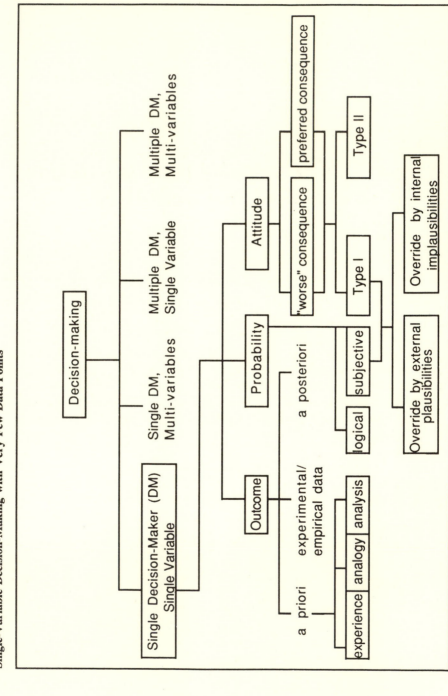

1 Irrevocable Commitment with Incomplete Data

OVERVIEW: Annihilate the Soviet Union, or be annihilated by the Soviet Union. These appeared to be the only two choices open to the Deputy Commander of North American Air Defense (NORAD) on October 5, 1960, when the computers flashed the warning: "It is 99.9 percent certain that you are under ICBM [Intercontinental Ballistic Missile] attack!" It was not a drill; it was for real, as was made clear by the Duty Officer in the War Room: "Coca Color actual!"*

Decisions under uncertainty—*certainty that one of several outcomes will occur, but which one is not known or knowable—are governed by the decision-maker's attitude toward* risk—*the occurrence of an outcome other than the one specified.*

Thus, if the approaching flying objects were not Soviet ICBMs, then the United States would have launched World War III unprovoked. If they were indeed Soviet ICBMs and the United States did not retaliate, it chose to be wiped out by the aggressor. Which is "worse" of the two evils? The answer determines the NORAD Commander's decision.

The stakes on this one-of-a-kind decision are astronomical. In preparation for handling such enormities, we study a less awesome, but quite grave, situation under uncertainty: first-degree murder trials. Western jurisprudence considers hanging an innocent man "worse" (Type I error) than letting a first-degree murderer go free, postulating the Null Hypothesis: *The accused is innocent until proved guilty. Null Hypothesis (NH) is a statement that something is zero.*

When it comes to guilt, we need to distinguish, say, jaywalking from first-degree murder. On a scale of 1 to 100, let us say that first-degree murder is 98. Innocence of first-degree murder means that the Guilt Index of the accused is −98. Because the NH must state something as zero, Guilt Index − −98 = 0; or Guilt Index + 98 = 0.

We apply the same procedure to construct the NH of the NORAD Commander on October 5, 1960. To reduce the risk of miscalculation, let us consider the launching of one missile an accident, but the launching of two or more missiles as deliberate. If the Soviet Union did not launch two missiles, or launched −2 missiles against the United States, the NH of Soviet innocence would be: number of Soviet missiles launched against the United States − −2 = 0, or number of Soviet missiles launched against the United States + 2 = 0. Falsely rejecting this "truth" of Soviet innocence would lead the United States to launch World War III unprovoked, which is considered the "worse" consequence than being wiped out by a Soviet attack, making unprovoked launching the Type I error for NORAD.

On that fateful day, the decision-maker rejected both the NH. His rejection in the face of overwhelming evidence (saving the world) was based on logical probability, *which we examine in chapter 2.*

MILITARY MISSION APPLICATION 1: "IT IS 99.9 PERCENT CERTAIN THAT YOU ARE UNDER ICBM ATTACK!"

At 3:15 P.M. on October 5, 1960, the War Room at NORAD watched the alarm level indicator rise rapidly from the lowest (1) to the highest (5). The alarm level mirrors the *defense condition* (DEFCON).

DEFCON 5

An unclassified report of the actual event states:

At 3:15 P.M. last October 5 the red telephone rang, and the Battle Staff got a bone-chilling message from the general duty officer in the War Room, Air Force Col. Robert L. Gould: "Coca Color *actual!*" This was for real!

In the War Room, the Battle Staff found the alarm level indicator flashing at "3". It went quickly to "4", then "5", indicating that a massive ICBM attack was under way. . . . Alarm level "5" means: "It is 99.9 percent certain that you are under ICBM attack!" . . . It was a tense and frightening moment. And there was not a second to spare for conjecture: if an attack had been launched against us, defense weaponry must be flushed into the air, and the retaliatory forces must be unleashed, right *now!*[1]

Uncertainty and the Decision Imperative

Uncertainty is not the ignorance of outcomes. As a matter of fact, when a coin is tossed, we are certain that one of two outcomes will occur. What is not known is heads or tails? Again, when a die is tossed, it is certain that 1, 2, 3, 4, 5, or 6 will turn up. What is not known is which of the six numbers?

The future outcome of a coin toss or die toss is not only unknown but also not knowable in advance. We define *uncertainty* as *the certainty that one of several outcomes will occur; but which one is unknown and unknowable.*

Although the future outcome—whether the future event is in the next second, day, month, year, or millennium—is unknown and unknowable, decision(s) have to be made now. It could be a decision to launch a retaliatory strike against the incoming ICBMs; it could be a decision to commit $3.9 billion to research the feasibility of a non-nuclear defense in space against incoming ICBMs; it could be a decision to invest $1 million in a business strategy; it could be a decision to buy a house for $97,500. *Decision-making, whether for missions or markets, is the irrevocable commitment of resources today for results tomorrow.*

Risk-Taking and Decision-Making

Because the results will not be known until tomorrow (or the next instant, day, month, or millennium), at the time the decision-maker makes an irrevocable resource commitment, he (she) has to decide how to cope with an unexpected outcome. We define *risk* as *the occurrence of an outcome other than the one specified.*

For instance, it will rain whether one carries rain gear or not. The weather is uncertain; therefore, one takes a risk in carrying rain gear. It is an inconvenience if one carries rain gear and it never rains. It is more than an inconvenience if one gets caught in a downpour without rain gear. One's decision to *pre*-commit the resources (carry rain gear or not carry rain gear) depends on one's set of perceived alternative outcomes and attitudes toward risk. We define *attitude* as *the preparedness to accept [adverse] outcome[s].*

Nuclear Retaliatory Decision within 15 Minutes

On October 5, 1960, the fateful decision had to be made and made fast. From the time the Ballistic Missile Early Warning System (BMEWS) reports that enemy ICBMs have been launched, there is a maximum response time of under fifteen minutes. When DEFCON 3 is reached, the NORAD commander is required to request permission to launch a retaliatory strike from the president of the United States. At DEFCON 4, the president should be airborne in his National Emergency Airborne Command Post (NEACP, pronounced "Kneecap" for phonetic ease) aircraft. At DEFCON 5, all is over but the shouting and then deafening silence.

The NORAD commander did not know if the flying objects reported by the computers were indeed Soviet ICBMs heading toward U.S. targets. Could the computers that flashed rapidly rising DEFCON numbers be in error? They found that the computations were flawless.

Nuclear Annihilation: Accept or Initiate Strategic Nuclear War

If the Soviet ICBMs were zooming in on the United States, and if the NORAD commander did not request presidential authority to launch a retaliatory strike, it would mean that the United States allowed itself to be wiped out. On the other hand, if the objects reportedly fast approaching the United States were not in fact Soviet ICBMs, and if the NORAD commander requested and was granted presidential authority to launch retaliatory strike, it would mean that the United States initiated World War III unprovoked.

The consequences are not the mirror images of each other. Both are unthinkable. But given that it was not known and not knowable if Soviet ICBMs were indeed launched against the United States, the decision would have to be based on the attitude toward the risk of either the United States being annihilated or the United States initiating unprovoked nuclear annihilation.

To work our way toward handling such enormities, let us start with extremely grave, but less global, consequences. Let us stipulate that the person found guilty of first-degree murder will in fact be electrocuted; if found innocent, he (she) will go free.

SOCIAL MISSION APPLICATION 1: UPHOLDING JUSTICE IN FIRST-DEGREE MURDER TRIALS

In a first-degree murder case, the truth may never be known. If one were omniscient, one could know for sure if the accused was innocent or guilty. Barring omniscience, errors are bound to occur: some first-degree murderers will go free, and some innocent people will be electrocuted under mandatory electrocution for first-degree murder convictions. If errors cannot be avoided, we could try to commit the grave error as few times as possible. Which of the two consequences is worse than the other in (1) modern society under Western jurisprudence and (2) in the Wild West?

If the modern society abhors electrocuting an innocent man, it will create an NH of innocence. If the Wild West abhorred letting the guilty go free, it would create an NH of guilt. If the truth is that the accused is innocent, then falsely denying that truth would be the error that will cause the worse of the two consequences, as far as modern society is concerned, as shown in Table 1.1. Notice that the worse of the two consequences determines the NH. If the truth is that the accused is guilty, then falsely denying that truth would be the error that will cause the worse of the two consequences, as far as the Wild West is concerned, as shown in Table 1.2.

Developing a Null Hypothesis

First, choose the worse of the two bad consequences of making the wrong decision. A decision is wrong when the true hypothesis is falsely rejected (Type I error—false rejection of the true as false): or when a false hypothesis is wrongly accepted as true (Type II error—false acceptance of the false as true).

Second, identify that the truth when denied, gives rise to the worse consequences. In Western jurisprudence, the worse consequence is hanging an inno-

Table 1.1
Western Jurisprudence: Hypothesis of Innocence

Truth / Perception	Null Hypothesis: The accused is innocent of first-degree murder	
	TRUE	FALSE
TRUE	OK	Type II error: False acceptance of the False as True = Let a first-degree murderer go free
FALSE	Type I error: False rejection of the True as False = Hang an innocent man	OK

Table 1.2
"Wild West" Jurisprudence: Hypothesis of Guilt

Truth / Perception	Null Hypothesis: The accused is guilty of first-degree murder	
	TRUE	FALSE
TRUE	OK	Type II error: False acceptance of the False as True = Hang an innocent man
FALSE	Type I error: False rejection of the True as False = Let a first-degree murderer go free	OK

cent man; therefore, the truth is that the accused is innocent. In the Wild West, the truth is that the accused is guilty. It considers the guilty going free as the worse consequence. The opposite of the worse consequence defines the truth: the accused is guilty.

Third, *quantify* the critical element of the truth in such a way that a null statement can be developed. When the truth is innocence, what is zero? "Guilt." Similarly, when the truth is guilt, what is zero? "Innocence."

Null Hypothesis 1: The Accused Is Innocent

To make an operational measure out of "zero guilt" or "zero innocence," express the given crime as a quantity. If first-degree murder ranks as 98 on a scale of 1 to 100, the absence of that guilt means that Guilt Index $= -98$. When a $=$ b, a $-$ b $= 0$. Guilt Index $- (-98) = 0$, or, NH: Guilt Index $+ 98 = 0$.

WOrse TRUth QUantify (WOTRUQU) specifies the three steps:

1. WOrse of the two consequences: Hang an innocent man.

2. TRUth denied in (1): Hanged man is innocent.

3. QUantify the essence of truth: Innocence means that the Guilt Index is zero. Add something to the Guilt Index to make it zero; or subtract something from the Guilt Index to make it zero. Adding 98 to the Guilt Index makes it zero. NH: Guilt Index $+ 98 = 0$.

Null Hypothesis 2: The Accused Is Guilty

If the truth is that the accused is guilty, or his Guilt Index is 98, what is the NH? Applying WOTRUQU,

1. WOrse of two consequences: Letting the murderer go free.

2. TRUth denied in (1): Freed man is a murderer.

3. QUantify the essence of truth: guilt means that innocence is zero. To make the Guilt Index zero, what should be added to (subtracted from) the Guild Index? NH: Guilt Index $- 98 = 0$.

Developing the Null Hypthesis of DEFCON 5

On October 5, 1960, the issue was very real: Strategic Nuclear War (SNW). What were the two applicable alternate NHs?

Null Hypothesis 1: Innocence $=$ Soviet Union
Launched -2 Missiles

1. WOrse of two consequences: United States initiating SNW unprovoked.

2. TRUth denied in (1): No nuclear provocation by the Soviet Union.

3. QUantify the essence of truth: No provocation means no (or zero) missiles were

launched against the United States by the Soviet Union. How do we make the SNW Initiation Index zero (as we did the Guilt Index)? Let us say that if one missile is launched by the Soviet Union, it could be an accidental launch—no provocation intended. If, however, two missiles are launched, then we count it as nuclear provocation. The truth is that no Soviet missiles were launched, or -2 Soviet missiles were launched against the United States. By selecting the number of Soviet missiles launched against the United States as our SNW Index, we construct the NH: Number of Soviet missiles launched against the United States $- (-2) = 0$, or (Soviet SNW Initiation Index $+ 2$) $= 0$ (Table 1.3).

Null Hypothesis 2: Guilt = Soviet Union Launched 2 Missiles

If, on the other hand, the Soviet Union did indeed launch 2 (or more) missiles against the United States, we have:

1. WOrse of the two consequences: Soviet annihilation of the United States.

2. TRUth denied in (1): Soviet Union initiated SNW unprovoked.

3. QUantify the essence of truth: Initiation of SNW by the Soviet Union means that the number of Soviet missiles launched against the United States $= 2$, giving us the NH: Number of Soviet missiles launched against the United States $- 2 = 0$, or (Soviet SNW Initiation Index $- 2$) $= 0$ (Table 1.4).

Table 1.3
Strategic Missile Launching: Hypothesis of Soviet Innocence

Truth / Perception	Null Hypothesis: No. of Soviet Misiles launched against the United States - (-2)=0	
	TRUE	FALSE
TRUE	OK	Type II error: False acceptance of the False as True = US not retaliating against Soviet launch
FALSE	Type I error: False rejection of the True as False = US initiates strategic nuclear war	OK

Table 1.4
Strategic Missile Launching: Hypothesis of Soviet Guilt

Truth / Perception	Null Hypothesis: No. of Soviet missiles launched against the United States -(2)=0	
	TRUE	FALSE
TRUE	O K	Type II error: False acceptance of the False as True= US initiates strategic nuclear war
FALSE	Type I error: False rejection of the True as False = US not retaliating against Soviet launch	O K

ONE-OF-A-KIND VERSUS MANY-OF-A-KIND DECISIONS

The October 5, 1960, decision was one-of-a-kind. It was a situation in which the fate of the world literally hung by a very slender thread. The deputy commander of NORAD had to opt for one of the two NHs. Both held disastrous consequences for the whole world if proved wrong.

Safeguards in Many-of-a-Kind Decision Situations

To prepare ourselves to consider the enormity of wrongly annihilating the whole world, we look at the problem of wrongly killing a single human being. One wrongly executed person is one too many. However, it is inevitable that we make such a mistake. How often should we tolerate such a mistake? One in a million times; one in ten million times; one in a billion times?

We choose the frequency of committing such a grave error as wrongly executing an innocent person. Whether the preferred frequency is one in a million or one in a billion, the fact is that it is not zero. There is a penalty associated with our passion for justice: the lower the frequency of Type I error, the higher the frequency of Type II error. In other words, in order to ensure that no more than one in a million is wrongly executed, we have to risk letting up to 999,999 first-degree murderers go free!

First-Degree Murder Trials Repeated Ad Infinitum

How highly does society value the life of the accused? So highly that it is willing to risk letting up to 999,999 first-degree murderers go free. To society, a first-degree murder trial of an accused person is a single instance of a continuing process of millions of trials. In a million first-degree murder trials held in all the courts of the land, could we be sure that no more than one defendant is falsely executed?

Institutional Safeguards

No two first-degree murder trials are alike. No two juries are alike. Yet society takes extreme care to ensure that an innocent person is hardly ever executed. It is incumbent on the prosecution to show that the accused did in fact willfully commit the first-degree murder. The defense is not required to prove that the accused is innocent; it only has to create "reasonable doubt" in a *single juror's* mind. The judge decides what evidence is admissible and what is not. He (she) rules on every objection raised by either set of lawyers. The entire procedural due process is designed to ensure that the accused is given a fair hearing before a jury of his (her) peers. If convicted, he (she) still has a series of appeals. And even if he (she) gets to death row, last-minute appeals delay the actual execution.

It is the large number of trials that makes it possible for us to specify a preferred frequency of error of, say, one in a million. Each trial is indeed unique; however, the society considers each trial to be part of an unending stream of similar trials. In the context of *infinite trials,* Type I error in first-degree murder trials can be targeted to approach the preferred frequency of, say, one in a million.

Unique Events with No Repetitive Trials

Although the first-degree murder trial is a many-of-a-kind event, the DEFCON 5 decision was one-of-a-kind. It could not have been considered a single instance of a stream of SNW decisions. Because the October 5, 1960, event was unique, few institutional safeguards could have been instituted beforehand. The NORAD commander had to keep his own counsel and choose one of the two NHs: innocence or guilt of the Soviet Union.

NORAD Deputy Commander's Rejection of the Evidence

The deputy commander did not choose either NH. He was not ruling out either; but he decided to go beyond both of them.

Factor 1: Locating the Indispensable Decision-Maker

In the face of seemingly incontrovertible evidence of massive Soviet ICBM attack on the United States, the deputy commander had to be convinced: "It is 99.9 percent certain that you are NOT under ICBM attack."

The Commander in chief of NORAD, Air Force Gen. Laurence S. Kuter, was in his C-118, 18,000 feet over South Dakota, en route home from an inspection trip. He had left NORAD's deputy commander in chief, Canada's Air Marshall C. Roy Slemon, in charge.

Slemon's first question was directed at Air Force Brig. Gen. Harris B. Hull, NORAD's chief of intelligence: "Where is Khrushchev?"

"In New York City," Hull replied.

"Do you have any intelligence indications that would tend to confirm the radar reports?"

"None, sir."[2]

Factor 2: Tracking the Indispensable Precedent Activity

There were two factors that led Slemon to suspend belief in both NHs. The first was political, pertaining to the single person with authority to "push the button." The second was technical, pertaining to the indispensable elements preceding an ICBM launch.

Regarding the first, Slemon decided that unless Khrushchev himself gave the order, the ICBMs would not be launched. Regarding the second, Slemon knew that there were some steps in launching as indispensable as knee bends are to sprinting. Absent the "knee bends," no launch.

Logical Constructs of Criticality: (1) Necessary and (2) Sufficient Conditions

Faced with incontrovertible evidence that a massive ICBM attack against the United States was in progress, Slemon essentially stepped back from that evidence and raised the questions: *Who* must order the ICBM launch; and *What* must precede the ICBM launch? We could consider the latter a *necessary* condition, and the former a *sufficient* condition.

Without Khrushchev in Moscow, there could be no massive ICBM launch command. Absent that condition, the evidence of DEFCON 5 falls to the ground. Again, without the knee bends that must precede ICBM launches, there can be no launches. Absent that condition, the evidence of DEFCON 5 is seriously questionable.

These two logical constructs of the necessary condition of knee bends and the sufficient condition of Khrushchev's presence in Moscow to authorize the ICBM launch made Marshall Slemon set aside the powerful and apparently conclusive evidence that the computers presented. In other words, *logical probability* overrode the empirical data. We will examine logical probability in the next chapter.

CONCLUDING OBSERVATIONS

A single one-of-a-kind decision situation was examined in this chapter. On October 5, 1960, the computers at NORAD flashed: "It is 99.9 percent certain that you are under ICBM attack!" It was for real; it was not an exercise.

The NORAD commander had to either assume that the incoming objects were

Soviet ICBMs and launch a retaliatory strike, or not launch a retaliatory strike and face the possibility of being wiped out. The decision depended on his Type I error—that which produced the worse of the two evil consequences of either initiating World War III or being wiped out by the aggressor.

To prepare to select the NORAD commander's Type I error, we considered a less awesome, but still quite grave, situation: first-degree murder trials, which are many-of-a-kind. Western jurisprudence considers hanging an innocent person worse than letting a first-degree murderer go free. Therefore, it asserts that the accused is innocent until proved guilty. If, on a scale of 1 to 100, first-degree murder is 98, the presumption of innocence of the accused says that the Guilt Index $= -98$. The NH is (Guilt Index $- -98$) $=$ Guilt Index $+ 98 = 0$.

Similarly, we constructed an NH for Soviet innocence and an NH for Soviet guilt. Allowing that a single missile could be accidentally launched, we set 2 as the number of Soviet missiles launched against the United States that would constitute a nuclear attack. If the Soviets are innocent, then no missiles were launched against the United States, or the number of missiles launched was -2. The NH is: Number of Soviet missiles launched $- -2 = 0$, or Soviet SNW Initiation Index $+ 2 = 0$. The NORAD commander rejected both the NHs. He did so in the face of overwhelming evidence. What he did could be understood as an exercise of logical probability, which will be discussed in chapter 2.

QUESTIONS: CONCEPTS AND COMPUTATIONS
FOR COMMITMENT

Our focus is decision-making, not number-crunching. Therefore, we divide the reinforcement of the text material into six categories: (1) Concepts: Foundational, (2) Concepts: Formulational, (3) Computations, (4) Conclusions, (5) [Resource] Commitments, and (6) Caveats. See chapter 11 for answers to questions for this chapter.

Concepts: Foundational

1. "Give me all the facts before I make my decision," says the decision-maker. How do you answer him (her)?

2. Actions are irrevocable commitment of resources today for results tomorrow. What type of data are most germane to taking actions?

The Problem: Ammunition Acceptance

3. During World War II, when the United States became the "arsenal of democracy," the U.S. Army was quite upset with the statement of statisticians that 100% acceptability could never be guaranteed. How would you explain to a nonstatistician why this is so? What practical steps would you recommend that the Army decision-makers take?

Concepts: Formulational

The Problem: Nuclear Freeze

4. The U.S. Senate passed by a sizable majority a resolution on "nuclear freeze." If you were a senator who voted for the resolution, what was your Null Hypothesis (NH)?

5. If you voted against the resolution, what was your NH?

6. If you were sent by the president to persuade a key senator to change his vote from yea to nay, what would be your strategy?

The Problem: Reinstatement of the Death Penalty

7. Many states in the Union have repealed the death penalty. About a third of them have reinstated the death penalty. Formulate your NH if you favor the *reinstatement* of the death penalty. (Note that this is *not* the question discussed in chapter 1.)

8. If you are against the reinstatement of the death penalty, what is your NH?

Computations

The Problem: Reinstatement of the Death Penalty

9. What variable would you select to decide on *reinstating* capital punishment? What frequency of results *opposed to what you desire* would you allow as the criterion for reinstating the death penalty?

Conclusions

The Problem: DEFCON 5

10. You are Marshall Slemon, being court-martialed for not following the established procedure in which the NORAD commander is mandated to request presidential authority to launch a retaliatory nuclear strike at DEFCON 3. Defend yourself.

The Problem: Anti-Recidivism

11. Psychologists may emphasize nature (hereditary factors) or nurture (environmental factors) in explaining major criminal behavior. Recidivism (repeat criminal behavior) is an election issue in the race for district attorney in your state. Why would you vote for a candidate who stands for a strong anti-recidivism platform? (Note that *repeat* criminality is the issue, not criminality itself.)

[Resource] Commitments

The Problem: Hanging an Innocent Person

12. Setting the preferred frequency of wrongly hanging an innocent person at 1 in a million costs, say, 25 times as much as a frequency of 1 in 100,000. Argue for spending 25 times as much resources for the first frequency.

13. Argue for the second frequency.

Caveats

The Problem: DEFCON 5

14. Why did Marshall Slemon set aside the incontrovertible evidence?

The Problem: Reinstatement of the Death Penalty

15. Why is the state governor given the power of stay of execution in first-degree murders? Why is he (she) given the power to commute the death sentence?

NOTES

1. J. G. Hubbell, "You are Under Attack!" *Reader's Digest*, April 1961, p. 39.
2. Ibid.

2   Decision-Making with Very Few Data Points

OVERVIEW: The one-of-a-kind decision situations such as the flashing by the NORAD computers in real-life conditions, "It is 99.9 percent certain that you are under ICBM attack!" calls for the use of logical probability. NORAD deputy commander Slemon presumably used logical probability concepts to set aside the compelling conclusions of a massive Soviet ICBM launch.

Logical probability is the degree of belief in propositions, which associates one set of premises with one set of conclusions. In logical probability, this relationship is unique. But given the same evidence, subjective probability can deny the uniqueness of the (premise-conclusion) relationship and assign a different value to the probability, p.

Faced with $p = 1$ for death in office of American presidents elected in a year ending in zero from 1840 through 1960, in 1980 candidates Reagan and Carter had to override the logical probability value of 1 with a very low value, such as $p = .1$.

Not only in national political life, but also in everyday personal life, would-be spouses override logical probability. When the logical probability assigns a high $p = .8$ for failure of a marriage with a spouse who grew up in an unaccepting environment, this may well be set aside by a determined spouse-to-be who says that in his (her) particular instance, "We will make it work," making the probability of failure very small, say, $p = .1$.

A third example of overriding logical probability by subjective probability is found in the Cuban Missile Crisis. With overwhelming evidence supporting the conclusion that the Soviets were getting ready to do battle, $p = 1$, Robert Kennedy urged President Kennedy to assign a low p, and ignore Khrushchev's strident second letter and answer the first letter, thus setting the stage for solving the crisis.

Although extremely important, logical probability and the non-repeatable sub-jective probability do not enjoy the guarantee offered by the relative frequency concept of probability that a random sample can specify the population value(s) within limits with specified levels of confidence. This we explore in the next chapter.

POLITICAL MISSION APPLICATION 1: "THE FUTURE WILL HAVE TO NECESSARILY ANSWER . . . BOTH AS TO MY ASPIRATIONS AND MY FATE, SHOULD I HAVE THE PRIVILEGE OF OCCUPYING THE WHITE HOUSE"

Former congressman Seymour Halpern, Democrat, who represented New York from 1959 to 1973, is a collector of documents and manuscripts. One of the documents he has collected is a "Letter from John F. Kennedy as U.S. senator."

The Zero Factor

Halpern was contacted by Al Aronowitz, a free-lance writer, in the course of his research on the phenomenon of every U.S. president elected in a year ending in zero from 1840 through 1960 dying in office. Because John F. Kennedy was elected president in November 1960, his reply *a year-and-a-half earlier,* on May 27, 1959, to Henry Squires of Lakewood, California, is of considerable interest:

The historical curiosity which you related in your letter of May 4 is, indeed thought-provoking: "Since 1840, every man who has entered the White House in a year ending with a zero has not lived to leave the White House alive." Since you are writing an article on this topic and have asked for my view, I'm afraid I can be of little help. I must, candidly, admit that I've really never reflected on this bit of Americana.

As to "What effect, if any, this will have on your Presidential aspirations," I feel that the future will have to necessarily answer this for itself—both as to my aspirations and my fate, should I have the privilege of occupying the White House.

On face value, I daresay, should anyone take this phenomenon to heart . . . anyone, that is, who aspires to change his address to 1600 Pennsylvania Avenue . . . that most probably the landlord would be left from 1960–64 with a "For Rent" sign hanging on the gatehouse door.

With every good wish I am sincerely,

John F. Kennedy[1]

A Population of Seven

In chapter 1 we discussed one-of-a-kind and many-of-a-kind situations, DEF-CON 5 on October 5, 1960, being an example of the former and the trial of those accused of first-degree murder an example of the latter. In the latter case, statements can be made about all first-degree murder trials—past, present, and future—on the basis of data from a small number of such trials, suitably chosen.

Population

We choose the characteristic(s) that defines the population. We choose it according to our purpose(s). Thus, if our interest is in the first-degree murder trials, then all first-degree murder trials—past, present, and future—constitute the *population*. If our interest is in the first occurrence of NORAD computers flashing: "It is 99.9 percent certain that you are under ICBM attack!" then the *population* comprises only one element. If our interest is in U.S. presidents elected in a year ending in zero from 1840 through 1960, our *population* has seven elements. If our interest is in the presidents who died in office from 1840 through 1960, that *population*, too, has seven elements. Both populations are shown in Table 2.1.

Probability as Unique Logical Relationship

Given that seven out of seven U.S. presidents elected to office in a year ending in zero died in office, what *logical relationship(s)* can be deduced? In chapter 1, we found that Marshall Slemon rejected the overwhelming evidence of a massive

Table 2.1
U.S. Presidents Elected to Office in Years Ending in Zero, 1840–1960

Year in which Elected President	The U.S. President	Year in which Died in The White House
1840	William H. Harrison	1841
1860	Abraham Lincoln	1865
1880	James A. Garfield	1881
1900	William McKinley	1901
1920	Warren G. Harding	1923
1940	Franklin D. Roosevelt	1945
1960	John F. Kennedy	1963

Soviet ICBM launch against the United States because he used *logical probability*.

LOGICAL PROBABILITY

Jacques Bernoulli pointed out in *Ars Conjectandi*[2] in 1713 that probability is an aspect of incomplete knowledge.

Probability as Degree of Confidence

Because we cannot usually know with certainty whether or not an event will occur, we can only have a "degree of confidence" in the truth of the proposition that asserts its occurrence:

The *"degree of confidence"* is identified with the probability of an event. It depends on the knowledge that the individual has at his disposal. Therefore, it can *vary from individual to individual*. The art of guessing (*Ars Conjectandi*) consists in estimating as precisely as possible the best values of probabilities [emphasis added].[3]

Causality and Probability

Bernoulli's concept of probability was taken up in 1921 by John Maynard Keynes (1883–1946), who was attracted to David Hume (1711–76)'s idea of causality. Causality postulates relationships between *events* ("The stone broke the glass") and *propositions* ("Red sky at night, sailor's delight [next morning]"). Probability verifies the causal postulates by experiment/experience.

Hume said that we attribute causality when all we observe is association. It is impossible to prove causality between event A and event B because they occur in conjunction:

For, when we regard any events as causally connected, all that we do and can observe is that they frequently and uniformly go together. Now in this sort of togetherness it is a fact that the impression or idea of the one event brings with it the idea of the other. A habitual association is set up in the mind; and as in other forms of habit, so in this one, the working of the association is felt as a compulsion. This *feeling*, Hume concludes, is the only discoverable impressional source of the idea of causality: in other words, when we assert, however carefully (as in natural science), a causal connection between any two objects the sole experience or evidenced necessitation is not in them but in the habituated mind.[4]

Probability: Unique Logical Relationship between Propositions

Under the influence of Bertrand Russell, Keynes adopted a *proposition* (instead of an event) "as that which carries the attribute of probability." In *A Treatise on Probability*, Keynes says that probability is an undefinable *logical relationship* between (1) a proposition and a body of knowledge, (2) between one statement and another statement(s) representing evidence, a relation associated with the rational *degree of belief* in the propositions:

Let our premises consist of any set of propositions *h* and our conclusion consists of any set of propositions *a*, then if a knowledge of *h* justifies a rational degree of belief in *a* of degree A, we may say that there is a probability-relation of degree A between *a* and *h*.[5]

Kyburg and Smokler paraphrase Keynes as follows: "Given a statement *S* and a body of evidence *E*, there is one and only one real number *p* such that it may correctly be said that the probability of *S* relative to *E* is *p*.[6]

LOGICAL PROBABILITY APPLIED TO DEFCON 5

Marshall Slemon's logical constructs, by which he rejected overwhelming evidence, were logical probability concepts.

Indispensable Decision-Maker Presence in Moscow

Logical Premise (*h*1): The general secretary of the Communist Party of the Soviet Union must be present in Moscow.

Logical Conclusion (*a*1): To order a massive ICBM launch against the United States.

What are the empirical values of *h* and *a?* We will distinguish the *empirical* premise and conclusion with a *prime*, *h*1′ and *a*1′.

Empirical Premise (*h*1′): Khrushchev is not in the Soviet Union.

Empirical Conclusion (*a*1′): There is no massive Soviet ICBM launch.

What is the probability relation of degree A? It is 1. Slemon is certain that there is no massive Soviet ICBM launch. Given the logical premise, the logical conclusion is inevitable. So also, given the denial of the logical premise, the logical conclusion is denied.

Indispensable Precedent Activity

Logical Premise (*h*2): Certain "knee bends."

Logical Conclusion (*a*2): Must occur before massive ICBM launches.

Empirical Premise (*h*2′): No "knee bends" have occurred.

Empirical Conclusion (*a*2′): There is no massive ICBM launch.

Again, Slemon is certain, or $p = 1$. However, *p* does not have to be 1. As Kyburg and Smokler point out, "there is one and only one real number *p*." The relationship between premise and conclusion is of the form "If-Then." By the same token, "If not-Then not," as we saw in DEFCON 5. Although not necessarily 1, we would expect the "one and only real number *p*" to be higher than .5. Given the same situation, can someone else conclude differently from Slemon?

SUBJECTIVE PROBABILITY

The answer is yes.

Probability: Nonunique Relationship between Propositions

Conclusions are uniquely drawn from evidence in logical probability; but not so in subjective probability. Kyburg says:

On the subjectivistic view, probability represents a relation between a statement and a body of evidence, but it is not a purely logical relation. It is a *quasilogical relation* and the numerical values attached to it represent a degree of belief. On the subjectivistic view, this value is *not uniquely determined:* a given statement may have any probability between 0 and 1, on given evidence, *according to the inclination of the person whose degree of belief that probability represents* [emphasis added].[7]

Probability: Degree of Belief

It was De Morgan who first defined probability in terms of "degrees of belief":

By degree of probability, we really mean, or ought to mean, *degree of belief.* Probability, then, refers to and implies belief, more or less, and belief is but another name for imperfect knowledge, or it may be, expresses the mind in a state of imperfect knowledge [emphasis added].[8]

LOGICAL AND SUBJECTIVE PROBABILITIES APPLIED TO THE "ZERO FACTOR"

We will first apply logical probability to the "Zero Factor."

Election to Presidency in Year Ending in Zero

Logical Premise (*h*3): The person elected to the U.S. presidency in a year ending in zero from 1840 through 1960.

Logical Conclusion (*a*3): Does not leave the White House alive.

Empirical Premise (*h*3′): Candidate Reagan/Carter elected to the U.S. presidency in 1980.

Empirical Conclusion (*a*3′): Will not leave the White House alive.

Nonunique Relationship between Propositions: Kennedy

Twenty years earlier, Candidate Kennedy had found the *logical* probability compelling: "For Rent" sign . . . from 1960 to 1964." However, his *subjective* probability assigned a negligible value of *p*. "I must candidly admit that I've really never reflected on this bit of Americana." In other words, whatever may be the value of *logical* probability *p*, say, 1, for certain death in office of all the six men elected president in a year ending in zero during the preceding 120 years, Candidate Kennedy, running for the presidency, considered the *subjective* probability *p* to be, say, .1. Being subjective, his reasoning, such as "luck of the Irish," would not have to be repeatable: nobody else needs to be able to arrive at the same subjective probability.

Nonunique Relationship between Propositions: Reagan

Two decades later, two candidates offer themselves for the presidency. They have had to come to terms with the logical probability of 1 for certain death in office. And they both have had to convince themselves that the subjective probability was negligible. Reagan could have claimed the "luck of the Irish" or "the Teflon president(cy)" to make the subjective probability negligible enough to run for the presidency. The nation and the world breathed a collective sigh of relief when President Reagan left the hospital two weeks after a bullet lodged only about an inch from his heart on March 30, 1981, which occurred in the first presidency to which the "zero factor" would apply. And when he left the office on January 20, 1989, Reagan would become the first president to defy the logical probability of the "zero factor."

SOCIAL MISSION APPLICATION 2: CHOOSING ONE'S SPOUSE FOR THE FIRST TIME

For Candidate Kennedy and Candidate Nixon in 1960, and for Candidate Reagan and Candidate Carter in 1980, running for the presidency in a year ending in zero was a unique event. So, also, the selection of a spouse for the first time is a unique event. How do we go about choosing a spouse for the first time? We will see how, in this dramatically important single decision in life, logical probability underlies our choice. However, the most compelling conclusions that logical probability offers can be, and often are, set aside by subjective probability, as was done by Kennedy and Reagan.

A Measurable Criterion of Success of Marriage

To explore what concept of probability underlies our choice of a spouse for the first time, we must first define a *measurable criterion* of marriage. How is the outcome of marriage going to be measured? "Happiness" is an obvious answer;

however, it is not measurable. We could find surrogates of happiness and measure the surrogates. Let us say that duration of the marriage is a surrogate, and a specific duration of the marriage, such as 10 or more years, is a measure of the "success" of the marriage. To arrive at the conclusion "Survival of marriage for 10 or more years," what are the plausible premises?

Factor 1: Nature

Psychologists divide the factors that influence behavior into two groups: nature and nurture. Genetic elements are nature factors, whereas social elements, such as the environment of one's upbringing, are nurture factors. How much do nature and nurture contribute to human behavior? How do these interacting factors contribute to behavior?

Concerning the extent of genetic determination in human intelligence, most investigations have yielded heritability estimates between 70–80 percent. . . . Major, independent studies concur in showing that specific aspects of intelligent behavior (verbal ability, spatial intelligence, and word fluency) have strong genetic dependence.[9]

Psychologists tell us that they do not know what intelligence is. However, they are able to tell us that "the more intelligent a person, the higher his verbal ability; the more intelligent a person, the higher his quantitative ability; the more intelligent a person, the higher his analytical ability, etc." This does not necessarily mean that all three manifestations will be higher in the more intelligent. One or two areas of ability could be high with the other area(s) registering average or even below average values.

In the spouse selection, we implicitly postulate a logical probability relationship between two propositions:

Logical Premise ($h4$): The more intelligent the spouse.

Logical Conclusion ($a4$): The more successful the marriage.

Notice that we have no precise definition of intelligence; we do not know what "more intelligent" really means. Scores on the Scholastic Aptitude Test (SAT) and Scholastic Achievement Test give little clues on how successful the spouses would be in their marriage because SAT scores only try to predict how successful the student would be in college as measured by the first-year grades. Nevertheless, we associate intelligence with success in marriage and elsewhere. To know how well we accept this logical probability, consider how vehemently we reject the opposite:

Logical Premise ($h5$): The less intelligent the spouse.

Logical Conclusions ($a5$): The more successful the marriage.

On the other hand, we associate the intelligence of parents of the spouses with the success of the marriage of their children:

Logical Premise (*h*6): The more intelligent the parents of the spouse.

Logical Conclusions (*a*6): The more successful the marriage.

Factor 2: Nurture

If we do not know what intelligence is, we know even less about love. Although definitions of love vary, we implicitly accept that the more loving the environment of upbringing, the better adjusted the child (Table 2.2); and the better adjusted the child, the better the chances of the marriage being a success.

Logical Premise (*h*7): The more accepting the environment in which the spouse was brought up.

Logical Conclusion (*a*7): The more successful the marriage.

Factor 1: Subjective Probability Override

It will be recalled that subjective probability differs from the logical in precisely denying the unique relation between *h* and *a*. We could assign a value to the probability higher than .5; say, .8 for Factor 1 and .9 for Factor 2.

Each child born to the same father and mother is not equally intelligent. We do not know how important the intelligence of the spouses' parents is to the success of the marriage. Irrespective of the *logical* relationship between parents' intel-

Table 2.2
Children Learn What They Live

If a child lives with criticism, he learns to condemn.
If a child lives with hostility, he learns to fight.
If a child lives with fear, he learns to be apprehensive.
If a child lives with pity, he learns to be sorry for himself.
If a child lives with jealousy, he learns to feel guilty.

If a child lives with tolerance, he learns to be patient.
If a child lives with encouragement, he learns to be confident.
If a child lives with praise, he learns to be appreciative.
If a child lives with recognition, he learns it is good to have a goal.

If a child lives with approval, he learns to like himself.
If a child lives with honesty, he learns what truth is.
If a child lives with fairness, he learns justice.
If a child lives with acceptance, he learns to love.

ligence and success of children's marriage, the parties to the marriage can assign a higher or lower *subjective* value to the *p*. Thus:

Logical Premise (*h*8): The more intelligent the parents of the spouses.

Logical Conclusion (*a*8): The more successful the marriage.

Logical probability of this (premise-conclusion) relation is, say, $p = .8$.

Empirical Premise: (*h*8′): In this marriage, spouses' parents are quite intelligent.

Empirical Conclusion (*a*8′): But the gut feeling is that the children's marriage is not likely to be successful.

Subjective probability of this empirical (premise-conclusion) is, say, $p = .4$.

Notice that no reason has been given. Gut feeling is unverifiable and unchallengeable. It is similar to the declaration "My left knee hurts; therefore it is going to rain tomorrow."

Factor 2: Subjective Probability Override

The subjective probability comes into play even more in Factor 2. The converse of the (premise 7, conclusion 7) combination is:

Logical Premise (*h*9): The less accepting the environment in which the spouse was brought up.

Logical Conclusion: (*a*9): The less successful the marriage.

Logical probability of this (premise-conclusion) is, say, $p = .9$.

The compelling conclusion of the logical probability can be set aside by subjective probability by Spouse X and Spouse Y, who have a gut feeling that despite adverse odds, they will make their marriage a success.

Empirical Premise (*h*9′): Spouse was brought up in an unaccepting environment.

Empirical Conclusion (*a*9′): But this particular pair will make their marriage a success.

Subjective probability of failure of marriage is, say, $p = .1$.

As we saw earlier with respect to the zero factor in the U.S. presidential elections, the parties to the marriage can, and indeed do, defy the logical probability by using a subjective probability override.

MILITARY MISSION APPLICATION 2: "THIS WOULD MEAN WAR"

We have seen how logical probability led Marshall Slemon to reject the overwhelming evidence of an ICBM attack on October 5, 1960. We will now see how three years later logical probability played a crucial role in the awesome decision-making at the only nuclear brinkmanship in recorded history, the Cuban Missile Crisis.

Two Contradictory Letters in 12 Hours

At 6 P.M. Friday, October 26, 1962, a letter came to President Kennedy from Premier Khrushchev. The rambling style was unmistakably Khrushchevean. Robert Kennedy says in his memoirs, *Thirteen Days,* "This is my proposal, he said. No more weapons to Cuba and those within Cuba withdrawn or destroyed, and you reciprocate by withdrawing your blockade and also agree not to invade Cuba."[10]

After examining and re-examining the message late into the morning hours, the Executive Committee of the National Security Council (ExComm) asked the State Department to analyze and make recommendations. But the next morning, Robert Kennedy received a memo from Federal Bureau of Investigation director J. Edgar Hoover suggesting that the Soviets were preparing for war:

He had received information the night before that certain Soviet personnel in New York were apparently preparing to destroy all sensitive documents on the basis that the U.S. would probably be taking military action against Cuba or Soviet ships and *this would mean war.* I asked myself as I drove to the White House: If the Soviets were anxious to find an answer to the crisis, why this conduct on the part of the Soviet personnel? Did the Khrushchev letter really indicate a solution could be found? [emphasis added].[11]

Now comes a second letter from Khrushchev:

It was obviously no longer Mr. Khrushchev personally who was writing, but the Foreign Office of the Kremlin. *The letter was quite different from the letter received twelve hours before.* "We will remove our missiles from Cuba, you will remove yours from Turkey. . . . The Soviet Union will pledge not to invade or interfere with the internal affairs of Turkey; the U.S. to make the same pledge regarding Cuba" [emphasis added].[12]

Logical Probability Constructs

Both letters were from Khrushchev to Kennedy. The first was not published; but Moscow published the second letter, showing to the world Soviet determination to have its way. In the meantime, Secretary McNamara reported that the Russians and Cubans were working round the clock at the missile installations. And on Saturday morning came word that Major Rudolf Anderson's U-2 plane was hit by a surface-to-air missile (SAM) in Cuba, that his plane had crashed, and that he was killed.

Logical Premise ($h10$): The second letter was composed by hawks who overruled Khrushchev.

Logical Conclusion ($a10$): Khrushchev is not in control of the crisis.

Logical probability is low, since this was the first indication, say, $p = .7$.

Recall that Keynes' definition of logical probability refers not to a single proposition, but to "any set of propositions h" as premises and "any set of propositions *a*" as conclusions. In other words, we can indeed provide premises 1,2, . . . , n; and conclusions 1,2, . . . , m. Let us incorporate the three premises staring at the ExComm on Saturday morning, October 27:

Logical Premise (*h*11): The second letter was composed by hawks who overruled Khrushchev.

Logical Conclusions (*a*11): Khrushchev is not in control of the crisis.

Logical probability, say, $p = .7$.

Logical Premise (*h*12): The same night that Khrushchev's first letter reached ExComm, Soviet consular personnel in New York were preparing to destroy sensitive documents anticipating US-USSR war over Cuba.

Logical Conclusion (*a*12): The real intent of the Soviets is war. The Khrushchev letter is intended to mislead the United States. Therefore, Khrushchev is not in control.

Logical probability, say, $p = .8$.

Logical Premise (*h*13): Soviet SAM killed the U.S. pilot of a U-2 over Cuba.

Logical Conclusion (*a*13): USSR is really preparing for war.

Logical probability, say, $p = .9$.

Whether taken one at a time or together, the three premises demand a significant degree of belief (probability) that Khrushchev is not in control of the crisis.

Joint Chiefs of Staff: Air Strike Monday, followed by Invasion

Even before the grave news of the shooting down of the U-2 by a SAM in Cuba, killing the pilot, Major Anderson, the Joint Chiefs of Staff (JCS), who joined the ExComm meeting on Saturday, made their recommendations:

The Joint Chiefs of Staff joined the meeting and recommended their solution. It had the attraction of being a very simple next step—an air strike on Monday, followed shortly afterward by an invasion. They pointed out to the President that they had always felt the blockade to be far too weak a course and that military steps were the only ones the Soviet Union would understand. They were not at all surprised that nothing had been achieved by limited force, for this is exactly what they had predicted.[13]

The JCS recommendations would indicate a logical probability of $p = 1$ that hawks were in control in Moscow, overriding Khrushchev.

Robert Kennedy: Subjective Probability

In the face of overwhelming logical probability of, say, 1 that Khrushchev is overruled by the hawks in the Kremlin, Robert Kennedy sets aside the compelling conclusion from the logical premises, and opts for a low p for the conclusion that Khrushchev is not in control. The State Department had already prepared a response to the second letter, rejecting the demand that the United States remove the missiles from Turkey. Recalls Kennedy:

I suggested, and was supported by Ted Sorensen and others, that we *ignore the latest Khrushchev letter* and respond to his *earlier letter's* proposal, as refined in the *offer made to John Scali* that the Soviet missiles and offensive weapons would be removed from Cuba under UN inspection and verification, if, on its side, the United States would agree with the rest of the Western Hemisphere not to invade Cuba [emphasis added].[14]

What were the gut feelings of Robert Kennedy that led him to set aside the overwhelming evidence that the Soviets were ready to do battle? Perhaps he felt that Khrushchev was strong enough to withstand any coup d'état. Perhaps he thought that the USSR's taking the unorthodox step of communicating through ABC newsman John Scali that they would remove the missiles under U.N. supervision if the United States would not invade Cuba was a small, but significant, ray of hope. In terms of probability, Robert Kennedy overruled the logical $p = 1$ with, say, a subjective $p = .1$.

CONCLUDING OBSERVATIONS

In this chapter, we discussed one-of-a-kind decisions, as opposed to many-of-a-kind decisions in the stream of first-degree murder trials—past, present, and future. The relative frequency concept applies to the latter, whereas logical and subjective probability concepts apply to the former.

Faced with a 100% chance of death in office for U.S. presidents elected to office in a year ending in zero from 1840 through 1960, the logical probability of death in office for the person elected to the presidency in 1980 is 1. Subjective probability, however, can deny the logical probability. Candidates Reagan and Carter had to set aside the logical probability of 1 by the subjective probability of, say, .1 to run for the presidency.

This setting aside of logical probability is frequently observed in choosing one's spouse for the first time. The child growing up in an unaccepting environment is unlikely to love. Nevertheless, the marriage with a spouse so brought up may be assigned a high subjective probability of success by the spouse who says, "Our uniqueness overrides the logical probability."

A third instance in which subjective probability set aside logical probability is the Cuban Missile Crisis, which we discussed using the firsthand account of a principal player, Robert Kennedy. His subjective probability led President Kennedy to ignore Khrushchev's second letter, much more strident than the first, and accept Khrushchev's "offer" to withdraw Soviet missiles from Cuba under U.N. supervision, and assure that the United States would not invade Cuba. When Khrushchev accepted that letter, the Cuban Missile Crisis was virtually over. Had it not been for that letter, war was a very real possibility. And that letter was drafted by Robert Kennedy (and presidential speech writer Ted Sorensen), whose subjective probability set aside the logical probability of 1.

Logical and subjective probability govern the more important decisions in personal, national, and international life. The premise and conclusions themselves are subjectively selected; therefore, the wrong (premise-conclusion) pairs could be selected. However, their associations would demand that one and only one conclusion could be drawn. That logical imperative is set aside for cause or no cause in subjective probability.

Subjective probability is nonrepeatable and nonverifiable; but relative frequency is the opposite. Unlike subjective and logical probability, which deal with propositions, relative frequency deals with events and the occurrence of specified outcomes in infinite trials, which we turn to in chapter 3.

QUESTIONS: CONCEPTS AND COMPUTATIONS
FOR COMMITMENT

Our focus is decision-making, not number-crunching. Therefore, we divide the reinforcement of the text material into six categories: (1) Concepts: Foundational, (2) Concepts: Formulational, (3) Computations, (4) Conclusions, (5) [Resource] Commitments, and (6) Caveats. See chapter 11 for answers to questions for this chapter.

Concepts: Foundational

1. Differentiate between logical and subjective probability.
2. What defines a population? Who defines it?

The Problem: DEFCON 5

3. Given the same situation at NORAD as faced by Marshall Slemon on October 5, 1960, why would someone else conclude differently?
4. Give, with reasoning, another conclusion and justify the accompanying resource commitment.

Concepts: Formulational

The Problem: Cuban Missile Crisis

5. Defend probabilistically the recommendation of the JCS given in the text.

The Problem: Spouse Selection

6. Defend probabilistically your second marriage to a two-time divorcee.
7. Develop three primary criteria in choosing a job, and identify the specific types of probability that you use, and their acceptable critical values.

Computations

The Problem: Cuban Missile Crisis

8. Kennedy biographer Sorensen says: "The odds that the Soviets would go all the way to war, [President Kennedy] later said, seemed to him *then* [Cuban Missile Crisis, 1963] somewhere between *one out of three and even.*" Another Kennedy biographer, Arthur Schlesinger, reports that Kennedy told him that the probability of war over the Berlin Wall (1981) was one-third. Give your reasoning for Kennedy's probabilities.

The Problem: Spouse Selection

9. The marriages of three out of four of your close friends from grade school through college ended in divorce in less than five years. You are planning to marry for the first time. Develop your specific types of probabilities and their critical values.

Conclusions

The Problem: Cuban Missile Crisis

10. Give three reasons why (a) the shooting down of the U-2 over Cuba on Saturday morning and (b) the second letter from Khrushchev demanding U.S. withdrawal of missiles from Turkey, *together,* should not be taken as Soviet readiness to fight.

The Problem: Spouse Selection

11. Give three reasons why you should set aside the divorces of three out of four of your longtime friends in deciding to marry your choice.

[Resource] Commitments

The Problem: Crisis Communication

12. The hot line between Moscow and Washington was set up to reduce the possibility of war by miscalculation. How much is the presidential translator of the hot line worth? Why?

The Problem: Premarital Counseling

13. One out of two marriages ends in divorce. How much would you spend for a premarriage counselor? Why?

Caveats

The Problem: Applicable Marriage Parallel

14. In any important problem, the most critical aspects are one-of-a-kind. The skill in constructing a valid parallel is crucial. Develop, with reasoning, the parallel(s) you use for your first marriage.

The Problem: Cuban Missile Crisis

15. Develop Robert Kennedy's parallel(s) and/or logical constructs to override the obvious pointers to imminent war by the Soviets.

NOTES

1. Seymour Halpern, "Letter from John F. Kennedy as U.S. Senator," May 27, 1959, New York, N.Y.

2. Jacques Bernoulli, *Ars Conjectandi* (Basel, 1713).

3. D. van Dantzig, "Statistical Priesthood (Savage on Probabilities)", *Statist. Neerl.* 2 (1957): 1–16.

4. Thomas E. Jessop, "Hume, David," *Encyclopedia Britannica* 11 (1960), p. 882B.

5. John M. Keynes, *A Treatise on Probability* (London: Macmillan, 1921), p. 4.

6. Henry E. Kyburg, Jr., and Howard E. Smokler, *Studies in Subjective Probability* (New York: Wiley, 1964), p. 5.

7. Ibid., pp. 5–6.

8. Augustus De Morgan, *Formal Logic,* (London: Taylor & Walton, 1847), pp. 171–73.

9. William R. Thompson, "Human Behavior, Innate Factors," *Encyclopedia Britannica* 8 (1975), p. 1148.

10. Robert F. Kennedy, *Thirteen Days: A Memoir of the Cuban Missile Crisis* (New York: New American Library, 1969), p. 89.

11. Ibid., p. 93.

12. Ibid., pp. 94–95.

13. Ibid., pp. 96–97.

14. Ibid., pp. 101–2.

*Part II Single-Variable Decision-Making
with Very Many Data Points*

Part II
Single-Variable Decision-Making with Very Many Data Points

3 Decision-Making with Very Many Data Points

OVERVIEW: Although extremely important to decision-making, logical and sub-jective probability do not enjoy the guarantee offered by the relative frequency concept of probability: The ratio of the number of specified outcomes *(tails) to* the number of possible outcomes *(heads and tails) tends closer and closer to a specified value as the number of trials tends to infinity. If the finite observations are a random sample of coin tosses, we can say with a level (95.0%, . . . 99.9%) of confidence that no matter how many similar small samples are taken, their results will lie in a range based on the single sample.*

If half of 22,071 male physicians aged 40 to 84 (screened for prior incidence of heart attacks and particular disposition to heart attack) were to take aspirin and the other half placebo, they could be considered a random sample with respect to the characteristic of interest: disposition to having heart attacks. Some of those who took aspirin did have heart attacks, and some did not. These observed frequencies *are compared with* frequencies expected *if the aspirin-taking had no effect on heart attack incidence. Therefore, the sum of the square of the (observed—expected) frequencies divided by the expected will be lower than the table* χ^2 *value if aspirin-taking and heart attacks are not related, and higher if related.*

The observed frequencies *of heads in 100 throws of ten coins are quite close to* expected frequencies *of three theoretical probability distributions—binomial, normal, and Pearsonian Type I.*

SOCIAL MISSION APPLICATION 3: AN ASPIRIN EVERY OTHER DAY KEEPS THE HEART ATTACK AWAY

Does aspirin reduce the risk of heart attacks? To find the answer, the American Medical Association (AMA) conducted a study for more than five years. The results were so encouraging that they terminated the study earlier than originally planned in order to publicize the decisively beneficial results.

The Population

We said in chapter 2 that the population comprises all elements with specified common characteristic(s). The characteristics of the population for the aspirin study were as follows: (a) member of the AMA, (b) male, (c) age 40 to 84 years, (d) volunteer for the study of the effect of aspirin-taking on heart attacks, (e) able to tolerate aspirin, (f) no prior history of heart disease, and (g) no prior history of gout or of liver or kidney disease.

The Control Group

To determine the effect of any "treatment"—which is a generic term for deliberate change through changes in fertilizers (e.g., fertilizer X versus fertilizer Y), changes in instruction methods (e.g., teaching method 1 versus teaching method 2), or changes in diet (e.g., skimmed milk versus whole milk)—there has to be two groups similar in all essential characteristics except that of the change agent.

The Treatment

One-half of the 22,071 male physicians who shared the seven characteristics took a placebo every other day (*control group*); the other half took an aspirin every other day (*experimental group*).

The Results

Of the 11,034 who took an aspirin every other day for more than five years, 104 had heart attacks. Of the 11,037 who took placebos, 189 had heart attacks.

STATISTICALLY SIGNIFICANTLY DIFFERENT

Clearly, 104 is numerically different from 189. We can say that (189 − 104 =) 85 fewer heart attacks were experienced by the experimental group, and that this represented 45% less heart attacks.

Observe the Random Sample: Make Statements about the Population

These two statements are about the sample of 22,071 male physicians who participated in the study. Can we make any statements about any larger group of which the 22,071 are a part?

Consider all the physicians who fulfill the seven specified common characteristics, not only in the present, but also in the future. If similar groups of 22,071 physicians undertook similar aspirin-taking experiments over similar time periods in the future, hundreds and thousands of times, can we say anything about their results?

If we can consider the 22,071 to be a random sample of the population of physicians with the seven specified characteristics, *then* we can observe the random sample, and make statements about the population with specified levels of confidence. We define:

Randomness: Equal chance of occurrence of every outcome in each trial. A simple random sample is a portion (≤100%) of the population, the characteristic of interest of which has an equal chance of occurrence in every element selected each time.

Ensuring Randomness: The Characteristic of Interest

What is the "characteristic of interest"? The incidence of heart attacks. Does each one of the 22,071 have an equal chance of having a heart attack? Yes, because the AMA excluded from the sample those who had a greater chance of heart attacks: (a) those who already had heart attacks; (b) those who because of aspirin tolerance variations could have a greater chance of heart attacks, and (c) those who had a history of other diseases that could result in a greater chance of heart attacks.

Is the sample a random sample of *all* AMA physicians aged 40 to 84? No. Notice that characteristic (d) was "volunteer for the study of the effect of aspirin-taking on heart attacks." The self-selection process would exclude those who did not volunteer. Did those who did not volunteer differ materially from those who did, with respect to disposition to having heart attacks? If nothing in the design of the study purposely excluded those who were materially different in their disposition to having heart attacks, we could reasonably rule out that the nonvolunteers were not dissimilar in their disposition to having heart attacks.

By excluding those with a greater chance of heart attacks through screening, and by not having made volunteering dependent on disposition to having heart attacks, we could consider the 22,071 to be a random sample with respect to the characteristic of interest: disposition to having a heart attack.

The Four Exclusive and Exhaustive Groups

To determine if aspirin-taking reduces heart attacks, we have to (a) identify the exclusive and exhaustive outcomes, (b) determine the "expected" frequency of occurrence of events in each group if there were no association between treatment and results, (c) compute the extent to which each observed value differs from the "expected," and (d) determine if the index of the sum of the entries in (c) could have occurred by chance. If the observed result could *not* have occurred by chance, say, 95% of the time, then it is *statistically significantly different* (SSD) from chance occurrence 95% of the time. There are four steps in determining SSD results. We will specify them with reference to the heart attack study.

Step 1: Groups: In terms of the characteristic of interest, there are four possibilities:

1. (Take aspirin) and (Have no heart attack)
2. (Take aspirin) and (Have heart attack)
3. (Take no aspirin) and (Have no heart attack)
4. (Take no aspirin) and (Have heart attack)

We can use a generic classification system by considering the treatment as the *Condition*. The Condition can be yes (Take aspirin) or no (Take no aspirin).

Similarly, we can consider the result as the *Effect*. The Effect can be yes (Have no heart attack) or no (Have heart attack). The groups can then be generically represented as *Joint Events:*

1. (Condition yes) and (Effect yes)   (yes-yes)
2. (Condition yes) and (Effect no)   (yes-no)
3. (Condition no) and (Effect yes)   (no-yes)
4. (Condition no) and (Effect no)   (no-no)

Steps 2 through 4 require the Relative Frequency *Concept* of Probability and the *Operations* of Marginal and Joint Probabilities.

RELATIVE FREQUENCY

We start with the grand total: 22,071.

Relative Frequencies of the Margin: Rows

We will enter the *Condition* in the rows. Thus Condition yes is Row 1; Condition no is Row 2.

Our condition is aspirin-taking. Of the 22,071 physicians, 11,034 took an aspirin every other day for more than five years. The total of the Condition yes is 11,034, and the total of Condition no is 11,037, as seen in Table 3.1.

Our *Effect* is the incidence of heart attack. *We chose* which effect is yes and which effect is no according to our own interest. No heart attack is the yes effect, and heart attack is the no effect, as stated earlier.

Of the 11,034 with Condition yes, 10,930 had no heart attacks, or Effect yes, and 104 had heart attacks, or Effect no. Of the 11,037 with Condition no, 10,848 had no heart attacks, or Effect yes, and 189 had heart attacks, or Effect no.

Relative Frequencies of the Margin: Columns

The *effect* is presented in columns in Table 3.2.

RELATIVE FREQUENCY CONCEPT OF PROBABILITY

To compute the expected frequency of events in each of the four cells, we need the relative frequency concept of probability.

Table 3.1
Heart Attack Contingency Table: Condition

Effect Condition	YES	NO	TOTAL
Row 1 YES			11,034
Row 2 No			11,037
TOTAL			22,071

Table 3.2
Heart Attack Contingency Table: Condition and Effect

Effect / Condition	YES Column 1	NO Column 2	TOTAL
Row 1 YES	YY 10,930	YN 104	11,034
Row 2 No	NY 10,848	NN 189	11,037
TOTAL	21,778	293	22,071

Probability: Relative Frequency of Events

In a coin toss, the exclusive and exhaustive outcomes are heads and tails. The probability of heads is ½; tails is ½. If the event of interest to us is tails, the probability of the exclusive outcome of heads is (1 minus the probability of the other exclusive outcome: tails, which is ½, giving us 1 − ½ =) ½.

Similarly, if we choose the outcome of 4 on the face of a die as the event of interest to us, all the other outcomes—1, 2, 3, 5, and 6—constitute the other exclusive outcome. The probability of 4 is ⅙; hence the probability of the other exclusive outcome is (1 minus the probability of 4, which is ⅙, giving us 1 − ⅙ =) ⅚.

$$\text{Relative Frequency} = \frac{\text{Number of specified outcomes}}{\text{Number of possible outcomes}}$$

Requirement 1: Infinite Trials

Two conditions underlie the relative frequency concept of probability. One is that probability is a *tendency* that is evident as the number of trials increases enormously, going beyond all finite numbers into infinity. Because we never reach infinity, probability forever approaches, but never reaches, 1.

The sun is a medium star around which the earth, a small planet, has been revolving for about 5 billion years. Although astronomically inaccurate, we are used to saying, "The sun rises in the east." If the sun did not "rise in the east," just for once, that would mean that the earth would be out of its orbit around the sun. Therefore, we can say that out of 5 billion × 365 = 1,825 billion *possible outcomes* of sunrise (ignoring the leap year days), 1,825 billion *specified outcomes* of the the sun "rising in the east" have indeed taken place. But the probability of the sunrise is *not* 1; it *tends to* 1 as the number of trials, *n*, tends to infinity. The evidence to date is based on 1,825 billion observations; but 1,825 billion is not infinity. The sun is expected to last another 5 billion years. Even 3,650 billion is not infinity. Therefore, at the end of 10 billion years of daily "sunrise," we still have to say that the probability of the sunrise *tends to* 1.

$$\text{Probability} = \frac{\text{Number of specified outcomes}}{\text{Number of possible outcomes, } n} \text{ as } n \text{ tends to infinity}$$

$$p = 0.4 \Rightarrow \text{(implies) } p \rightarrow \text{(tends to) } 0.4 \text{ as } n \rightarrow \text{(tends to) } \infty \text{ (infinity)}$$

Requirement 2: Convergence

As *n* tends to *infinity*, probability *tends to* .1, .99, etc. If 48 heads occurred in 100 coin tosses, the *estimate* of *p* = .48. As *n* tends to infinity, heads and tails are equally likely to occur, or *p* = .5. In other words, *p* gets closer and closer to .5 as *n* gets larger and larger, as shown in Table 3.3.

Convergence means that the difference between the *p* and the ratio gets closer and closer to zero. In Table 3.3, we show a straightforward progression to the .5 ratio. However, in real life, the departure from zero could be on either the plus side or the minus side, but the departures from zero will get smaller and smaller as *n* increases.

Variations of the Relative Frequency Concept

In 1866 John Venn formulated an event's probability as the limiting value of its relative frequency as the number of events is indefinitely increased.[1] Variations on the theme have been made by Richard von Mises (probability is not a simple limit, but the event ought to be irregularly distributed),[2] A. H. Copeland,[3] Abraham Wald,[4] Hans Reichenbach (three alternative definitions of the randomness of the distribution of the event),[5] Jerzy Neyman,[6] R. A. Fisher,[7] and others. This concept of probability gives us a test of *statistical independence:* Are the rows (aspirin-taking) and columns (heart attack) independent of each other? In other words, do the rows have no effect on the columns?

Decision-Making under Uncertainty

Table 3.3
Convergence Illustration

No. of Tosses	No. of Heads	Heads/Tosses	p-(Heads/Tosses) p = 0.500000
100	48	0.480000	0.020000
1,000	492	0.492000	0.008000
10,000	4958	0.495800	0.004200
100,000	49,875	0.498750	0.001250
1,000,000	499,995	0.499995	0.000005
10,000,000	4,999,999	0.4999999	0.0000001

STATISTICAL INDEPENDENCE

Rows and columns are independent of each other if

Joint Probability = Product of Corresponding Marginal Probabilities

We will transcribe the cell names for the Joint Events in Table 3.4. It should be noted that the cells represent Joint Events (Condition and Effect) combinations. The values, such as YY = 0.495, are relative frequencies (Number of specified outcomes/Number of possible outcomes). We have discussed earlier the randomness of the cell entries with respect to the characteristic of interest, disposition toward having a heart attack. Assuming that the 22,017 physicians are a random sample of the population with the seven specified common characteristics, the relative frequencies are probabilities, e.g., Joint Probability of (Y,Y) is .495. *Sum of Joint Probabilities = Marginal Probability.*

If the rows and columns are independent of each other, i.e., if the aspirin-taking has no effect on heart attacks, then:

Row 1 Marginal Probability × Column 1 Marginal Probability = Joint Prob. of cell (1,1)
.500 × .986 = .493 for Y-Y

Row 1 Marginal Probability × Column 2 Marginal Probability = Joint Prob. of cell (1,2)
.500 × .014 = .007 for Y-N

Row 2 Marginal Probability × Column 1 Marginal Probability = Joint Prob. of cell (2,1)
.500 × .986 = .493 for N-Y

Row 2 Marginal Probability × Column 2 Marginal Probability = Joint Prob. of cell (2,2)
.500 × .014 = .007 for N-N

The *observed* joint probability of cell (1,1) is .495.

The *expected* joint probability of cell (1,1) is .493.

Statistical independence is denied if a *single* observed joint probability differs from the expected joint probability. Since .495 is not equal to .493, statistical independence is denied; or independence of rows and columns is denied. In other words, aspirin-taking may have an effect on heart attacks.

This denial is similar to a grand jury indictment. The indictment only says that there is enough evidence to believe that a crime has been committed. In the aspirin study, it means that there is evidence to suggest that aspirin-taking may have some effect on heart attacks. How strong an effect? In which direction? The answers require a statistical test, just as the indictment calls for a trial.

Table 3.4
Heart Attack Contingency Table: Joint and Marginal Probabilities

Effect / Condition	YES Column 1	NO Column 2	TOTAL
Row 1 YES	Jt. prob. YY 0.495	Jt. prob. YN 0.005	Row 1 Marg. probability 0.500
Row 2 NO	Jt. prob. NY 0.491	Jt. prob. NN 0.009	Row 2 Marg. probability 0.500
TOTAL	Col 1 Marg. probability 0.986	Col. 2 Marg probability 0.014	1.000

CHI-SQUARED (χ^2) TEST

Step 1: Identify the exclusive and exhaustive outcomes.

Step 2: Determine the expected frequency of occurrences if there were no association between *treatment* and *results*.

Step 3: Compute the extent to which each *observed* value differs from the *expected*.

Step 4: Determine if the index of the sum of the entries in Step 3 occurred by chance.

$$\text{Chi-squared } (\chi^2) = (\text{Observed} - \text{Expected})^2/\text{Expected}$$

We know that the observed frequency in cell (1,1) is 10,930. What is the expected frequency if *there were no relation* between aspirin-taking and heart attacks? The joint probability is .493. Multiplying the grand total of 22,071 by the joint probability, we get $22,071 \times .493 = 10,881$.

Observed $-$ Expected $= 10,930 - 10,881 = 49$. Squaring 49 and dividing it by the expected frequency of 10,881, we get .2206 for cell (1,1).

For cell (1,2) the expected frequency is $22,071 \times .007 = 154$. The observed frequency is 104. Observed $-$ Expected $= 104 - 154 = -50$. Squaring -50 and dividing it by the expected frequency of $154 = 16.2338$.

For cell (2,1), the expected frequency is $22,071 \times .493 = 10,881$. The observed frequency is 10,848; $(10,848 - 10,881) = -33$. Squaring -33 and dividing it by the expected frequency, we get .1001.

For cell (2,2), the expected frequency is $22,017 \times .007 = 154$. The observed frequency is 189; $(189 - 154) = 35$. Squaring 35 and dividing it by the expected frequency of 154, we get 7.9545.

What is the sum of the χ^2 for cells (1,1), (1,2), (2,1), and (2,2)? We get $.2206 + 16.2338 + .1001 + 7.9545 = 24.5090$.

CHI-SQUARED (χ^2) TABLE

We compare the computed value of 24.5090 against the appropriate table value. *If computed value $>$ table value, reject the Null Hypothesis (NH) of the table.* What is the NH of the χ^2 table?

Known Population Probabilities: Pearson

Karl Pearson used the symbol χ^2 for the first time in 1900. He wanted to test whether a sequence of n observed values came from a parent population of known properties. How far off could the observed values be before we conclude that they are SSD from the parent population?

Let the parent population be divided into separate r parts—$R_1, R_2, \ldots R_r$—with no overlapping. Let the probability of R_i be designated p_i; thus $p_i = P(R_i)$. Since the entire population is divided into r parts and only r parts, the total of the probabilities for all the r parts together should equal 1. $\Sigma p_i = 1 \ (i = 1, 2, \ldots n)$

The population p_i can be estimated from the sample of size n. If v_i members of the sample exhibit the property, $P(R_i) = (v_i/n)$. If the sample sequence of n observed values came from the parent population of known properties, the quantity, observed − expected, must be close to zero. Karl Pearson showed that if we take $c_i = n/p_i$, the resulting measure will have simple properties. He called the measure χ^2. Substituting $c_i = n/p_i$, $(i = 1,2, \ldots n)$

$$\chi^2 = \Sigma \, n/p_i \, [v_i - np_i/n]^2$$
$$= n/p_i \, [v_i - np_i]^2/n^2 = \Sigma_1 \, [v_i - np_i]^2/np_i,$$

where v_i are the *observed frequencies* and np_i are the *expected frequencies* for all r groups.[8]

Estimated Population Probabilities: Fisher

Pearson assumed that the theoretical distribution of the population probabilities is *known*. Generally, the *estimates* of the population measures are made from the observed distribution. These estimates, $\hat{p}$, replace the probabilities, p, as follows:

$$\chi^2 = \Sigma[v_i - np_i]^2/np_i \quad (i = 2, \ldots ,n) \quad \chi^2 = \Sigma[v_i - n\hat{p}_i]^2/np_i$$
$$\text{(Pearson)} \qquad\qquad\qquad\qquad\qquad \text{(Fisher)[9]}$$

Degrees of Freedom

To calculate the expected frequencies on the basis of known theoretical distribution, we used the total of the frequencies. If we specify that the sum of three numbers is 127, we can choose the first number freely; we choose, say, 43. So, also, we can choose the second number freely, say, 95. But we *lose the freedom* to choose the third number because we have to observe the *restriction* that the sum of the three should equal 127. The restriction is a *linear restriction* of the form: $x_1 + x_2 + x_3 = 127$.

To calculate the expected frequencies, we multiplied the row marginal probability by the column marginal probability. The Row 1 total was specified: .50; the Column 1 total was specified: .986. The linear restriction of the row total made each row lose 1 degree of freedom, leaving it with $(r - 1)$ degree of freedom. Similarly, the linear restriction of the column total made each column lose 1 degree of freedom, leaving it with $(c - 1)$ degree of freedom. Thus, the degrees of freedom of the table made up of R rows and C columns is $(r - 1)(c - 1)$. In the heart attack study, there are two rows and two columns. Therefore, the degrees of freedom $(2 - 1)(2 - 1) = 1$.

Table Value

The NH of the χ^2 table is that the difference between the observed and expected frequencies is zero. In our study, we obtained the expected frequencies assuming statistical independence: the rows and columns are independent of each other. *If computed X^2 value > Table X^2 value, reject the NH; otherwise, accept.*

Levels of Significance

The χ^2 table shows NH values corresponding to (a) degrees of freedom (DF) and (b) levels of significance.

χ^2 for 1 DF and 95% level of significance is 3.8

1	98%	5.4
1	99%	6.6
1	99.9%	10.8

The computed value in the heart attack study is 24.5090 (Table 3.5), which is >10.8. Therefore, we *reject* the NH that aspirin-taking has *no effect* on heart attacks (*note the double negative*) at the 99.9% significance level (or with 99.9% confidence). The computed value is SSD from the table value 99.9% of the time, or 999 out of 1,000 times. The difference between the computed value (24.5090) and the expected value (table value of 10.8) could have occurred by chance only 1 out of 1,000 times.

Table 3.5
Heart Attack: Observed and Expected Frequencies

Effect \ Condition	YES	NO
YES	Observed : 10,930 - Expected : 10,881 (O-E) = 49 $(O-E)^2/E = 49^2/10,881$ = 0.2206	Observed : 104 - Expected : 154 (O-E) = -50 $(O-E)^2/E = -50^2/154$ = 16.233
NO	Observed : 10,848 - Expected : 10,881 (O-E) = -33 $(O-E)^2/E = -33^2/10,881$ = 0.1001	Observed: 189 - Expected: 154 (O-E) = 35 $(O-E)^2/E = 35^2/154$ = 7.9545

Chi-Squared = 0.2206 + 16.2338 + 0.100⁻ 7.9545
= 24.5090

Conclusion Format

To avoid the mistake in dealing with the double negatives of the NH, we use three steps: (1) *the conclusion:* Write out the NH; (2) *The cancellation:* Cancel the (no/not/zero) in the NH if it is rejected; and (3) *the frequency of error:* (100 − level of confidence/significance) stated as 1 in 100, 1,000, and so on.

Accept NH: The conclusion that there *is no relationship.* . . .

Reject NH: The conclusion that there *is {no} [some] relationship* between aspirin-taking and heart attacks may be wrong 1 in 1,000 times.

PHYSICAL APPLICATION 1: 100 TOSSES OF 10 COINS

In the heart attack study, the χ^2 applied to rows *and* columns. In coin toss, the expected frequencies depend only on the columns.

Expected Frequencies

The number of heads in a throw of ten coins can be 0, 1, . . . , 10. Each coin can produce heads or tails, the probability of heads being .5. Therefore, the probability of r success (specified outcome—heads) and $n - r$ failures (not specified outcome—tails) is $p^r.q^{n-r}$. Choosing r successes out of n trials is given by the number of combinations of n things taken r at a time. The probability of r success ($r = 1$ head, $r = 2$ heads, . . . , $r = 10$ heads) is given by [10]

$$ {}^nC_r\, p^r\, q^{n-r} $$

Cumulative binomial distribution table gives the probability of "r or more successes," "success" being the specified outcome, say, heads. Reading from the table with $n = 10$, for ten coins in a throw, we find that the probability of one or more heads in one throw of ten coins is .9990; and the probability of two or more heads is .9893. The exact probability of occurrence of one head is, therefore, (.9990 − .9893 =) .0097. Because there are 100 such throws, the *expected frequency* of one head is $100 \times .0097 = .97$, as shown in Table 3.6. The *observed frequency* is 0.

Similarly, the probability of occurrence of three or more heads in a toss of ten coins is .9453, giving the exact probability of occurrence of three heads as (.9893 − .9453 =) .0440. Multiplying this probability of occurrence in 1 throw by the total number of 100 throws, we get the *expected frequency* of $100 \times .0440 = 4.40$. The *observed frequency* is three.

Computed χ^2

As we did in the heart attack study, we find the χ^2 for each expected frequency. *Cells with expected frequencies <5 are combined into a single cell.* Thus cells

Decision-Making under Uncertainty

Table 3.6
Binomial Distribution Fit to Coin Toss Data

(1) x_i	(2) $P(r > x_i)$	(3) $P(r > x_{i-1})$	(4) (2) - (3)	(5) exp y 100 X (4)	(6) obs. y	(7) (6) - (5)	(8) $\frac{[(6) - (5)]^2}{(5)}$ Chi-Squared
0	1.0000	0.9990	0.0010	0.10*	0**		
1	0.9990	0.9893	0.0097	0.97*	0**	0.97	0.9700
2	0.9893	0.9453	0.0440	4.40*	3**	-1.40	0.4455
3	0.9453	0.8281	0.1172	11.72	10	-1.72	0.1573
4	0.8281	0.6230	0.2051	20.51	24	-3.49	0.5939
5	0.6230	0.3770-	0.2460	24.60	22	-2.60	0.2748
6	0.3770	0.1719	0.2051	20.51	21	0.49	0.0117
7	0.1719	0.0547	0.1172	11.72	11	-0.72	0.0442
8	0.0547	0.0107	0.0440	4.40*	5**	0.60	0.0818
9	0.0107	0.0010	0.0097	0.97*	4**	3.03	9.4648
10	0.0010		0.0010	0.10*	0**	-0.10	0.1000

DF 10 - (1) = 9; or 10- (4) =6	Computed Chi-Squared Table value 99.9%	10 DF / 6 DF 12.144 / 4.293 21.666 / 16.812
Combining cells with expected frequencies < 5	Cells (0,1,2) Expected 5.47* Observed 3.0** / Cells (8,9,10) Expected 5.47* Observed 9.0**	Revised Chi-Sq. 0.9325 2.2783

for $r = 0$, $r = 1$, and $r = 2$ are combined into a single cell with the expected frequency of 5.47. Similarly, cells for $r = 8$, $r = 9$, and $r = 10$ are combined into a single cell with the expected frequency of 5.47. The total number of cells is 7, with DF $(7 - 1 =)$ 6.

Computed χ^2 for 6 DF	4.293
Table χ^2 with 95% significance	12.6
Table χ^2 with 99% significance	16.8
Table χ^2 with 99.9% significance	22.5

The conclusion that the difference between the binomial distribution and the observed distribution is zero may be wrong 1 in 1,000 times.

NORMAL CURVE AND PEARSONIAN CURVE I FIT TO THE COIN TOSS DATA

Karl Pearson developed solutions to a family of curves that can fit any set of data. The curve may be rectangular, J-shaped, U-shaped, bell-shaped, and so on. Which of the Pearsonian curve fits the data best is determined by κ, which is a function of *4 moments about the mean*. Each observation is measured from the mean. The distance is squared, cubed, and raised to the fourth power to give, respectively, the 2nd, 3rd, and 4th moments about the mean. A detailed discussion appears elsewhere.[11] Suffice it for the present to note that the familiar bell-shaped normal curve is appropriate when $\kappa = 0$.

$\kappa = -\infty$	$\kappa < 0$	$\kappa = 0$	$\kappa > 0, < 1$	$\kappa = 1$	$\kappa > 1$	$\kappa = \infty$
:	:	:	:	:	:	:
Type III	Type I	Normal $\beta_2 = 3$ Type II $\beta_2 < 3$ Type VII $\beta_2 > 3$	Type IV	Type V	Type VI	Type III

We present in Table 3.7 three theoretical distributions fitted to the observed coin toss data. The computed χ^2 for the normal curve is 6.1107; for Pearsonian Type I it is 3.42709; both of which are $<$ the table χ^2 value for 6 DF at 99.9% level of significance.

The conclusion that the difference between the normal distribution and the observed distribution is zero may be wrong 1 in 1,000 times.
The conclusion that the difference between the Pearsonian I distribution and the observed distribution is zero may be wrong 1 in 1,000 times.

CONCLUDING OBSERVATIONS

What statements can we make on the heart attack experience of 22,071 physicians aged 40 to 84, half of whom took an aspirin every other day, while the other half did not?

We identified seven characteristics that were specific to the population of physicians who participated in the heart attack study. We considered the characteristic of interest—disposition to having heart attacks—with respect to which the sample of 22,071 could be considered random, insofar as those who took aspirin and those who did not were chosen on the basis of their disposition to having heart attacks. The object of the study was to determine if aspirin-taking had any impact on the first heart attack.

How many would be expected to have heart attacks among those who took aspirin and those who did not? The product of the marginal probabilities gives the expected frequencies if the rows (aspirin-taking) and the columns (heart

Table 3.7
Pearsonian, Normal, and Binomial Fits to Coin Toss Data

(1)	(2)	(3)	(4)	(5)	(6)	(7)	(8)
		Expected Frequencies and Contribution to Chi-Squared					
Heads	Frequency	Pearsonian		Normal		Binomial	
1	0	0.0035	0.0035	0.748	0.7479	0.97	0.9700
2	3	2.0935	0.3925	3.257	0.0203	4.40	0.4455
3	10	10.5414	0.0278	9.538	0.0224	11.72	0.1573
4	24	19.6175	0.9790	18.786	1.4471	20.51	0.5939
5	22	22.2530	0.0029	24.894	0.3364	24.60	0.2748
6	21	17.2839	0.7990	22.190	0.6381	20.51	0.0117
7	11	11.0885	0.0007	13.307	0.3999	11.72	0.0442
8	5	5.2297	0.0101	5.162	0.0051	4.40	0.0818
9	4	1.8531	2.4873	1.457	4.4383	0.97	9.9648
10	0	0.4659	0.4659	0.266	0.2657	0.10	0.1000
			5.1687		8.3212		12.1440
Chi-Squared with combined cells			3.4270		6.1107		4.2933

attacks) had no effect on each other. For each cell, the square of the (observed −
expected) frequencies was divided by the expected frequency to give the χ^2 −
value. The sum of the computed χ^2 was compared with table χ^2. Because the
former was higher than the latter, we rejected the NH. The conclusion that
aspirin-taking and heart attacks were unrelated was rejected (implying that the
aspirin-taking does have an effect on heart attack); the rejection could be wrong 1
in 1,000 times.

The expected frequency in the heart attack study uses a *joint probability,*
probability of a joint event, whereas the expected frequency of heads in a toss of
ten coins uses a *single-event probability*. Binomial distribution specifies the
expected frequency of 0, 1, . . . , 10 heads (or that of tails, if *you* defined
success as tails instead of heads) in each throw of ten coins, which we multiply
by 100 to determine the expected frequency of 0, 1, . . . , 10 heads in 100
throws of ten coins. They are compared with the *observed frequency*. The computed χ^2 < table χ^2; the conclusion that the difference between the binomial and
the observed distribution is zero may be wrong 1 in 1,000 times. Similar results
for normal and Pearsonian Type I curves attest to their excellent fit to the data.

From the NH underlying the χ^2 table, we turn in chapter 4 to the NH underlying other statistical tables.

QUESTIONS: CONCEPTS AND COMPUTATIONS
FOR COMMITMENT

Our focus is decision-making, not number-crunching. Therefore, we divide the reinforcement of the text material into six categories: (1) Concepts: Foundational, (2) Concepts: Formulational, (3) Computations, (4) Conclusions, (5) [Resource] Commitments, and (6) Caveats. See chapter 11 for answers to questions for this chapter.

Concepts: Foundational

1. What is the NH of the χ^2 table?
2. What is the advantage(s) offered by relative frequency concept of probability over the other concepts?
3. What statements can you make about "sunrise tomorrow morning" using the different concepts of probability? Why is each different? Which do you use for your decision about tomorrow? Why?
4. Statistical statements are not proofs; but *dis*proofs. Why? Illustrate.

Concepts: Formulational

Mr. Frederick T. Rope of Teachers College, Columbia University, reported in his 1941 book, *Opinion Conflict and School Support,* the survey responses by 1,464 adult residents of Pittsburgh, Pennsylvania (707 men and 757 women). We will discuss two of the questions.

The Problem: Higher School Taxes

Question 1: Some say that in future years, the only way that schools can keep up the services they are giving today is to increase taxes. If this is true, should school services be cut, or taxes increased?

The Data: Of the men, 296 were for increasing the taxes, 228 against, and 183 had no opinion. Of the women, 236 were for increasing the taxes, 226 against, and 295 had no opinion.

5. Formulate the NH of Question 1.
6. State the rule of statistical independence with reference to the data.

The Problem: Tax Support for Nursery Schools

Question 2: Do you think tax money should, or should not, be spent on nursery school for children under four and a half years old?

The Data: There were 400 favorable responses, 954 unfavorable, and 110 "no opinion."

The respondents were divided into three age categories: 20 to 34 (565 respondents), 34 to 54 (649 respondents), and over 54 (250 respondents). In the first age group, 153 were favorable, 377 were unfavorable, and 35 had no opinion. In the second group, 182 were favorable, 417 were unfavorable, and 50 had no opinion. In the third group, 65 were favorable, 160 were unfavorable, and 110 had no opinion.

7. Formulate the NH of Question 2.
8. State the rule of statistical independence with reference to the data.

Computations

The Problem: Higher School Taxes

9. Set up the marginal totals for Question 1: (1) of the rows; (2) of the columns. (See Table 3.1. Use the principle that the sum of the cells must equal the marginal row totals *and* column totals.)
10. Compute the joint and marginal probabilities (see Table 3.4).
11. Compute the expected frequencies in each cell (see Table 3.5).
12. Compute the χ^2 value in each cell (see Table 3.5).
13. Determine the degrees of freedom.
14. Choose two levels of significance; record the table values χ^2.

The Problem: Tax Support for Nursery Schools

15. Set up the marginal totals for Question 2: (1) of the rows; (2) of the columns. (See Table 3.1. Use the principle that the sum of the cells must equal the marginal row totals *and* column totals.)
16. Compute the joint and marginal probabilities (see Table 3.4).
17. Compute the expected frequencies in each cell (see Table 3.5).
18. Compute the χ^2 value in each cell (see Table 3.5).
19. Determine the degrees of freedom.
20. Choose two levels of significance; record the table values of χ^2.

Conclusions

The Problem: Higher School Taxes

21. Develop the conclusion of Question 1 following the three steps specified in this chapter to develop the Conclusion Format.

The Problem: Tax Support for Nursery Schools

22. Develop the conclusion of Question 2, following the three steps specified in this chapter to develop the Conclusion Format.
23. State the conclusion of Question 1; interpret it for a lay person.
24. State the conclusion of Question 2; interpret it for a lay person.

[Resource] Commitments

The Problem: School Services versus Tax Increase

25. As chairman of the school board will you, (1) increase taxes, or (2) cut school services? Why?

26. As chairman of the school board will you (1) spend tax money on nursery-school children under four and a half years, or (2) not. Why?

27. If you wanted to change the minds of the population, whose vote would you work on to (1) increase the support for school taxes or (2) institute tax support to nursery school? Why?

Caveats

28. What was the basis of the data for Question 1? Question 2?

The Problem: Higher School Taxes

29. Specify the characteristic of the Pittsburgh group that you would survey to reinforce the support for taxes?

30. What are the limitations of your conclusions?

NOTES

1. John Venn, *The Logic of Chance* (London: Macmillan, 1888), ch. VI.

2. Richard von Mises, *Probability, Statistics, and Truth* (London: Hodge, 1939).

3. A. H. Copeland, "The Theory of Probability from the Point of View of Admissible Numbers," *Ann. Math. Statis.* 3 (1932): 143.

4. Abraham Wald, "Die Wiederspruchfreiheit des Kollektivbegriffes," *Actualities Sci. Indust.* 735 (1938): 79.

5. Hans Reichenbach, *The Theory of Probability* (Berkeley: University of California Press, 1949).

6. Jerzy Neyman, *First Course in Probability and Statistics* (New York: Holt, Winston and Reinhart, 1950).

7. Ronald A. Fisher, *Statistical Methods and Scientific Inference* (New York: Hafner, 1956), p. 109.

8. Karl Pearson, "On the Criterion That a Given System of Deviations from the Probable in the Case of a Correlated System of Variables Is Such That It Can Be Reasonably Supposed to Have Arisen from Random Sampling," *Phil. Mag.* 50, Ser. 5 (1900): 157–75.

9. Ronald A. Fisher, "The Conditions under Which χ^2 Measures the Discrepancy between Observation and Hypothesis," *J. Roy. Statist. Soc.* 87 (1924): 442–49.

10. George K. Chacko, *Applied Statistics in Decision-Making* (New York: Elsevier, 1971), ch. 11.

11. Ibid., ch. 8.

4 Null Hypothesis Foundations of Standard Statistical Tables

OVERVIEW: The χ^2 table provides the values if (observed − expected) frequencies are zero. The expected frequencies are based on two conditions: (1) population of mutually exclusive and exhaustive outcomes (2) that are unrelated to each other, whether they are two faces of a coin or condition-effect combinations such as aspirin-taking and heart attacks or cigarette-smoking and cancer. When the possible outcomes are only two, the binomial distribution is appropriate; when there are more, the multinomial distribution is appropriate.

When n is large, the binomial and the χ^2 distributions tend toward the normal distribution. With n = 22,071, the normal distribution is used to reject the null hypothesis (NH) that there is no difference in heart attack incidence between those who took aspirin and those who took placebo.

The normal distribution is specified by the mean and standard deviation. The motivation for the originators of the normal curve was theological (De Moivre) or astronomical (Gauss). Their premise was that orderliness predominates—be it in the creation of the world or in the motion of the heavenly bodies. They found that the law of error, or the normal curve of error, attested to the preponderance of zero error. Error is (ideal − actual). The mean of the standard normal distribution is zero, and it occurs with the highest frequency. In other words, orderliness is the rule of the universe, deviations in the form of errors being the exception; the greater the error, the smaller its frequency.

We use the value in the form of mean, or variation in the form of standard deviation, to identify the populations from which the observed data come 95%, 99%, etc. of the time. We accept the NH that there is no difference between the mean personal income of the population from which the New England Region sample came and the population of the 1973 mean personal income in the United States. We also use t to reject the NH that there is no difference between the mean *personal income in the New England Region in 1973 and in the year 2000.*

In the case of personal income, our characteristic of interest is the central value, *obtained by summing the personal income and dividing it by the total number of people. We did not add and divide heart attacks to get the mean, but we studied the* variations *in the heart attack incidence between aspirin-takers and placebo-takers. These variations come to the fore when we compare* several means. *When four different diets are administered to four samples of animals, we test the variations among the treatments against the variations among the subjects and reject the NH of zero difference.*

HEAVENLY MISSION APPLICATION 1: "IRREGULARITIES WILL BEAR NO PROPORTION TO THE RECURRENCY OF THAT ORDER WHICH NATURALLY RESULTS FROM ORIGINAL DESIGN"

In chapter 3, we found that when ten coins were thrown 100 times, the frequencies expected of 0 heads, 1 heads, 2 heads, . . . , 10 heads calculated on the basis of a normal curve corresponds so closely to the observed frequencies that they could well have been generated by a normal curve. Called the "curve of the facility of errors," the normal curve was developed by De Moivre to establish that the universe displayed an original design of orderliness.

n, the Foundation of the Differences in Null Hypotheses

We should note the fundamental difference in the NH between logical and subjective probability and the relative frequency probability. In the Cuban Missile Crisis, Robert Kennedy's NH that Khrushchev was in control referred to a unique event, population $n = 1$. What logical probability persuaded him to reject the overwhelming evidence to the contrary? We offered several applicable propositions, in each of which n was definitely *small*.

By contrast, in chapter 3, where we considered 100 tosses of ten coins, the population n was *infinite*. The expected frequencies were based on $n = \infty$, whether they were derived from the binomial, normal, or Pearsonian distribution. We asked, which population produced this sample—binomial, normal, or Pearsonian? For instance, the NH postulating the binomial distribution for the coin toss was:

(The expected frequencies of the population from which this sample of coin toss data came *minus* the expected frequencies of the population, which is a binomial distribution with p = 0.5) = 0.

When the NH was accepted, we could say, Yes, this sample came from a binomial population, with a certain degree of confidence:

The conclusion that the difference between the binomial distribution and the observed distribution is zero may be wrong 1 in 1,000 times.

Distributions: Discrete and Continuous

The expected frequencies have been calculated elsewhere.[1] In fact, three sets of expected frequencies were calculated in Table 3.7 on the basis of three probability distributions: binomial, Pearsonian Type I, and normal. These distributions are *not* the fit to the *sample* of ten coins thrown 100 times; but they are the fit to the *population* from which the data on the 100 throws each of the ten coins could have come, as *n* tends to infinity. We have used the words "curve" and "distribution" interchangeably. The latter is the formal basis for the geometric figure of the former. We define:

Distribution is the probability that a random variable X assumes a value $\leqq$ a specified value.

A variable is an entity (event, relationship, object, instance) that assumes different values in a prescribed manner. A random variable is an entity, each of whose values has an equal chance of occurrence in every trial.

A coin toss is an entity. It assumes the values heads and tails. All the outcomes (two in this instance) have an equal chance of occurrence in every trial, which makes the coin toss a random variable. Similarly, a die is an entity, assuming values 1, 2, . . . , 6. All the six outcomes have an equal chance of occurrence in every trial, making the die toss a random variable.

In a coin toss and die toss, the values are discrete. Either one or two heads or *n* heads occurs, not 1.113 heads. However, barometric pressure values are continuous (e.g., 29.496 inches). Decimal values appear in continuous distributions but not in discrete distributions. The binomial distribution is discrete, whereas the normal and Pearsonian distributions are smooth, as seen from Figure 4.1. To draw the normal curve, we need to know its *mean* and *standard deviation,* which are its *parameters*.

Parameter (parametric constant) is a *variable constant:* it is a value that is *constant* for a group, but *varies* from group to group.

The mean is the average, the *central value*. The standard deviation is the *spread* of the data; its square is the variance.

The mean (income) is a constant for a group (e.g., $4,998 for the New England Region in 1973), but varies from group to group (e.g., $4,998 for the New England Region, $5,100 for the Pacific Region). The spread of the data would also vary; the larger the disparity in income, the larger the spread from the highest to the lowest, as reflected in the standard deviation.

Figure 4.1
Pearsonian, Binomial, and Normal Distribution Fits to Coin Toss Data

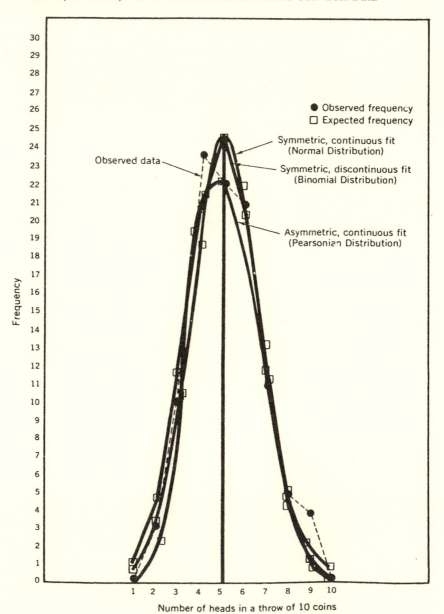

$$\text{Mean } \bar{X} = (\Sigma\ X_i/n)\ (i = 1, 2, \ldots, n)$$
$$\text{Variance} = \text{square of the standard deviation}$$
$$\text{Standard deviation} = \sqrt{s^2} = \sqrt{n\ \Sigma\ X_i^2 - (\Sigma\ X_i)^2/\ (n)\ (n - 1)}$$

Normal Approximation to Binomial

We found that the normal curve was a good approximation to the binomial distribution, which is the precise fit for the coin toss data. We saw that the probability of r successes in n trials is given by $\binom{n}{r} p^r \cdot q^{n-r}$.

As n becomes large, in this instance 1,000, we find that the straight lines of the binomial distribution are extremely close to the smooth curve of the normal. We are familiar with the rounding up of decimals 0.6 and higher to the next larger integer, and the rounding down of decimals 0.5 and lower to the next smaller integer. In rounding 9.6 to 10.0, we add 0.4; in rounding 9.5 to 9.0, we subtract 0.5. Both are inaccurate, but the inaccuracies balance out in the long run. So also, the *smooth* (normal) curve balances out the (binomial) *straight* lines.

Normal Approximation to the χ^2 Distribution

In chapter 3, we presented the number of people with Condition yes, Effect yes (YY), and the other combinations YN, NY, and NN. Their DF was 1. The sample size, n, was large at 22,071.

As n for χ^2 with 1 DF becomes large, $\sqrt{\chi^2}$ is distributed normally.

We will demonstrate this result using the heart attack data. Earlier we *rejected* the NH that there was no difference between the incidence of heart attack in those who took aspirin and those who took placebo.

SOCIAL MISSION APPLICATION 4: NORMAL CURVE ANALYSIS OF HEART ATTACK STUDY

We express in Table 4.1 the fractions not in the terms of the grand total as we did for χ^2 in Table 3.4, but in terms of the *marginal* totals. Thus, $p_1 = a/N_1$, 10,930/21,778 = .50188 (compared with .495 in cell 11 of Table 3.4). Similarly, $p_2 = b/N_2$, 104/293 = .35495. The pooled estimate $p = a + b/\ N_1 + N_2\ (= N)$ is obtained as 11,034/22,071 = .49993.

The normal distribution gives the area under the normal curve from the mean to the ordinate, z. The ordinate is the distance of the given value divided by the standard deviation.

$$z^2 = (p_1 - p_2)^2/[(p(1 - p)(N_1 + N_2)/(N_1 N_2)] = \chi^2$$
$$= (.021588)/(5,517.7279)/(6,380,954) = 24.965355$$
$$\sqrt{z^2} = \sqrt{24.965355} = 4.996534 = \sqrt{\chi^2}\ \text{(which is distributed normally)}.$$

Table 4.1
Heart Attack Contingency Table Data: Normal Approximation to Chi-Squared

Effect / Condition	YES	NO	TOTAL
Row 1 YES	10,930 (a)	104 (b)	11,034
Row 2 No	10,848 (c)	189 (d)	11,037
TOTAL	21,778(N_1)	293(N_2)	22,071(N)

Normal Table

We find that the normal curve values are all positive. Because the curve is symmetrical, the left half is exactly the same as the right half, only with the reverse sign. The area under the normal curve in the normal table is .5.

We find that when $z = 1$, the area from the mean to that ordinate is .3413. Similarly, the area from the mean to the ordinate $z = -1$ is also .3413. In the *standardized (unit) normal curve*, mean $= 0$, and standard deviation $= 1$. Therefore, when $z = +1$, the ordinate is 1 standard deviation to the right of the mean, and when $z = -1$, the ordinate is 1 standard deviation to the left of the mean. Together, the mean ± 1 standard deviation covers .3413 + .3413 = .6826 of the area (about two-thirds).

When $z = 2$, the area is .4772 to the right of the mean; when $z = -2$, the area is .4772 to the left of the mean. Together, the mean ± 2 standard deviations = .4772 + .4772 = .9544 (roughly 95% of the area). When $z = 1.96$, mean ± 1.96 standard deviations = 95% of the area. If the computed value of $z >$ table value of z, *reject* the NH that the difference between p_1 and p_2 is zero. If the computed value is higher than the table value of $z = 1.96$, reject the NH with 95% confidence.

Normal Curve Conclusion on the Heart Attack Study

Let us call the *z* value for the heart attack study 4.999997. If $z = 1.96$ represents 95%, what does $z = 4.999997$ represent? 99.9999994. So we reject the NH that there is zero difference in the fraction that suffers heart attack between those who take aspirin and those who take placebo:

The conclusion that *there is a difference* in the fraction suffering heart attack between those who take aspirin and those who do not may be wrong 1 in 100,000,000 times.

LAW OF ERROR: CONCLUSION OF HEAVENLY MISSION APPLICATION 1

The origin of the normal curve dates back to November 12, 1733, when De Moivre[2] developed the "approximation for the value of factorial x," which is used to derive the equation to the normal curve from the binomial expansion. It is interesting to note that without any tables of the probability integral—let alone modern computers—De Moivre found that the total area between the middle term and 1 standard deviation in either direction was .682688.[3]

Error: Theological Motivation

In 1738 De Moivre published his own translation of his *Approximatio* in the second edition of another book, *The Doctrine of Chances*. We will see in chapter 7 how the latter influenced Thomas Bayes to use conditional probability to derive the conclusion of a Creator from the evidence of Creation. In both instances, the motivation was theological:

The *causes* which led De Moivre to his "Approximation" or Bayes to his theorem were more *theological* and sociological than purely mathematical, and until one recognises that the post-Newtonian English mathematicians were more influenced by *Newton's theology* than by his mathematics, the history of science in the eighteenth century—in particular that of the scientists who were members of the Royal Society—must remain obscure [emphasis added].[4]

What De Moivre found in the "curve of the facility of errors" was that the probability of the minimum error (or zero error) was the maximum. In a unit normal curve, the mean is 0 and standard deviation is 1, as pointed out earlier. If we define *error* = (*Ideal* − *Actual*), then we can see that the error is minimum (zero) at the central value. The minimum error has the maximum probability; and the higher the error, the lower the probability. This tells De Moivre that "Irregularities" are minor compared with the "Order[liness] of the Universe":

And thus in all cases it will be found, that although Chance produces irregularities, still the Odds will be infinitely great, that in process of Time, those *Irregularities will bear no proportion to the recurrency of that Order* which naturally results from *Original Design.* . . . Again, as it is thus demonstrable that there are, in the constitution of things, certain *Laws according to which Events happen*, it is no less evident from Observation, that these Laws serve to wise, useful and beneficial purposes, to *preserve the steadfast Order of the Universe*, to propagate the several Species of Beings, and furnish to the sentient Kind such degree of happiness are as suited to their State [emphasis added].[5]

Error: Astronomical Motivation

If theology motivated De Moivre, astronomy motivated Gauss. Helen M. Walker, whose *Studies in the History of Statistical Method* makes available careful translations of original works, points out how Gauss used probability of errors to determine the orbit of a planet from a number of observations:

Acknowledging his debt to Laplace,[6] Gauss made use of the law of probability in Section III of Book II of his great work on the theory of the *motions of the heavenly bodies*,[7] and also reached the *principle of least squares*, which had first been published by Legendre in 1805. This section of the book relates to the *determination of the orbit of a planet from any number of observations*. . . . The work of Gauss . . . established the theory of *errors of observation*, of which modern statistical theory is the direct descendant [emphasis added].[8]

TWO BASES OF NULL HYPOTHESIS: [CENTRAL] VALUE AND VARIANCE

Both types of errors—(1) "Irregularities" from the "recurrency of that Order" (De Moivre) and (2) "errors of observation" of "the orbit of a planet from any number of observations" (Gauss)—were based not on the value of the characteristic of interest, but on the *variations* from the value.

Basis 1: [Central] Value

Unlike the pioneers of the law of error, we often use not the variations from a value, but the value itself as the characteristic of interest. We use the *central value* to specify the *substantive characteristic of interest*, such as the 1986 U.S. per capita income. The central value is $14,461, which is obtained by dividing the sum of the incomes by the total number of people.

Basis 2: Variances from the [Central] Value

On the other hand, in the heart attack study, we did not take the sum and divide by the number of people. Instead, we measured the *square of the difference* between the observed values and the expected values. We were not looking for the number of people suffering heart attacks, but their *variations from the (ex-*

pected) values. By how much did the heart attack incidence of those who took aspirin vary from the expected values; and by how much did the heart attack incidence of those who did not take aspirin vary from the expected values?

Basis 1: Value (= Mean); Basis 2: Variance (= Standard Deviation)

We know that mean is one of the two parameters of the normal distribution, the other parameter being standard deviation, which is the square root of variance. *Mean* can be the arithmetic mean of a series of numbers; or it can be the fraction of specified occurrences over possible occurrences (e.g., heads in a coin toss). Similarly, we may use *variance* itself, or its variations, such as *standard deviation,* to test the NH.

NULL HYPOTHESIS OF VALUE AND VARIANCE

The values observed can be absolute or relative; the sample size, n, can be large or small. In all instances, we observe the sample and ask the question, What population(s) could this sample have come from 95%, 99%, etc. of the time?

Absolute Values: Mean (Small Sample)

In 1908 the British statistician William Sealy Gossett published a paper, pointing out that the normal distribution does not calibrate well the ratio of mean to standard error in small samples. He had to publish it under a pseudonym, "Student," because the Guiness Brewery in Dublin, to which he was adviser, forbade its employees from publishing research results.

As in the case of the normal distribution, the NH of the t-distribution is (*sample mean minus population mean) is zero.* Actually, the reference is to the mean of the population that could have generated this sample mean, as we pointed out at the beginning of this chapter. The numerator is identical: $\bar{X} - \mu$. The only difference in the denominator is that the sample standard deviation is used as an estimate of the population standard deviation, which is unknown:

$$t = \bar{X} - \mu \, / s_x / \sqrt{n}, \text{ where } n \text{ is the DF}$$

What is the relation of t to z? In the case of the unit normal distribution, mean = 0 and variance = 1. Substituting those values, t reduces to $\bar{X}/1/\sqrt{n}$. If Xs are normally distributed, then the t-distribution reduces to $\sqrt{n}$. $\bar{X}$. The distribution is unchanged when multiplied by a constant, making the t-distribution normal, which states the NH for large samples, even as the t-distribution states it for the small samples.

Relative Values: Variance and Different Forms of Variance

We stated earlier that in the heart attack study, the focus was not on the absolute values, but on the relative values of the change in performance. The change was measured by the sum of squares of (observed *minus* expected) in terms of the expected frequencies of heart attack incidence if the (condition) had no impact (effect).

What happens when there are more than two conditions and two effects? Consider the choice of the best of three fertilizers. They can be tried on, say, four equal plots of land adjacent to one another. By choosing physically contiguous areas, we hold constant the several major factors that affect the yield per acre, such as sunshine and rainfall; the yield is the result of the fertilizers.

The "treatment" is the fertilizers (three); the "subject" is each different plot of land (four). We consider four plots of land, each treated with three different fertilizers. We compare the differences in the yield owing to the "treatment" expressed in terms of the differences in the yield owing to the "subject." NH says that there are no differences among the "treatments."

There is no difference between the variations owing to the "treatment" and the variations owing to the "subjects."

Unless this NH can be rejected, the "treatment" is ineffective. Notice that our test basis is not the absolute value of the yields, but their relative variances (see Biological Mission Application 1).

MARKET APPLICATION 1: PER CAPITA PERSONAL INCOME IN 1973, 1983, 2000

We will apply absolute values to identify SSD populations based on small sample values.

Data Set 1

We present in Table 4.2 the per capita personal income in constant (1972) dollars for 1973 and the projection for 2000 for the United States, for the New England region, and for the six states of the region.

The Null Hypothesis

There are six states in the New England region. The sum of the personal income for the six states in 1973 is 27.7 (in thousand of dollars), yielding a mean of 4.62, as shown in Table 4.3. However, this is different from the per capita personal income for the region of 5.0 shown in Table 4.2. The reason for the difference is that we are giving *equal* weight to the average of each state in the region, the largest (Massachusetts) and the smallest (Rhode Island) getting the same weight.

Table 4.2
Per Capita Personal Income in Constant (1972) Dollars

Region, And State	1973	2000
U.S.	4,740	7,369
New England	4,998	8,073
Maine	3,902	6,187
New Hampshire	4,436	7,413
Vermont	4,059	6,606
Massachusetts	5,075	8,207
Rhode Island	4,516	7,305
Connecticut	5,670	9,134

Table 4.3
Test of Significance of Difference between 1973 Per Capita Income: New England Region and the United States

U.S. per capita income (Population Mean) 4.7 (in $ Thousands)

	X_i	X_i^2
New England	5.0	
Maine	3.9	15.21
New Hampshire	4.4	19.36
Vermont	4.1	16.81
Massachusetts	5.1	26.01
Rhode Island	4.5	20.25
Connecticut	5.7	32.49
Total	27.7	130.13

$\overline{X}$ = 4.62 (in $ Thousands)
====

$$t = \frac{\overline{X} - \mu}{s_{\overline{x}} / \sqrt{n}} = \frac{4.62 - 4.70}{.6706* / 2.2361}$$

$$= \frac{-0.08 \times 2.2361}{.6706}$$

$$= \underline{-0.26676}$$

$$s_i^2 = N(\Sigma X_i^2) - (\Sigma X_i)^2 / N(N-1)$$

$$= \frac{6 \times 130.13 - (27.7)^2}{6 \times 5}$$

$$= 0.449667$$

$$s_i = 0.6706*$$

However, in Table 4.2 the census data arrive at the per capita income for the region by dividing the sum of the total personal income ($60.7 million) by the total population of the region (12.144 million), giving *unequal* weights to Massachusetts and Rhode Island.

$\bar{X} = 4.62$; $\mu = 4.7$. Can the population from which the $\bar{X}$ could have come be the same as the population with mean 4.7? In other words, could the New England region per capita personal income have come from the U.S. population per capita personal income?

There is no difference between the mean personal income (in 1972 dollars) of the population from which this sample could have come, and the 1973 mean personal income (in 1972 dollars) of the United States.

The Computation

In Table 4.3 we compute t, which comes to $-.26676$. The DF for the sample size $n = 6$ is $(6 - 1)$, or 5. From the t-table we find that the table value of t with 5 DF with 95% confidence is 2.57; with 99% confidence is 4.03. The computed t is $-.26676$. We ignore the sign in comparing the computed t with the table t because the t distribution, like the normal distribution, is symmetrical, and only the values of the right-hand side of the curve, the positive values, are shown in the statistical tables. We see that $-.26676$ is less than 2.57 (or 4.03). The computed $t <$ table t; accept the NH.

The Conclusion

The conclusion that there is no difference between the mean personal income (in 1972 dollars) of the New England region, and the United States may be wrong 1 in 100 times.

Data Set 2

We can compare the sample and population means; we can also compare two sample means. The comparison is really not between two sample means, but between the two population means that could have given rise to two sample means.

In Table 4.4 we find that the mean personal income $\bar{X}$ for the New England region in the year 2000 is 7.47, compared with 4.62 for the year 1973 in Table 4.3.

The Computation

We compute t. The numerator is the difference between $\bar{X}_1$ and $\bar{X}_2$ (instead of $\bar{X}_1$ and μ). The denominator is the square root of the weighted sum of the variances. The DF is $n_1 + n_2 - 2 = 6 + 6 - 2 = 10$. Computed t is -10.9033 As we did in Table 4.3, we ignore the sign of the value for the same reason. Computed t: $10.9033 >$ table t with 99.9% confidence: 4.59. Reject NH.

Table 4.4
Test of Significance of Difference between Per Capita Income in 1973 and 2000: New England Region

	X_i	X_i^2	
New England	8.1		
Maine	6.2	38.44	
New Hampshire	7.4	54.76	$t = \dfrac{\bar{X}_1 - \bar{X}_2}{s^2\left(\dfrac{n_1 + n_2}{n_1 \cdot n_2}\right)} = \dfrac{4.62 - 7.47}{0.7841670 \ast \times 12/36}$
Vermont	6.6	43.56	
Massachusetts	8.2	67.24	$= -10.9033$
Rhode Island	7.3	53.29	$s^2 = \dfrac{(n_1 s_1^2 + n_2 s_2^2)}{n_1 + n_2 - 2}$ $\dfrac{(5 \times 0.449667) + (5 \times 1.118667)}{6 + 6 - 2}$
Connecticut	9.1	82.81	
Total	44.8	340.10	$= 0.7841670 \ast$
$\bar{X} = 7.47$ (in \$Thousands)			

The Conclusion

The conclusion that *there is a difference* between the population of mean personal income in 1973 from which the sample could have come, and the population of mean personal income in 2,000 from which the same could have come may be wrong 1 in 1,000 times.

Meaning: Mean personal income (in 1972 dollars) in the New England region in 2000 will be statistically significantly higher than in 1973.

BIOLOGICAL MISSION APPLICATION 1: THE TIME FOR BLOOD COAGULATION WITH FOUR DIFFERENT DIETS

We will apply variations to determine SSD populations.

The Data

Does diet influence the time it takes blood to coagulate? The "treatments" are the "diets"; the "subjects" are "animals." Are the variations among the treatments SSD from those among the subjects? We will use the data from Box et al.:

The diets [A, B, C, and D] were randomly allocated to the [24] animals, and the blood samples were taken and tested in random order. [Analysis of Variance] can be precisely justified on the supposition that the data can be treated as random samples from four normal populations having the same variance and differing, if at all, only on their means.[9]

The Computation

We compute the F value in Table 4.5, which presents the data on the time it takes for the blood of 24 animals randomly selected for treatment by four diets to coagulate. The F value is the ratio of the variations *between treatments* (the diets) to variations *within treatments* (between animals). This test of variations is known as analysis of variance (ANOVA).

To find the *numerator,* we start with the mean value of each treatment and the grand mean. It is advisable to calculate the grand mean by *adding every value and dividing by the total number.* The average of the means will not necessarily be identical with the grand mean calculated directly from the total of all values.

The difference of each mean from the grand mean is squared, and multiplied by the number of subjects in each sample. For treatment A, $(64 - 61)^2 \times 4 = 36$; for B, $(64 - 66)^2 \times 6 = 24$; for C, $(64 - 68)^2 \times 6 = 96$; and for D, $(61 - 64)^2 \times 8 = 72$. The sum of the squares for treatments A, B, C, and D is $(36 + 24 + 96 + 72) = 228$. Because the sum is obtained over four treatments, the DF are $(4 - 1 =)$ 3, the mean square is $228/3 = 76$.

To find the *denominator,* we measure the variations among the subjects by summing for each treatment, the square of the difference between each subject and the mean value of the treatment. For diet A, $(60 - 61)^2 + (59 - 61)^2 + (63 - 61)^2 + (62 - 61)^2 = 10$; for B, $(65 - 66)^2 + (66 - 66)^2 + (67 - 66)^2 + (63 - 66)^2 + (64 - 66)^2 + (71 - 66)^2 = 40$; for C, $(71 - 68)^2 + (66 - 68)^2 + (68 - 68)^2 + (68 - 68)^2 + (67 - 68)^2 + (68 - 68)^2 = 14$; for D, $(62 - 61)^2 + (63 - 61)^2 + (60 - 61)^2 + (61 - 61)^2 + (64 - 61)^2 + (63 - 61)^2 + (56 - 61)^2 + (59 - 61)^2 = 48$. The sum of squares for subjects 1 through 24 is $(10 + 40 + 14 + 48 =)$ 112. The DF is the total number of observations (24) minus the total number of treatments (4), or 20. The mean square is $112/20 = 5.6$

The ratio of the numerator to the denominator is $76/5.6 = 14.8$. The table value of F for (3 DF in the columns and 20 DF in the rows) is 3.10 at 95% confidence and 4.94 at 99% confidence. Because the computed value > table value, reject the NH.

The Conclusion

The conclusion that *there is a difference* among the treatments may be wrong 1 in 100 times.

Meaning: The treatments may have differences in effect. Since treatment C registered the highest mean value of 68 seconds, that diet is most effective for delayed blood coagulation.

Table 4.5
Time for Blood to Coagulate of 24 Animals Randomly Allocated to Four Different Diets

Subjects \ Treatment	Diet A	Diet B	Diet C	Diet D
1			71	
2	60			
3				62
4		65		
5				63
6				60
7			66	
8		66		
9		67		
10	59			
11	63			
12		63		
13			68	
14		64		
15		71		
16			68	
17			67	
18				61
19				64
20	62			
21			68	
22				63
23				56
24				59
Total	244	396	408	488
No. of Subjects	4	6	6	8
Treatment Mean	61	66	68	61

Grand
Mean 64

CONCLUDING OBSERVATIONS

In chapter 3 we found that the NH underlying the χ^2 table was that the difference: (observed minus expected frequencies) is zero. When n is large, χ^2 tends toward the normal, as does the binomial. In chapter 3 we used the χ^2 distribution to reject the NH of no difference in the incidence of heart attack between those who took aspirin and those who took placebo. Because the n (= 22,071) is large, we now use the normal distribution instead.

What is the NH underlying the normal curve? In the standardized normal curve, mean = 0 and standard deviation = 1. De Moivre, who invented the "curve of the facility of errors" wanted to show that the original design of the universe was order[liness]. If we consider error as (ideal minus actual), an orderly universe would have the minimum error, or the maximum probability for the minimum error: mean 0 has the highest probability. To both De Moivre and Gauss, the *variation* from the central value was the deciding criterion: the higher the variation, the lower its probability, the very high and the very low being very few. However, we often use the central *value* to specify the substantive characteristic of interest, such as the 1986 per capita income. Thus the NH of the t distribution is (sample mean minus population mean) is zero.

While t illustrates NH based on *value*, ANOVA illustrates NH based on *variation*. When "subjects" are given different "treatments," the NH is that there is zero difference between "treatments." The F test measures the ratio of the variation owing to "treatment" to the variation owing to "subjects."

Per capita personal income and the time to coagulate of the blood of animals ("subjects") under different diets ("treatments") are *single* variables. Next, we turn to *multiple* variables: One or more variables (X_1 by itself or $X_1, X_2, \ldots, X_n$ together) account for the value of Y. The NH is that the change in Y corresponding to a change in X_1 ($i = 1$, or $i = 1, 2, \ldots, n$) is zero.

QUESTIONS: CONCEPTS AND COMPUTATIONS
FOR COMMITMENT

Our focus is decision-making, not number-crunching. Therefore, we divide the reinforcement of the text material into six categories: (1) Concepts: Foundational, (2) Concepts: Formulational, (3) Computations, (4) Conclusions, (5) [Resource] Commitments, and (6) Caveats. See chapter 11 for answers to questions for this chapter.

Concepts: Foundational

1. Distinguish between values and variations as the basis of NH.
2. What is the NH of (1) t table; F table?
3. State the conclusion about (1) the binomial fit to the coin toss data; (2) Pearsonian fit to the coin toss data; and (3) normal fit.
4. What was the basis of the NH in (3)—value or variation?

The Problem: Aspirin and Heart Attacks

5. We used the χ^2 table to test the heart attack data in chapter 3, and the normal curve table in chapter 4. Which test would you prefer? Why?

Concepts: Formulational

The Problem: "The Rich Getting Richer"

Is it true that the rich get richer and the poor get poorer? How would you test the proposition, given the data in Table 4.6?

6. Select two regions from the United States for comparison, giving reasons.
7. What minimum period would you choose? Why?
8. What is your NH?

The Problem: Admission Test Scores

The entrance examination scores of 447 college students have a mean of 121.6 and a standard deviation of 37.15. Tests of the data show that they are normally distributed.

9. How would you determine the minimum score for admission to a special program?
10. How would you determine the score to ensure that you select 17% of the top-scoring students?

The Problem: Selecting the Text

11. How would you choose one textbook from four, given the following final course grade of 20 students: Textbook 1: 66, 88, 77, 72; Textbook 2: 88, 89, 80, 77, 82, 79; Textbook 3: 100, 86, 96, 81, 95; Textbook 4: 73, 92, 99, 85, 67?

Computations

The Problem: "The Rich Getting Richer"

12. To test the proposition that the rich get richer and the poor get poorer, there has to be a minimum of four sets of values:

The "rich" income in time 1	income in time 2
The "poor" income in time 1	income in time 2

Which region is the richest in time 1 (1973)? The poorest? We see that the poorest region in 1973 remains the poorest in 2000, while the richest region in 1973 is the fourth richest in 2000, although its per capita personal income is 97.2% of the richest region in 2000.

13. Compute the mean and standard deviation of the two regions in 1973 and in 2000 (see Table 4.3).

Table 4.6
Per Capita Personal Income in Constant (1972) Dollars and Projections

Region and State	Actual 1973	Actual 1983	Projection 1990	Projection 2000
U.S.	4,750	5,470	6,434	7,369
South Atlantic	4,437	5,203	6,102	7,010
Delaware	5,370	5,905	6,830	7,709
Maryland	5,170	6,116	7,147	8,112
Dist. Columbia	5,735	7,339	8,453	9,467
Virginia	4,582	5,668	6,573	7,515
W.Virginia	3,692	4,295	5,127	5,996
North Carolina	4,012	4,594	5,490	6,373
South Carolina	3,692	4,302	5,155	6,054
Georgia	4,135	4,864	5,761	6,719
Florida	4,684	5,396	6,252	7,120
West S. Central	4,038	5,185	6,160	7,108
Arkansas	3,587	4,189	5,097	5,982
Louisiana	3,647	4,802	5,718	6,719
Oklahoma	4,053	5,126	6,120	7,121
Texas	4,235	5,452	6,435	7,356
Mountain	4,441	5,100	6,045	6,971
Montana	4,505	4,665	5,599	6,506
Idaho	4,277	4,473	5,365	6,290
Wyoming	4,768	5,562	6,752	7,928
Colorado	4,805	5,966	6,918	7,829
New Mexico	3,731	4,522	5,344	6,217
Arizona	4,445	4,976	5,971	6,891
Utah	3,852	4,217	5,026	5,899
Nevada	5,342	5,787	6,787	7,652
Pacific	5,110	6,057	6,978	7,906
Washington	4,826	5,692	6,624	7,492
Oregon	4,574	5,048	6,019	7,046
California	5,200	6,203	7,112	8,035
Alaska	5,774	8,023	9,025	9,958
Hawaii	5,226	5,701	6,517	7,461

Table 4.6—Continued

Region and State	Actual 1973	Actual 1983	Projection 1990	Projection 2000
U.S.	4,750	5,470	6,434	7,369
New England	4,998	6,099	7,108	8,073
Maine	3,902	4,619	5,341	6,187
New Hampshire	4,436	5,674	6,498	7,413
Vermont	4,059	4,664	5,679	6,606
Massachusetts	5,075	6,212	7,236	8,207
Rhode Island	4,516	5,472	6,371	7,305
Connecticut	5,670	6,993	8,146	9,134
Mid Atlantic	5,168	5,956	6,898	7,847
New York	5,351	6,094	6,979	7,854
New Jersey	5,534	6,558	7,663	8,662
Pennsylvania	4,662	5,372	6,271	7,256
East No.Central	4,975	5,403	6,462	7,402
Ohio	4,741	5,256	6,315	7,267
Indiana	4,695	4,955	6,069	7,042
Illinois	5,442	5,812	6,836	7,763
Milwauke	5,046	5,384	6,503	7,419
Wisconsin	4,556	5,297	6,276	7,232
West N. Central	4,888	5,303	6,322	7,262
Minnesotta	4,961	5,572	6,609	7,509
Iowa	5,110	5,009	6,151	7,132
Montana	4,469	5,171	6,078	6,984
North Dakota	6,088	5,456	6,359	7,288
South Dakota	4,756	4,617	5,495	6,435
Nebraska	5,016	5,236	6,257	7,244
Kansas	4,985	5,664	6,785	7,750
East So. Cent.	3,681	4,299	5,202	6,143
Kentucky	3,782	4,400	5,333	6,285
Tennessee	3,889	4,463	5,416	6,305
Alabama	3,619	4,318	5,192	6,170
Mississippi	3,267	3,827	4,649	5,601

Whether you choose the richest region in 1973 and the richest in 2000, or you choose the richest in 1973 and its value in 2000, you find that the n is different for the poorest region and the richest. You need Fisher's $t =$

$$(\bar{X}_1 - \bar{X}_2)\,(\sqrt{n_1 + n_2 - 2}).\,\sqrt{n_1 n_2 / n_1 + n_2} / \sqrt{s_1^2 + s_2^2}$$

Fisher's t is distributed as Student's t with $n_1 + n_2 - 2$ DF

s_1 is the standard deviation of X_1 whose sample size is n_1

s_2 is the standard deviation of X_2 whose sample size is n_2

14. Compute the t for time 1 (1973).
15. Compute the t for time 2 (2000).
16. Choose two levels of significance.

The Problem: Admissions Test Scores

17. Set the percentage of students you want for the special program, say, top 8%. Because the data are normally distributed, we use the normal curve table. Let the minimum score for admission to the special program be X. We know that the distance of X from the mean has to be expressed in standard deviation units: (X − mean/standard dev.). Substituting the values, we have (X − 121.6/37.15) = 8% of the area under the normal curve. Because the tables show only the positive half of the curve, should we take half of the 8%? *No, because we want only the top 8%,* not total 8% from the very high and the very low. So the computed z value should equal (.5000 − .0800 = .4200). We see that $z = 1.41$. The area from the mean to $z = 1.41$ is .4207, leaving the area to the right of $z = 1.41$ as .0793.

$$Z = \frac{X - 121.6}{37.15} = 1.41 \quad X = 173.98$$

To check our result, let us see what percentage of the students will score 173.98 or above. (173.98 − 121.6/37.15) gives a z value of 1.4099. From the table, the area from the mean to $z = 1.4099$ is .4207. The percentage of students scoring at or above 173.98 is (.5000 − .4207 =) .0793.

18. Follow the same procedure as in #17 for problem #10.

The Problem: Selecting the Text

19. What is the "treatment"? What is the "subject"?
20. What is the NH?
21. Develop a table of correspondence to randomly allocate course grades.
22. Set up the table of "subjects" and "treatment" (see Table 4.5).
23. Determine the numerator (see Biological Mission Application 1).
24. Determine the denominator (see Biological Mission Application 1).
25. Select two levels of significance of the F values.

Conclusions

The Problem: "The Rich Getting Richer"

26. Develop the conclusion of 1973 data comparison following the three steps specified in chapter 3 to develop the conclusion format.
27. Develop similarly the conclusion of 2000 data comparison.
28. State the conclusion of the 1973 data comparison; interpret.
29. State the conclusion of the 2000 data comparison; interpret.
30. Develop the conclusion of the textbook problem per format.
31. State the conclusion; interpret.

[Resource] Commitments

The Problem: "The Rich Getting Richer"

32. As chairman of the Presidential Blue Ribbon Commission on Abolition of Poverty, develop three operational recommendations to reduce the gap between the rich and the poor states.

The Problem: Selecting the Text

33. Which textbook would you adopt? Why?

Caveats

The Problem: "The Rich Getting Richer"

34. Are the data on per capita income random for your purposes?

The Problem: Admission Test Scores

35. Are the entrance exam scores random for your purposes?

The Problem: Selecting the Text

36. Are the data on the course grade of students random for your purposes?
37. To what extent are your results and recommendations invalid?

NOTES

1. George K. Chacko, *Applied Statistics in Decision-making* (New York: Elsevier, 1971), ch. 11.
2. Abraham De Moivre, *Approximatio Ad Summam Terminorum Binomii* (London: 1733).
3. Helen M. Walker, *Studies in the History of Statistical Method* (Baltimore: Williams & Wilkins, 1931), p. 16.

4. Karl Pearson, communication in *Nature,* April 17, 1926.

5. Abraham De Moivre, *The Doctrine of Chances: Or a Method of Calculating the Probability of Events in Play* (London: 1718).

6. Pierre-Simon, Marquis De Laplace, *A Philosophical Essay on Probabilities,* tr. from the 6th French ed. by Truescott and Emory. (New York: 1901).

7. Carl Friedrich Gauss, *Theoria Motus,* tr. by Charles Henry Davis (Washington, D.C.: 1857).

8. Walker, *Studies,* pp. 22, 24.

9. George E. P. Box, William G. Hunter, and J. Stuart Hunter, *Statistics for Experimenters* (New York: Wiley, 1978), p. 165.

Part III Multiple-Variable Decision-Making with Very Many Data Points

Part III
Multiple-Variable Decision-Making with Very Many Data Points

5 Pairwise and Groupwise Togetherness

OVERVIEW: From single variables, such as per capita income and the time for blood to coagulate, we turn to multiple variables.

Sir Francis Galton contributed the concepts of regression and correlation in 1886 when he investigated the phenomenon of the general characteristics of the population remaining unchanged over generations. He studied the relation between the heights of fathers and sons, and postulated that the height regresses toward mediocrity (the middle), the taller parents producing shorter children and the shorter parents producing taller children, keeping the height steady at the middle level.

We study the relation between age and height of students in two sections of an upper division statistics class. The computational formulas for the regression equations are developed and applied with Y as the height and X as the age. Regression asks, given a value of X, what is the corresponding value of Y? Each value of Y is associated with a range, reflecting the error in estimating Y from X.

In multiple regression, Y is related to many variables, not just one. After introducing the basic concepts using illustrative numerical data, we consider a real-life universal problem: How to influence salesmanship to improve sales?

The sales of the top 25 out of a total of 55 salesmen of a durable goods company are chosen. The commission earned by the salesmen is based on a complicated formula, but that is the most tangible reward. Should the management raise the commission?

The sales by the salesmen and the commission they earn depend on the sales potentials of the sales territory. Through advertising, the company can make its name recognition easier for the customers. Should the management increase advertising? Unlike in multiple linear regression, where the effects of one variable can be added to the effects of the other variables, the effects of advertising and commission appear to interact. *This interaction is recognized in a nonlinear multiplicative model that is* linear in logarithms. *We find that the exponents add up to more than 1, indicating that when commission increases by 10%, sales increase by 14.64%.*

After studying decision-making with very many data points, we turn next to important decisions made with very few data points.

SOCIAL MISSION APPLICATION 5: "REGRESSION TOWARD MEDIOCRITY IN HEREDITARY STATURE"

The law of error (the normal curve) enormously influenced Sir Francis Galton, who originated the concepts of correlation and regression in his 1886 above-named paper.

Application of the Normal Curve to Moral Statistics

As we saw in chapter 4, Gauss was motivated to develop the normal curve because of his interest in the accuracy of orbital motion. The application of the normal curve to moral statistics was due to a Belgian royal astronomer named Adolphe Quetelet, whose "studies in moral statistics opened a new field of statistical research, the sphere of human actions. . . . The influence of such factors as sex, age, education, climate, and seasons on criminal tendencies . . . [were] significant in the development of the methods, concepts, and scope of statistics."[1]

Application of the Normal Curve to Human Stature

Galton was also quite interested in applying the law of error to the study of human measurements. In his words:

I need hardly remind the reader that the Law of Error upon which these Normal Values are based, was excogitated for the use of astronomers and others who are concerned with extreme accuracy of measurement and without the slightest idea until the time of Quetelet that they might be applicable to human measures. . . . The Law of Error finds a footing wherever the individual peculiarities are wholly due to the combined influence of a multitude of "accidents" in the sense in which the word has already been defined. . . . In particular, the *agreement of the Curve of Stature with the Normal Curve is very fair*, and forms the mainstay of my inquiry into the laws of Natural Inheritance. [emphasis added].[2]

Galton's Method

Galton's 1886 paper presents a correlation chart and both regression lines. He had asked J. D. Hamilton Dickson to "kindly investigate for me the Surface or

Frequency of Error that would result from these three data: [(i) the average regression of the stature of offspring from midparent, (ii) *variability Q* for the general population, and (iii) Q for the fraternity]."[3]

Galton wondered how it was possible for an entire population to remain alike in general features, as a whole, during many successive generations, if the *average* product of each couple resembles the parents. To study the inheritance of size, he raised sweet peas and asked his friends to do the same for him; and he noted the size of the seeds produced corresponding to the different sizes of the seeds sown. These studies suggested to him the law of *reversion*, his earlier name for *regression*, the heights of offsprings "regressing" toward the mean.

Galton called the average of the stature of the parents "mid-parent"; and of the offsprings, "mid-fraternity." He developed the correlation tables, "*Tables of Stature.*" He used Q for (1) general population, (2) mid-parents, and (3) for each co-fraternity, comprising all the adult sons and transmuted daughters of a *group* of mid-parents who had the same stature. He found that Q for the various co-fraternities to be about the same, whether the mid-parents were tall or short. "However paradoxical it may appear at first sight, it is theoretically a necessary fact, and one that is clearly confirmed by observation, that the Stature of the adult offspring must on the whole be more *mediocre* than the stature of their parents" (emphasis added).[4]

SOCIAL MISSION APPLICATION 6: SIMPLE REGRESSION OF HEIGHT ON AGE OF UPPER DIVISION STUDENTS

To Galton, the question was, given the stature of the mid-parent, what is the corresponding stature of the offspring?

We can generalize the problem of simple regression as:

Given a value of X, what is the corresponding value of Y?

Linear Relationship between X and Y

We postulate that Y (offspring stature) is related to X (mid-parent stature) linearly. Linear regression requirements are:

1. X and Y are independent normal random variables, and
2. Their effects are additive.

Additivity means that the effect of one variable can be added to that of another (others). They do *not* interact; There are no XY-, XZ-, or XYZ-type terms.

$Y = a + bX$ is the regression equation.

X and Y are variables and a and b are parameters. For each set of data, a specific a, and a specific b value have to be determined.

We want the expected values derived from the equation $Y = a + bX$ to be closest to the observed values. When the expected value is the same as the observed value, the quantity (observed minus expected) is zero. If we square it, the quantity (observed minus expected)^2 will also be zero if $Y = a + bX$ is a perfect fit to the data.

Empirical Data

Table 5.1 presents the data on age and height of 78 students in Section I of my statistics class, and Table 5.2, the same data of 52 students in Section II. Abate is Student No. 1 in Section I; Agran is Student No. 2. Abate's height is Y_1, and age X_1, the subscript denoting that the data are the values of the first subject. Similarly, the second subject's height and age are, respectively, Y_2 and X_2. We see that Y can have subscripts 1, 2, . . . , 78; so also X can have subscripts 1, 2, . . . , 78, since there are 78 pairs of observations for Section I.

Normal Equations

Given $X_1 = 25$, what is the corresponding Y? Again, given X_2, what is the corresponding Y_2? In other words, how can we derive 68 inches height from Abate's age of 25 years and Agran's 73 inches height from his age of 19 years? We can look on 68 as $(25 \times 2) + 18$, or $(25 \times 3) - 7$. We can look on 73 as $(19 \times 3) + 16$, or $(19 \times 4) - 3$. In other words, (X times a constant) + a remainder. We want to find the *same constant, b,* that will apply to all the 78 values; and similarly, the *same remainder, a.*

$Y_1 = bX_1 + a$	Abate:	$68 = b. 25 + a$
$Y_2 = bX_2 + a$	Agran:	$73 = b. 19 + a$
. . . .		
$Y_{78} = bX_{78} + a$	Redholtz:	$63 = b. 20 + a$

$$\overline{\Sigma Yi = b\ \Sigma Xi + n\ a} \quad (i = 1, 2, \ldots , n) \qquad \text{Normal Equation I}$$

Since there are 78 a's, their sum $= 78\ a$, or $n.a$. What may not be obvious is the sum of 78 $b.x._i$. If b were 3, we would apply it to the ages of Abate and Agran as $(3 \times 25) + (3 \times 19)$. Their sum is *not* $(3 + 3)(25 + 1)$. The common multiple is factored out and applied to each X- value: $(3)(25 + 19) = (3)(44) = 132$, which we verify is the same as $(75 + 57)$.

We now derive normal equation II by applying the principle that an equation

Table 5.1
Age and Height Data of Upper-Division Statistics Students: Section 1

No.	Name Male Students	X Age Years	Y Height Inches
1	Abate	25	68
2	Agran	19	73
3	Alexander	20	67
4	Banks	24	71
5	Barg	20	69
6	Barker	33	72
7	Berns	21	66
8	Berger	21	70
9	Blanchard	20	70
10	Blue	20	71
11	Brown	20	72
12	Chaleff	19	70
13	Cross	20	71
14	Cucher	20	68
15	Daniels	20	67
16	Davidson	20	73
17	De Renziz	21	71
18	Doesburg	19	74
19	Dolan	20	68
20	Doran	21	72
21	Drain	20	68
22	Dobkin	21	69
23	Ferber	20	69
24	Gleed	23	75
25	Goldberg	20	70
26	Gonor	19	71
27	Gonzales	20	64
28	Grossman	21	71
29	Grotch	19	73
30	Gutierrez	25	72
31	Haden	20	66

Table 5.1—Continued

No.	Name Male Students	X Age Years	Y Height Inches
32	Hausner	21	71
33	Havert	19	68
34	Hongis	19	66
35	Hori	22	62
36	Jacobs	21	72
37	Kaufman	19	72
38	Kent	20	70
39	Kevany	22	70
40	Lainer	19	66
41	Levitz	20	72
42	Lucha	37	70
43	Mahan	19	68
44	Maron	19	67
45	Merrill	22	70
46	Morrison	19	71
47	Nehamen	19	69
48	Newson	21	73
49	Polen	22	70
50	Poll	20	68
51	Popkoff	18	74
52	Ritchey	24	74
53	Ross	21	71
54	Ruth	22	69
55	Schor	20	69
56	Shirk	21	73
57	Siegel	19	67
58	Spencer	20	71
59	Stern	22	68
60	Streetmaker	20	70
61	Stuman	19	72
62	Sussman	20	71
63	Taran	20	72

Table 5.1—Continued

No.	Name Male Students	X Age Years	Y Height Inches
64	Turner	19	73
65	Vincent	21	72
66	Weldon	22	72
67	Wells	21	70
68	Wessel	20	72
69	Williams	28	72
70	Wolfe	20	67
71	Wright	20	71
72	Zoss	19	66
No.	Name Female Students	X Age Years	Y Height Inches
73	Atherton	21	68
74	Bowser	21	72
75	Ferring	19	62
76	Janecek	20	67
77	Mader	19	66
78	Redholtz	20	63

remains unchanged if both sides are multiplied by the same quantity. We will multiply both sides of the equation by X_i.

$Y_1 = bX_1 + a$ when multiplied by X_1 yields:

$X_1Y_1 = bX_1X_1 + aX_1$ Similarly, for other X_i $(i = 2, \ldots, 78)$

$X_2Y_2 = bX_2X_2 + aX_2$

. . . .

$X_iY_i = bX_iX_i + aX_i$ $\cdots\cdots\cdots\cdots$ General Term

. . . .

$X_{78}Y_{78} = bX_{78}X_{78} + aX_{78}$

$\overline{\Sigma X_iY_i = b_i\Sigma X_i^2 + a\Sigma X_i}$ $(i = 1, 2, \ldots, n)$ Normal Equation II

Table 5.2
Age and Height Data of Upper-Division Statistics Students: Section 2

No.	Name Male Students	X Age Years	Y Height Inches
1	Adamoli	21	66
2	Ball	29	72
3	Bandich	20	68
4	Berger	20	70
5	Bowman	24	73
6	Brickman	19	66
7	Cassady	23	71
8	Cole	21	72
9	De Olden	24	72
10	Dicknirder	20	72
11	Elliott	19	70
12	Ford	27	60
13	Gingold	20	73
14	Goldstein	20	68
15	Gottlieb	21	71
16	Greines	20	72
17	Gross	22	72
18	Gutterman	24	69
19	Hagen	20	66
20	Hammond	20	72
21	Hellwig	20	73
22	Hemmersbach	27	73
23	Holl	21	73
24	Holloway	21	70
25	Holloway	20	68
26	Jackson	22	70
27	Luebbe	25	71
28	Maher	19	75
29	Masinter	20	72
30	Nicholasen	34	72
31	Nonak	23	71

Table 5.2—Continued

No.	Name Male Students	X Age Years	Y Height Inches
32	Ogasawka	22	68
33	Okura	20	67
34	Packer	19	66
35	Pepper	19	71
36	Peterson	21	70
37	Plummer	27	72
38	Richards	23	68
39	See	20	72
40	Shelley	20	69
41	Temmerman	22	73
42	Thomas	20	74
43	Tom	19	66
44	Torres	21	74
45	Waehrer	21	70
46	Youndt	20	70

No.	Name Female Students	X Age Years	Y Height Inches
47	Erickson	20	68
48	Foster	19	64
49	Greenwell	20	62
50	Keel	32	60
51	McNellis	20	68
52	Slattery	19	67

Normal equations I and II have to be simultaneously satisfied for a and b to have the property that the sum of the (observed minus expected) is a minimum for all the 78 observations. We are "observing" X and Y take successive values of 1, 2, . . . , 78. Or, X_i and Y_i are assuming values of $i = 1, 2, . . . , 78$. We are trying to make a function of (observed minus expected) as close to zero as possible. That function is the quantity (observed minus expected)^2. The *sum* of the *squares* for all the observations should be as close to zero, or the *least: Least [sum of] Squares.* The principle of least squares was first published by Legendre in 1805. We have developed the least squares solution to the age-height problem elsewhere.[5] The solution $(i = 1, 2, \ldots, n)$ is:

$$b = \frac{n \, \Sigma \, X_i Y_i \, - \, \Sigma X_i \, \Sigma Y_i}{n \, \Sigma (X_i)^2 \, - \, (\Sigma \, X_i)^2}$$

n. sum of products minus product of sums
divided by
n. sum of squares minus squares of sums

$$a = \Sigma \, Y_i - b \, \Sigma X_i / n \qquad (i = 1, 2, \ldots, n)$$

The Computation

The equation fitted to the age-height data of Section I is:

$$Y = 66.6188 + .1526 \, X$$

The corresponding equation fitted to Section II is:

$$Y = 71.4440 - .0740 \, X$$

The equation fitted to both the sections together is:

$$Y = 68.8260 + .0467 \, X$$

The Null Hypothesis

The regression coefficient *b* states by how much 1 unit of *X* changes *Y*. For Section I, $b = .1526$. When the age increases by 1, say from 19 to 20, the height increases by .1526 inch:

Age $X = 19$ Height $Y = 66.6188 + .1526 \times 19 = 69.52$ inches
Age $X = 20$ Height $Y = 66.6188 + .1526 \times 20 = 69.67$ inches

When age increases by 1, height increases by $(69.67 - 69.52 =) \, .15$ inch. Similarly, when age decreases, height decreases: $(69.67 - 69.52 =) \, .15$ inch.
The null hypothesis is that the rate of change is zero. Formally,

There is no difference between the population from which this sample regression coefficient could have come, and the population in which the regression coefficient is zero.

Test of Significance of the Regression Coefficient

The regression coefficient to estimate Y (height) from X (age) is b. The population regression coefficient is β. Their difference is divided by the sample *standard error of b*, which is a function of the standard error of estimate and the standard deviation of X.

Step 1: The *standard deviation of X* is computed as follows:

$$s_x = \sqrt{n \,(\Sigma X_i^2) - (\Sigma X_i)^2 \,/\, (n) \,(n - 1)} = 2.8409 \;(i = 1, 2, \ldots, n)$$

It stands to reason that the standard error of the rate of change of Y with respect to X would be the ratio of the spread of Y to the spread of X:

$$\frac{\text{the standard error of estimate of } Y \text{ from } X}{\text{the standard deviation of } X}$$

Step 2: The *standard error of estimate of Y from X* is computed as follows: When we estimated the expected height of a 19-year-old as 69.52 inches, the observed height of one particular 19-year-old, Agran, was found to be 73 inches, making the quantity: (observed − expected) to be (73.0 − 69.52 =) 3.48; its square 12.11.

The observed height of the first student, aged 20, Alexander, is 67.52 inches. The regression equation estimated his expected height to be 69.67 inches. The quantity: (observed − expected) is (67.5 − 69.67 =) − 2.17; its square, 4.71. The sum of all such squares using data expressed with one significant decimal for Section I is 566.78.

What we have done is to subtract from the observed Y (e.g., 73 for Agran, 67.5 for Alexander) the corresponding expected Y, obtained from the expression: $a + bx$. Thus,

$$Y_1 - (a + b_1 X_1) \quad \text{Agran: } 73 - (66.6188 + .1526 \times 19) = 3.48$$
$$Y_3 - (a + b_3 X_3) \quad \text{Alexander: } 67.5 - (66.6188 + .1526 \times 20) = -2.17$$

In general, $Y_i - (a + b_i X_i)$, obtained by using $Y_i = a + bX_i$.

If we multiply both sides of the equation by the identical quantity Y_i, the equation is unchanged. Multiplying and transposing,

$Y_1 Y_1$	$- Y_1$	$- bX_1 Y_1$	
$Y_2 Y_2$	$- aY_2$	$- X_2 a\, Y_2$	
. . . .			
$Y_i Y_i$	$- aY_i$	$- b\, X_i Y_i$	. . . . General Term
. . . .			
$Y_{78} Y_{78}$	$- aY_{78}$	$- bX_{78} \cdot Y_{78}$	

$$\Sigma Y_i^2 \qquad - a\Sigma Y_i \qquad - b\Sigma X_i Y_i \qquad (i = 1, 2, \ldots, n)$$

The standard error of estimates of Y from X is:

$$s_{Y.X} = \sqrt{\Sigma Y_i^2 - a\Sigma Y_i - b\Sigma X_i\, Y_i/n - 2}\ (i = 1, 2, \ldots, n)$$

What is the DF of the standard error of estimate? It depends on the number of independent linear restrictions imposed on the data. One linear restriction is that the sum of the X's be a specified quantity; another is that the sum of the Y's be another specified quantity. We subtract these two DF lost, owing to the independent linear restrictions, from the total number of observations, 78, to get 76. The sum of squares for Section I, 566.78, is divided by 76 to yield its square root 2.73 as the *standard error estimate*.

Step 3: The t value is computed to test if the sample came from a population whose regression coefficient is zero. The numerator is the (sample b minus the population β). The denominator is the *standard error of b*.

$$s_{b_{Y.X}} = s_{Y.X}/s_X \cdot \sqrt{n-1} = 2.73/2.8409. \ \sqrt{78-1}$$
$$= 2.73/24.9288 = .1095$$

The numerator is $b - \beta = .1526 - 0 = .1526$.

$t = .1526/.1095 = 1.3936$

Table t with $(78 - 2)$ DF with 95% confidence is 1.99.

Table t with $(78 - 2)$ DF with 99% confidence is 2.38.

Since (computed $t <$ table t), accept the NH.

The Conclusion

The conclusion that there is no difference between the population regression coefficient and zero may be wrong 1 in 20 times, or 1 in 100 times.

The reader may verify that the t for Section II is $-.5085$.

REGRESSION AND CORRELATION

The (X_1, Y_1), (X_2, Y_2), etc. relationship pairs the X and Y together; it is a *pairwise togetherness* relationship.

Correlation: Groupwise Togetherness

Instead of looking at each pair of values of the 2 variables, we could look at the X's and Y's as a group. How do all the data points cluster together as a group? Are they very close; or are they very far apart? The *groupwise togetherness* is correlation. It will be recalled that both the terms, regression and correlation, were coined by Karl Pearson in 1886.

Correlation being a mutual relationship between X and Y is reversible: $r_{(X,Y)} = r_{(Y,X)}$, unlike $b_{Y.X} \neq b_{X.Y}$. The range of values of correlation is -1 to $+1$, while b can take any value from $-\infty$ to $+\infty$.

Relationship between Correlation and Regression

Since r describes the collective relationship of $b_{Y.X}$ and $b_{X.Y}$, it is only logical that they be related to each other. As shown elsewhere, if we multiply the computational formulas for $b_{Y.X}$ and $b_{X.Y}$, its square root will yield the computational formula for r.[6]

$$r_{X,Y} = \sqrt{b_{Y.X} \cdot b_{X.Y}}$$

Test of Significance of the Correlation Coefficient

X and Y are independent normal random variables. We test if the population value of the correlation coefficient is zero, using t:

$$t = r\sqrt{n - 2} \ / \ \sqrt{1 - r^2} \text{ is distributed with } n - 2 \text{ DF.}$$

MULTIPLE REGRESSION

We have considered the linear relationships between age (X) and height (Y) in Tables 5.1 and 5.2; in fact, several variables such as age (X_1), weight (X_2), . . . , (X_n) could be related to height (Y).

Multiple Correlation, R

$R_{(X_1, X_2, \ldots, X_n, Y)}$ specifies the groupwise togetherness of n (*independent*) variables that affect the outcome of (*dependent*) variable Y. The range of R is from -1 to $+1$.

Illustrative Data

Table 5.3 presents illustrative data for multiple regression computation. The first set of values of X_1, X_2, X_3, and X_4 are, respectively, 3, 4, 5, and 6; the second set of values are 6, 7, 8, and 9. Corresponding to the first set of X values, Y is 10; and corresponding to the second set of X values, Y is 13.

Simple Correlations

The simple correlations between pairs of X's, such as (X_1, X_2) is .995466; (X_1, X_3) is .990057; (X_1, X_4) is .986446. This very high correlation means that X_1, for instance, explains 99.54% of X_2, making it superfluous to know both the variables; only one would do. Of course, the reason we get these high correlation values is because we have chosen the numbers sequentially: 3, 4, 5, 6, and 6, 7, 8, 9.

Table 5.3
Multiple Regression: Illustrative Numerical Data

X_1	X_2	X_3	X_4	Y
3	4	5	6	10
6	7	8	9	13
2	4	5	7	7
9	11	13	14	19
13	14	15	17	25
16	18	19	22	30

Multiple Correlation

The formula to compute R, the multiple correlation, is too cumbersome for manual calculations. However, we will discuss the results obtained from the computer calculations of Table 5.3 data. $R = .990205$. It means that 99.02% of Y is explained by X_i ($i = 1, 2, 3, 4$).

Partial Correlations

We found that the simple correlations indicate that the X_is are interdependent to such a degree that if we know one, the other is virtually completely known. What would happen if we held all the four variables, except one, say, X_3, constant, and then ask, How much of the Y is explained by that single variable? In the present case the question is moot because the simple correlations themselves are very close to 1. However, we will see in Market Application 2 that partial correlation is most useful in real-life instances.

> **Partial correlation: The association of one "independent" variable with the "dependent" variable Y, when the other "independent" variables are held constant. It is measured as the percentage of Y explained by one variable, when the remaining variables are held constant.**

Multiple Regression Equation

The multiple regression equation to the Table 5.3 data is:

$$Y = 2.0863 + 3.21794\, X_1 - 4.5237\, X_2 + 1.2622\, X_3 + 1.52234\, X_4.$$

This shows us that the variable that has the greatest influence on Y is X_2, although the effect is negative. For each unit increase in X_2, Y *decreases* by 4.5237 units. The next most influential variable is X_1: Each unit of increase in X_1 *increases* the value of Y by 3.21794 units. Slightly half as much influence is wielded by X_4; one unit increase in X_4 causes Y to *increase* by 1.52334. The least influential is X_3; one unit increase in X_3 increases Y by 1.2622 units.

MARKET APPLICATION 2: EFFECT OF SALES COMMISSION AND ADVERTISING OUTLAY ON SALES (BOOKINGS)

A perennial problem faced by corporations is, How should salesmen (saleswomen) spend their work hours? Time is in short supply; even more so is talent. Can multiple regression help?

How to Stimulate Sales (Bookings)?

Given that the salesperson effort is the most important element, what can corporate management do about it? Can we identify some things that the better salesmen do which may profitably be emulated by others?

Selecting the Y Variable

A durable goods manufacturer with five plants in the United States depends exclusively on 55 salesmen to "book" orders for the various products of the corporation. It takes months and even years to cultivate the customers who would place orders for hundreds and even thousands of units at one time. What is the appropriate system measure? We specify Y as *total bookings by state*.

Selecting the X Variables

Because the salesmen's commission depends on sales (actually, "*bookings,*" which are the *orders* placed; they do not become sales until the orders are met by shipment of products acceptable to the customers), it would be logical to consider commission as an X variable that influences the Y variable. What motivates the salesman most is his commission. So we specify X_1 as the *commission earned by state*. When a salesman sells in more than one state, his commission and bookings are prorated. We selected the 25 top salesmen, accounting for 46.89% of the commissions earned by all the salesmen in a given six-month period. Commissions are calculated on a complicated nonlinear formula.

Both the bookings and the commissions depend on the potential of the territory. *Advertising outlay* (X_2) would help the salesman better realize the sales potential of the territory (see Table 5.4).

Table 5.4
Multiple Regression of Commission Earned by State and Advertising Outlay on Bookings

State	logarithm of Bookings by State	logarithm of Commiss. by State	logarithm of Advertising by State
REGION I			
Connecticut	5.064083	3.885926	3.323252
New Jersey	5.274850	4.216957	3.665206
New York	5.405346	4.225051	3.226600
Massachusetts	5.249198	4.144263	3.282169
Washington,D.C.	5.082067	3.925570	2.881385
Maine, Vermont, NH	3.924072	3.203033	3.102434
Virginia	5.080626	3.887561	3.381837
Pennsylvania	4.960280	3.835120	3.308991
REGION II			
Minnesota	5.025715	3.903795	3.366610
Illinois	4.852541	3.725993	3.297761
Missouri	4.814714	3.669503	3.486855
Indiana	4.994977	3.922414	3.516535
Michigan-Salesman I	4.976533	3.816705	3.469380
Michigan-SM II	5.131619	4.023252	3.469380
Ohio	5.072617	3.959280	3.382917
REGION III			
California-SM I	4.794767	3.578754	3.381296
California-SM II	4.910624	3.854063	3.381296
California-SM III	4.767156	3.549861	3.381296
Arizona	4.674953	3.538197	2.888741
Wash.,Oreg.,Mont.,Ida.	5.114277	3.943890	3.468200
REGION IV			
Florida	5.056905	3.815910	3.483016
Alabama	4.812445	3.667826	2.932474
Georgia	4.961326	3.791340	3.350054
Tennessee	5.259594	4.034628	2.995196
REGION V			
Texas	5.015360	3.907841	3.497344

Nonadditive Effects

Let us say something called "*salesmanship*" is what accounts for the bookings by the salesmen. The better the "salesmanship," the higher the bookings as a fraction of the territory potential. To realize the potentials of the territory, the top management can invest in "salesmanship." Commission is one form of investment in "salesmanship"; advertising is another. We can consider the top management stimulating the salesmen to realize the potentials of their territory through *commission* and *advertising*.

The simplest assumption is that the effect of commission on bookings is *independent* of the effect of advertising on booking. *If* the two variables X and Y are independent, *then* their effects are *additive*. That is the meaning of the "+" sign in the equation $Y = a + b_1 X_1 + b_2 X_2$; the effect of X_1 is added to the effect of X_2.

But could we not say that the better the advertisement, the better the company name recognition by the customers, and therefore the more successful the salesmen's performance? In other words, the effects are *interactive,* not additive. We will see how this interactive effect can be handled by converting the nonlinear equation into linear form.

Douglas Production Function

A similar question was studied by Paul H. Douglas and his associates in 1928.[7] Their question was, By how much will the annual physical output of a firm increase when the labor is increased by 1%; when the capital is increased by 1%; and when both are increased by 1%? He found the answer was best represented by the equation $Y = A.X_1^{\alpha} . X_2^{\beta}$, where

Y denotes the annual physical output

X_1 denotes the manpower of the firm

X_2 denotes the capital of the firm

α denotes the elasticity of the output with respect to labor

β denotes the elasticity of output with respect to capital

Returns to Scale

Recall that the top management question is, By how much will bookings rise if commission is increased by 1%; if advertising is increased by 1%? If $\alpha + \beta = 1$, then the industry is operating under *constant returns* to scale. It means that a 10% increase in *each* of the *inputs,* labor and capital, will result in a 10% increase of the output. If, on the other hand, the sum were greater than 1 (*increasing returns*), say 1.5, then 10% increase in capital and labor would result in *15% increase in output.* If the sum were less than 1 (*decreasing returns*), say, 0.75, then 10% increase in capital and labor would result in a *25% decrease in the output*.

Linear in Logarithms

The relation of commission and advertising to bookings is: $Y = AX_1{}^\alpha \cdot X_2{}^\beta$. Taking logarithms, it reduces to an equation linear in logarithms:

$\log Y = \log A + \alpha \log X_1 + \beta \log X_2$, where

Y is the salesman bookings by state

X_1 is the salesman commission by state

X_2 is the advertising outlay by state

α is the elasticity of bookings with respect to commission

β is the elasticity of bookings with respect to advertising.

The Results

The multiple regression is:

$$Y = .5549 + 1.1708 \, X_1 + (-.0244) \, X_2.$$

The values are logarithms. $R_{Y.X_1X_2} = .9437$, which means that 94.37% of Y is explained by X_1 and X_2. The standard error of estimate of R is .0218. Assuming that the three variables are independent, normal, and random, between 90.01% and 98.73% of Y is explained by X_1 and X_2 two-thirds of the time.

Increasing Returns to Scale

The sum of the exponents of X_1 and $X_2 = 1.1708 - .0244 = 1.1464$. Because their sum > 1, 10% increase in the outlay on commission and advertising would increase bookings by 14.64%.

Partial Correlations

We find that $r_{Y_{X_1}X_2} = .9407$, $r_{Y_{X_2}X_1} = -.0527$.

Commission explains 94.07% of bookings when advertising is held constant, while advertising explains −5.27% when commission is held constant. The partial correlation of commission, 94.07%, is extremely close to the multiple correlation, 94.37%, lending credence to the conclusion that commission has the overwhelming role in explaining bookings. The negative sign of the partial correlation of advertising suggests that without commission, advertising would, if anything, *decrease* bookings.

CONCLUDING OBSERVATIONS

In chapter 4 we found that the standard statistical tables are founded on null hypotheses. We classified them into two groups: values and variations. When assessing a sample mean, we use the NH of *value*—that the *difference* between the value of the mean of the population from which the sample could have come and a given population mean value is zero. In other words, the sample came from the given population.

In chapter 5 we examined the NH based not on value, but on *variations about the value*. The Normal Curve of Error provided a continuing theme from the previous chapter. While the focus of Gauss and others was on the accuracy of astronomical observations, Galton and others focused on human measurements. He wondered what prevented the heights of succeeding generations from increasing indefinitely. He experimented with the size of successive generations of peas; and explained that pea size and human heights tend toward the mediocre (middle), the tall fathers producing shorter children and shorter fathers producing taller children, managing to keep the population height stable around the mean.

The general problem of regression is, Given a value of X, what is the corresponding value of Y? We examined the problem empirically with the data on 78 upper division students in one section of a statistics class, and 52 in the other: Given a value of X (age), what is the corresponding value of Y (height)? In Section I, when age increases by one year, height increases by .1526. This rate of increase is b, the regression coefficient. We test if b comes from a population with $\beta = 0$, or if age and height are *un*related to each other, by using the *variation* of height estimated from age and the variation of age around its mean value.

Regression specifies the Y corresponding to an X (*pairwise togetherness*), while correlation specifies the clustering of all the (X,Y) pairs (*groupwise togetherness*). Simple regression relates Y with X, while multiple regression relates Y with X_i ($i = 1, 2, \ldots, n$). We examined multiple regression concepts with the help of arbitrary data, and proceeded to a real-life application: How much should top management invest in salesmen's commission and how much in advertising?

The second variables—commission (X_1) and advertising (X_2)—could *not* be considered independent in their effect on sales ("bookings"). Their effects are *not additive:* they are *interactive.* Drawing on Paul Douglas's work in 1928 to establish by how much the output of a firm would rise if inputs of capital and labor were increased by 10%, we formulated the equation $Y = A. X_1^{\alpha} X_2^{\beta}$ and solved it using logarithms, obtaining an equation that is linear in logarithms: bookings would increase by 14.64% when outlay on commission and advertising is increased by 10%.

In chapters 3, 4, and 5 we considered decision-making with very many data points. However, many important decisions have to be made with very few data points. How can their content be improved by combining evidence is the question we address next.

QUESTIONS: CONCEPTS AND COMPUTATIONS
FOR COMMITMENT

Our focus is decision-making, not number-crunching. Therefore, we divide the reinforcement of the text material into six categories: (1) Concepts: Foundational, (2) Concepts: Formulational, (3) Computations, (4) Conclusions, (5) [Resource] Commitments, and (6) Caveats. See chapter 11 for answers to questions for this chapter.

Concepts: Foundational

1. What question does (1) simple regression answer? (2) multiple regression answer?
2. Who sets up the assumption of linear relationship in regression?
3. What is the primary weakness in the linearity assumption?
4. Why is partial correlation useful?
5. How does the Douglas function recognize interaction of variables?

Concepts: Formulational

The Problem: "Females Grow Taller"

6. How would you test the proposition "Females grow taller" from the data on ages and heights of upper division students?
7. What is your NH?

The Problem: Predicting Bookings by State

8. How would you set targets for bookings of salesmen by state?
9. Two logical candidate "independent" variables are (1) percentage of U.S. retail volume in the state urban trading center(s) and (2) percentage of U.S. effective buying income in the state. Should the actual dollar value of the bookings be used as the "dependent" variable? Or some other form of the dollar value of the bookings? Why?

Computations

The Problem: "Females Grow Taller"

10. Set up for Section 1 female students a computational table.
11. Set up a table of correspondence to match each female student by a randomly chosen male upper division student. For the comparison to be valid, we must take a random sample of six male students with ages matching the female students. There are two female students aged 21, two aged 19, and two aged 20. We can use the random number table (see ch. 6) to select the male students by

sequential number in the alphabetic order by name, since name or number has no direct relation with age or height. Let us select row 3, column 4, and read the first two digits down until we have found two 21-year-olds, two 19-year-olds, and two 20-year-olds, and note their respective heights.

The selected random numbers are 09, 67, 15, 58, 04, 78, 30, 56, 75, 75, 05, 49, 70, 25, 26, 10, 46, 16, 64, 72, 50, 15, 79, 22, 51, 01, 47, 88, 58, 43, 54, 73, 01, 30, 02, 26, 09, 21 . . . We see from Table 5.1 that Student No. *09 Blanchard is 20;* Student No. *67 Wells is 21;* Student No. *15 Daniels is 20;* Student No. 58 Spencer is 20 (not selected because we already have two 20-year-olds). Student No. 04 Banks is 24 (not selected because the age falls outside of 19 to 21); Student No. 78 is dropped because male student numbers stop with 72; Student No. 30 Gutierrez is 25 (not selected because the age falls outside of 19 to 21); *Student No. 56 Shirk is 21.* Student No. 75 falls outside of male student numbers 1 to 72; Student No. 75 again falls outside of 1 to 72; Student No. 05 Barg is 20, but the 20-year-old category is already filled; Student No. 49 Polen is 22 (not selected because age falls outside of 19 to 21); Student No. 70 Wolfe is 20; Student No. 25 Goldberg is 20; Student No. *26 Gonor is 19.* Student No. 10 Blue is 20; Student No. *46 Morrison is 19.* We now have the six matching males students.

12. Set up a computation table for the matching male students.
13. Compute *b* and *a* for the six female and six matching male students.
14. Use *t* to test the two regression coefficients in (13).

$$t = b_1 - b_2 \: / \: \sqrt{s_1{}^2/n_1 + s_2{}^2/n_2} \text{ with } n_1 + n_2 - 2 \text{ DF}$$

15. Follow the format of (10) through (14).

Table 5.5
Multiple Regression of Retail Volume and Effective Buying Income on Bookings by State

State	% of U.S. Bookings by State	% of U.S. Retail Volume in Urban Trading Center	%of U.S. Effective Buying Income in State
REGION 1			
Connecticut	1.7246	1.2571	0.4623
Massachusetts	4.9104	3.1122	2.6320
Rhode Isalnd	0.0010	0.4652	0.1613
New Jersey	3.0113	2.9218	0.5095
New York	15.2932	8.9340	6.7838
Pennsylvania	5.5654	4.8615	4.9254

Table 5.6
Observed Bookings and Expected Bookings

State & Region	% of U.S. Bookings by state (Observed)	Equation I (Expected)	Equation II (Expected)	Equation III (Expected)
REGION 1				
Connecitcut	1.7246	1.0104	1.2910	0.3676
Massachusetts	4.9104	4.2472	5.1793	4.3414
Rhode Island	0.0010	-0.3713	0.7506	0.1249
New Jersey	3.0113	3.9150	1.3756	3.9551
New York	15.2932	14.4050	15.6197	13.5606
Pennsylvania	5.5654	7.2993	9.2893	7.1562
TOTAL	30.3059	30.5056	33.5055	29.5058
REGION 2				
Illinois	10.8644	8.8718	9.4929	11.5463
Indiana	1.8033	2.2512	2.6279	2.4451
Michigan	5.1456	5.8480	5.3607	5.6085
Ohio	4.9612	7.3243	7.0021	7.2692
Wisconsin	1.2303	1.6666	1.8350	1.6687
Iowa	0.7984	0.7759	0.4635	0.4167
Minnesota	4.8692	2.4155	2.3577	2.3142
Nebraska	0.3758	0.9050	0.9080	0.7752
TOTAL	30.0482	30.0583	30.0478	32.0439

REGION 1

Equation I: $y = 1.1830 + 1.7448 x$
Equation II $y = 0.4625 + 1.7921 z$
Equation III $y = -0.6045 + 1.531 x + 0.0427 z$

REGION 2

Equation I: $y = 0.4322 + 1.8296 x$
Equation II $y = 0.3870 + 2.8237 z$
Equation III $y = 0.2466 + 0.6401 x + 1.9684 z$

FOR ALL U.S. $y = 0.4369 + 1.6252 x + (-0.2490) z$
$R_{y.xz} = 0.9026$ standard error of R = 0.0371

Partial Correlation Coefficients
$r_{yz.x} = -0.0108$, $r_{yx.z} = 0.6832$

The Problem: Predicting Bookings by State

16. Use a computer program or hand-held calculator to fit the multiple regression equation to the data for region 1 in Table 5.5.

Table 5.6 presents the observed data of y = percentage of U.S. bookings, and the expected bookings in each state in regions I and II based on equations I, II, and III for region I, region II and one equation for all United States, using X = percentage of U.S. retail volume in major state urban trading center(s) and Z = percentage of U.S. effective buying income in the state.

Conclusions

The Problem: "Females Grow Taller"

17. Develop the conclusion of the "females grow taller" problem following the three steps to develop the conclusion format (ch. 3).

The Problem: Predicting Bookings by State

18. Which equation would you choose for region 1; for region 2, to set binding sales quota by state?

[Resource] Commitments

The Problem: Predicting Bookings by State

19. How would you increase bookings, using the prediction of bookings by state: (1) From commissions and advertising? (2) From retail volume and effective buying income?

Caveats

The Problem: "Females Grow Taller"

20. How are your conclusions affected if the assumptions about the age and height variables are violated?

The Problem: Predicting Bookings by State

21. How does the linearity assumption reduce the validity of your conclusions about the means to increase bookings?

NOTES

1. F. H. Hankins, *Adolphe Quetlet as Statistician* (New York: 1908), p. 83.
2. Francis Galton, *Natural Inheritance* (London: 1888), pp. 54–57.

3. Francis Galton, Presidential Address to the Anthropological Section of the British Association, Aberdeen, Scotland, 1885.

4. Galton, *Natural Inheritance,* p. 95.

5. George K. Chacko, *Applied Statistics in Decision-Making* (New York: Elsevier, 1971), pp. 104–9.

6. Ibid., pp. 138–40.

7. Paul H. Douglas and C. W. Cobb, "A Theory of Production," *American Economic Review,* [(Suppl, 8, 1928): 139ff.

6 Dynamic Replication of Reality

OVERVIEW: In chapter 5, recognizing that the company outlay on advertising to develop consumer awareness and the company outlay on salesmen's commissions interact with each other, we used a multiplicative model. However, the model, linear in logarithms, treats the logarithms of the values of the two variables as independent.

We now turn to interacting variables, such as the wind pressure and thickness of the surface of aircraft wings. While a surface of average thickness could withstand average wind pressure, high wind pressure on a thin surface could crack it. How often such cracks could occur is determined by wind tunnel testing of aircraft models.

A gas station owner wants to know if the peak demand periods would cause unacceptably long lines of waiting customers. If he hires more attendants or installs more gas pumps, he would make a major commitment of funds. He would base such a decision on the balancing of customer waiting time against facility idle time.

To determine these two, he needs to perform a simulation(s) of arrivals of customers and their service time. The sequence of simulation steps is developed step by step: from the empirical data collection on critical variables to the expected value of customer waiting time and facility waiting time.

To justify installing an additional pump, how many customer arrivals should be simulated? How many times? Useful rules of thumb are developed. Further, a sequence of 12 simulation steps is applied to a perennial problem of determining and justifying the hiring of additional professional personnel in an office.

The computer has been used in simulation from the 1960s, when a journal was published by the Simulation Council. The General Purpose Systems Simulation (GPSS) Program developed at IBM in 1960 defines 43 specific block types, each of which represents a characteristic action. A GPSS simulator moves each entity through the system, and develops statistics on them. Within two years of GPSS, Rand developed SIMSCRIPT, which is a simulation language. The key elements are entities, attributes, sets, states, and events.

Monte Carlo simulation is an inexpensive but useful simulation method that can provide answers to questions about entities, the outcomes of which are produced by two or more interacting variables, for example, the arrival of customers at a gas station and the different types of service required by each customer.

From our discussion of multiple-variable decision-making with independent *and* interdependent *variables, we turn next to single- and multiple-variable decision-making with very few data points.*

DIFFERENT MODELS FOR DIFFERENT DECISIONS

A model is a representation of reality. How accurate and how detailed should the representation be? It depends on the decisions to be made on the basis of the model.

Static Models

A passport photograph is a representation of a person, perhaps not the most flattering, but a representation nevertheless, adequate for the purpose at hand. A portrait photograph is also a representation of the person; so is an oil portrait. Each serves a different purpose. One would not submit an oil portrait with the passport application, any more than send one's passport picture to the art gallery.

All three representations are static because they represent reality at a particular instant. They freeze time in its tracks, preserving the smile or scowl for posterity. Passport applications ask for recent photographs, sometimes specifying a time period, such as three months. The assumption is that the representation, the model, is valid for its purpose of visual identification.

A model is a representation of reality, appropriate to the subject matter and adequate for the purpose at hand.

Dynamic Models

The photograph of an airplane is a static model, freezing its features in time. However, when designing an airplane, it is necessary to know how the wings would withstand air pressure. To determine the breaking point, a model is made of the airplane. The model has to be quite precise with respect to the characteristic(s) about which a decision has to be made. The material, dimensions, structure, and so on of the model are dictated by the sensitivity of the decision to error. The criterion is, Can the decision based on the model be applied directly to the original entity?

Interacting Variables

In the wind tunnel test, variable 1, wing, interacts with variable 2, wind. The contours of the wing are subject to varying pressures from the wind. The outcome of the interaction depends on the combination of the values of the two variables: the value of variable 2 (e.g., 5,000 pounds per square inch [psi]) and the value of variable 1 (e.g., thin surface), producing the outcome, for example, crash. If, on the other hand, the value of variable 2 was 10 psi and the value of variable 1 was thick surface, the outcome would be no crash.

Probability Distributions of Each Variable

To ensure that the airplane can withstand wind pressure, the model should be subjected to the full range of wind pressures. The values of each variable is described by its probability distribution. We saw in chapter 4 that the mean and the standard deviation define the normal distribution. Furthermore, virtually all conceivable probability distributions can be specified by the four moments about the mean.

Two or More Interacting Variables

The probability distribution specifies the group behavior: how often each value or range of values of the variable occurs. But it does not, and cannot, specify which particular value will occur, and when. It could specify that the value of 5,000 psi could occur 1.4% of the time. Similarly, the contours of the airplane wing can be specified as being able to withstand 10 to 5,000 psi. When does the 5,000 psi hit the contour that can withstand, say, 10 psi?

Individual, Not Average, Value Critical to Real-Life Outcome

If we said that the mean wind pressure is 2,500 psi and the mean pressure that the wing can withstand is 3,000 psi, and therefore the airplane is safe, we would err grievously. The reason is that the individual values, not the average values, determine the outcome.

If the average values determined the outcome, the statistician who has his head in a block of ice and feet in boiling water should, on the average, feel comfortable! But the fact is that he is miserable everywhere: his head experiences the difference between body temperature and freezing, $(98.6 - 32.0 =)$ $66.6°$ Fahrenheit; and his feet experience the difference between body temperature and boiling, $(212 - 98.6 =)$ $113.4°$ Fahrenheit. When being scalded at one end and frozen at the other, the extremes do not "average out"; they aggravate each other because the central nervous system telegraphs extreme distress signals from both ends.

In the case of the wind pressure and the wing's ability to withstand, any pair of values may occur at any time, causing the wing to break or to survive. The "averages" do not apply. The individual values cannot be analytically determined in a given instance. On a die toss, we know that the value, say, "4" or "6" would occur one-sixth of the time in the long run. What we do not, and cannot, know is, in a particular throw, which value will occur?

Analytical Solution Impossible

The probability distribution specifies *group behavior*. It says how often a particular value or range of values will occur as *n* tends to infinity. It does *not* specify outcomes in *individual* trials; so we cannot apply group behavior to individual trials.

Experimental Solution the Only Feasible Approach

Analytic solution being impossible, we turn to experimental solution to determine the outcome of two or more interacting variables. We draw individual values from the distribution of each variable, and make them *interact* with each other.

MARKET APPLICATION 3: MUST I INSTALL AN ADDITIONAL GAS PUMP?

The owner of a gas station, like any businessman, has to balance demand and supply.

Variable 1: Demand

The gas station meets the demand for its services. The demand can be for products, like gas and oil; it can be for services, like oil change, minor repairs, or major repairs. We simplify the problem considerably by concentrating on one variable: demand for gas, D.

Usually, three kinds of gas are offered: regular (D_R), unleaded (D_U), and super-unleaded (D_S). Let us say that $D_R = 30\%$, $D_U = 60\%$, and $D_S = 10\%$. To simplify matters further, we will consider the decision-maker's (gas station owner) question: Must I install an additional unleaded gas pump?

Arrival of the customer at the gas station is the demand variable. Customers arrive in a steady stream (morning and evening rush hours), or they can be few and far between. We designate as *Variable 1: time between arrivals*.

Variable 2: Supply

Most of the time a customer stops by for gas. He may ask the attendant to check the oil and water. He may also ask for preliminary diagnostics of "funny noises from the dashboard." We can represent all these variations in demand in terms of the time spent by the customer at the gas station—*Variable 2: service time*. The customer *a*rrives, *w*aits, is *o*perated on, *l*eaves (AWOL).

To meet the customer demand, what does the gas station owner supply? His supply comprises *products* (different types of gas) and *services* (provided by the gas station attendants, including mechanics). We will assume that there is no self-service pump, and that all the service has to be performed by the attendant.

DECISION VARIABLES

The decision-maker has to recognize that he will lose some customers some of the time because he could not supply the products or attendants. When he increases the supply elements, they will meet the demand, but they are also likely to be idle outside of peak demand periods. He needs to consider two decision variables: (1) customer waiting time and (2) facility idle time.

Decision Variable 1: Customer Waiting Time

What would happen if on your way to work in the morning, or en route home after work, you found a long line at the gas station? Chances are that you would avoid going into that gas station and go elsewhere to fill gas. If it should happen a few times in a row, chances are that you would avoid that gas station altogether.

If you were the gas station owner, you would be worried about the long waiting lines at the pump, which drives away your customers. To avoid losing customers, you could install more pumps and hire more attendants.

Decision Variable 2: Facility Waiting Time (Idle Time)

Installing more pumps may shorten the customer waiting time, but it may also lead to several pumps being not used most of the time. At the peak hours all the pumps may be used, but at other times they may be mostly idle. The idle facility is not earning any returns for the gas station owner; on the contrary, he has to pay for them.

Similarly, if he hires a large number of attendants, all of them would probably be working during the peak hours, but most of them would be idle at other times. The idle attendant, like the idle facility, is not producing any revenue, but instead is adding to the cost.

Balancing Customer Waiting Time and Facility Idle Time

What the gas station owner has to do is balance the cost of the two waiting times: of the customer and of the facility (pumps and people). If the customer waiting time is too long, he will lose customers; if the facility waiting time (idle time) is too long, he will lose his investment. How should he trade one off against the other?

Determining the Population Values of Critical Variables

From his experience over time, let us say that he feels that the demand would support an additional pump. He would want to assure himself that such a demand is not transient, and that the long customer waiting time is sufficiently frequent to make the customers go away mad and not come back.

He should take valid random samples from which data on demand and supply are collected. The *sample data* have to be converted into *population characteristics*. As we said in chapter 4, a single random sample could yield a statement about the *entire population*. One major difference in the current instance is that there are two interacting variables: demand and supply.

SIMULATION: SEQUENCE AND DEFINITION

What the gas station owner needs to do (have done for him) is (1) determine the variables that are critical to his decision (e.g., *demand:* customer arrivals; *supply:* service time), (2) collect empirical data on the variables from a random sample(s) (e.g., 0800 to 1200 hours on the third Wednesday), (3) simulate the activity to develop the distribution of the interacting variables, and (4) establish the values of the critical variables (e.g., customer waiting time and facility idle time) with specified levels of confidence (95%, 99% of the time).

> **Simulation is the dynamic replication of reality when two or more interacting variables determine the outcome in such a way that the results of the replication are sufficient for decision-making purposes.**

It is the decision-maker who decides that the average customer *waiting time* of, say, seven minutes, is acceptable, or that the average length of the *waiting line,* say, five customers, is unacceptable, with which he compares the *expected* values of the customer waiting time, number of customers waiting, average facility idle time, and so on.

SIMULATION STEPS

Step 1: Empirical Data on Variables 1 and 2

Having identified the key interacting variables—the *demand* (time between arrivals) and *supply* (service time)—we need to collect data on a random sample. The purpose of the random sample is to so represent the whole that the conclusions based on the sample are within acceptable limits. Let us say that Wednesday 0800 to 1200 hours is a *random sample:* Each sample element meets the criterion that every value of each performance characteristic has an equal chance of occurrence.

On a sheet divided into minutes, the arrival of each car can be recorded in sequential order of arrival, #1, #2, . . . , #293 (*demand* variable). The service time of each car, #1, #2, . . . , #293, should also be carefully recorded (*supply* variable). The two sets of data have to be classified by appropriate class intervals. For instance, the time between arrivals can be five minutes; so also the service time can increase by five-minute intervals.

Step 2: Sample Data on Performance Characteristics

Let the collected data on 180 customers from 0800 to 1200 hours on a particular Wednesday be classified as shown in Table 6.1 (*demand*) and Table 6.2 (*supply*).

Step 3: Table of Correspondence

How do we represent the experience of the 180 customers? We draw the numbers from the random number (RN) table according to the empirical sample results. For instance, there were five minutes between arrivals of 10% of the customers, and ten minutes between arrivals of 15% of the customers. Or ten minutes or less time between arrivals was experienced by 25% of the customers. To reflect this sample result, we assign RNs as follows:

RN between 1 and 10 represents five minutes between arrivals.
RN between 11 and 25 represents ten minutes between arrivals.

Table 6.1
Sample Data on Performance Characteristics: Demand

Time Between Arrivals	No. of Arrivals	% of Arrivals	Cumulative %
5 minutes	18	10%	10%
10 minutes	27	15%	25%
15 minutes	9	5%	30%
20 minutes	36	20%	50%
25 minutes	45	25%	75%
30 minutes	45	25%	100%

Table 6.2
Sample Data on Performance Characteristics: Supply

Service time	Number of Customers	% of Customers	Cumulative %
5 minutes	9	5%	5%
10 minutes	36	20%	25%
15 minutes	72	40%	65%
20 minutes	18	10%	75%
25 minutes	36	20%	95%
30 minutes	9	5%	100%

We choose RNs from *another part* of the RN table to represent service time, so that we do *not* assume that the different variables are identically distributed. Let us present in Table 6.3 the *Table of Correspondence* between RNs and time between arrivals, on the one hand, and RNs and service time, on the other, at a gas station where we want to simulate 20 customers. We can represent 1% to 100% by three-digit random numbers, 001 to 100. However, if we designate 100 by the RN 00, then we represent the customer arrival and service by two digits instead of three.

Step 4: Prespecified Sequence of RN Selection

Unless the RNs are selected by a *prespecified sequence* that permits all the required number of RNs to be drawn, treating the RN table as a seamless fabric, the results will not be valid for the population. We illustrate the procedure for one variable:

1. Variable 1: Demand. Specify the *row* (e.g., 3) and *column* (e.g., 4).
2. Specify the *number of digits* (e.g., 2).
3. Specify the *order* (e.g., first two digits, fourth and fifth digits).
4. Specify the *initial direction* (e.g., down, up, across).
5. Specify the *subsequent direction* (e.g., right, up).
6. Specify the *end-point* (e.g., 20th customer).

Let us apply the prespecified sequence of RN selection to draw RNs for demand from *A Million Random Digits,* Rand Corporation, page 44 of which appears at the back of the book with the other standard statistical tables.

Table 6.3
Table of Correspondence for Service Station Data

DEMAND:	Time Between Arrivals	SUPPLY:	Service Time
RN 1-10	5 minutes	RN 1-5	5 min.
RN 11-25	10 minutes	RN 6-25	10 min.
RN 26-30	15 minutes	RN 26-65	15 min.
RN 31-50	20 minutes	RN 66-75	20 min.
RN 51-75	25 minutes	RN 76-95	25 min.
RN 76-00	30 minutes	RN 96-00	30 min.

1. *Row* 3, *column* 4 reads 09911.
2. *Number of digits* is two.
3. Let the *order* be the first two digits—09.
4. Let the *initial direction* be down—67, 15, 58, 04 . . .
5. Let the *subsequent direction be,* go to *column* 4, last row and then go *up*—02223, 00813, 91518, etc.

Similarly, the elements of the service time for Customers No. 1, No. 2, and so on would be chosen under a similar, prespecified sequence, but starting with a *different row and column* (e.g., row 5, column 1). If we choose the first two digits, going down the column we get 55, 69, 13, 17, 36, 81 as the RN for service time for Customers No. 1, No. 2, and so on, as shown in Table 6.4.

Step 5: Replication of Real-Life Interactions

Let us say that the gas station opens at 8:00 A.M. The time between the arrival of the 0th customer and the first customer is five minutes. Therefore, the first customer arrives at 0805 hours (Table 6.5).

How much service time does Customer No. 1 require? He (she) requires 15 minutes. Assuming that there is only one pump, it is occupied from 0805 to 0820 serving Customer No. 1.

Table 6.4
First Six Elements of Demand and Supply for Service Station Simulation

DEMAND:	Time Between Arrivals		SUPPLY:	Service Time	
Customer	R N	Time bet. Arrivals	Customer	RN	Serv. Time
1	09	5 minutes	1	55	15 m.
2	67	25 minutes	2	69	20 m.
3	15	10 minutes	3	13	10 m.
4	58	25 minutes	4	17	10 m.
5	04	5 minutes	5	36	15 m.
6	78	30 minutes	6	81	25 m.

Customer No. 2 arrives 25 minutes after No. 1, at (0805 + 0025 =) 0830 hours. The facility (pump) was idle from 0820 to 0830. How much service time does No. 2 require? He requires 20 minutes. He will be served from 0830 to 0850 at the single pump at the gas station.

Customer No. 3 arrives ten minutes after No. 2, at 0840 hours. He will have to wait from 0840 to 0850 hours before being served from 0850 to 0900 hours at the single pump at the gas station.

Customer No. 4 arrives 25 minutes after No. 3, at 0905, requiring ten minutes for service. He is promptly served from 0905 to 0915.

Table 6.5 is divided basically into (1) demand, (2) supply, (3) delay-customer, and (4) delay-facility. We complete the simulation for 20 customers and find that the total customer waiting time is 165 minutes, (average 8.25 minutes per customer) and the total facility idle time is 40 minutes.

REQUIRED NUMBER OF CUSTOMERS AND SIMULATIONS

Let us say that the gas pump costs $5,000. How many customers will it take for the gas station to earn that much in profit? If one gallon yields a profit of ten cents, it takes ten gallons to yield $1. If a customer buys ten gallons of gas, they yield $1 in profit. Our preceding simulation was only of 20 customers, who would yield an average profit of $20, which is too little compared with the $5,000 required for the additional gas pump.

The cost of the decision (e.g., $5,000) must be converted into the number of customers required to generate the resources. Thus we need 5,000 customers.

Table 6.5
Monte Carlo Simulation of 20 Customers at a Service Station

	DEMAND			SUPPLY				DELAY		
Customer Number	Time between Arrivals		Arrival Time	Service Time		Service Begins	Service Ends	Waiting Time		Waiting Customer
	RN	Time	00 min.	RN	Time			Customer	Attendant	
						05 min	20 m.	0 m.	5 min.	
1	09	5	05	55	15	05	20	0	5 min.	
2	67	25	30	69	20	30	50	0	10	1
3	15	10	40	13	10	50	60	10		
4	58	25	65	17	10	65	75	0	5	1
5	04	5	70	36	15	75	90	5		
6	78	30	100	81	25	100	125	0	10	1
7	30	15	115	84	25	125	150	10		2
8	56	25	140	63	15	150	165	10		
9	75	25	165	70	20	165	185	0		
10	05	5	170	06	10	185	195	15		1
11	49	20	190	20	10	195	205	5		2
12	70	25	215	41	15	215	230	0	10	
13	25	10	225	72	20	230	250	5		1
14	26	15	240	37	15	250	265	10		2
15	10	5	245	53	15	265	280	20		3
16	46	20	265	90	25	280	305	15		1
17	16	10	275	32	15	305	320	30		2
18	64	25	300	62	15	320	335	20		3
19	72	25	325	10	10	335	345	10		1
20	50	20	345	91	25	345	370	0		
							330 min.	165 min.	40 min.	

Average Customer Waiting Time = Total/ No. of Customers = 165/20 = 8.25 min.
Total Time Spent by the Customers = 330 + 165 = 495 min.
Attendant (Facility) Waiting Time = 40 min.

However, we need not simulate $n = 5,000$. A *strict rule of thumb is* $\sqrt{n}$. Our gas station owner needs to simulate $\sqrt{5,000} = 70.7$ customers.

How many times should he perform the simulation? Recall that we used *random sample* data and used the RN table to simulate the interaction between arrivals and service. If equal chance of occurrence of each outcome is obtained in each trial, then as n tends to infinity, the results would get closer and closer (converge; see Table 3.3) toward the true value of, say, seven minutes of customer waiting time.

If the convergence is strict, we would expect a random sample result *above* the true value, say ten, to be followed by another random sample result *below* the true value, say five, giving rise to an amplitude of $(10 - 5 =)$ 5; with shorter successive amplitudes like 3, 2 . . . Randomness does permit irregular amplitudes, but we assume successively shorter amplitudes in making the following rule of thumb:

> **If the average waiting time in Simulation No. 2, $w_2 > \pm 5\%$ w_1, the average waiting time in Simulation No. 1, perform Simulation No. 3, the average waiting time in which, w_3, should fall between w_1 and w_2.**

If w_3 falls outside w_1 and w_2, the assumption of randomness may need to be reexamined, with respect to the random sample data and/or the Table of Correspondence.

MARKET APPLICATION 4: JUSTIFYING 25% INCREASE IN PERSONNEL IN MY SECTION

A frequent requirement of any supervisor or manager is to justify additional personnel or equipment. How does the supervisor of eight justify hiring two more persons, a 25% increase?

Simulation to Determine If Personnel Increase Is Required

The *demand variable* in this instance is the arrival of tasks to be performed by the section. The *supply variable* is the number of professional people (in different categories, e.g., systems engineer, policy analyst, etc.), and the number of equipment (in different categories, e.g., third-generation computers, word processors, etc.). How many hours of the personnel, equipment, and so on are needed?

Does the office need more personnel? More equipment? Just as the gas station owner finds that the customer waiting time and/or waiting line is longer than he would like to see, I, as the section head, may find that time and again jobs have to be crashed with temporaries. The question is, Should I hire more permanent people?

A simulation would be a relatively easy and inexpensive way to determine if indeed the crash jobs are a recurring phenomena that call for permanent addition to the personnel. We will enumerate the steps of the simulation for decision-making on personnel hiring.

SIMULATION STEPS: $C^5R^4C^3$

Step C^5

1. C (concurrence) of the decision-maker on the sample period to generate simulation data (e.g., third Wednesday, 0800 to 1200 hours) (demand).
2. C (collect) data on arrival of tasks (demand).
3. C (cumulate) percentage of arrivals; develop the Table of Correspondence (demand).
4. C (conduct) simulation of n (e.g., 21) arrivals (demand).
5. C (conduct) simulation of n (e.g., 21) service (satisfaction of tasks, such as delivery of completed reports) (supply).

Step R^4

6. R (result) 1 = customer waiting time (total, average) (delay).
7. R (result) 2 = facility idle time (total, average) (delay).
8. R (repeat) simulation with 9, 10, or more if No. 6 is unacceptable (delay).
9. R (result) 3 = customer waiting time, facility idle time (total, average) (delay).

Step C^3

10. C (conduct) simulation of $\sqrt{n}$, where n is the additional hours of service (e.g., 1 (wo)man-year = 2,000 hours) represented by the additional investment in supply (delay). In this case, 2 man-years = 4,000 hours; $\sqrt{n} = \sqrt{4,000} = 63$.

    With only one day's worth of eight persons' work: ($8 \times 8 =$) 64 hours simulated, the need for two additional people for one year can be stated with 95% to 99% confidence.

11. C (convergence): Perform two simulations if $w_2 = \pm 5\% \ w_1$. If not, determine w_3 (which should fall between w_1 and w_2).
12. C (cost-effectiveness) of decrease from (6) to (9) justifies hiring two additional persons.

Monte Carlo Simulation

What we have discussed above are manual simulations, in particular, Monte Carlo simulation, a term coined by John von Neumann, circa 1942, when tackling the problem of atomic bomb radiation—certainly not amenable to experimentation. He had to identify the critical variables, develop appropriate empirical distributions based on reasoning, and study the interactions between the variables in a simulation.

COMPUTER AIDS TO SIMULATION

The appearance in 1961 of *Simulation,* the journal of the Simulation Council, underscored the use of computers in simulation. In an early volume of selected reprints from the journal, the 30 applications ranged from space trajectory simulations to flood simulation on the River Kitakami; from the hydrodynamics of the cardiovascular system to structural dynamics; and from nuclear reactor processes to the daily rhythm of nocturnal animals.

Computer Generation of Random Numbers

We have reproduced as Appendix Table A.6 a page from *A Million Random Digits*. Today the computer can generate RN and test if they are indeed random. We reproduced page 44 of Rand's RN table. The RN on another page would be different, but the results would be consistent. With the computer generation of RN, we can be as confident as we care to be about the randomness of the numbers.

General Purpose Systems Simulator Simulation

In the gas station example, we considered only one gas pump and one activity (in fact, several activities expressed as one activity with varying lengths of time). In the supermarket there is not one customer activity, but several, ranging from picking up a grocery cart and stopping at different grocery shelves to waiting at the checkout counter and unloading into the car.

One of the earliest attempts at using a simulation language that named these different activities was the General Purpose Systems Simulator (GPSS). GPSS defines 43 specific block types, each of which represents a characteristic action. The program user must draw a block diagram using only these 43 types.

A GPSS simulation moves each entity (transaction) through the system. A record is kept of each transaction, so that the appropriate ones are moved forward in time. On the basis of this record, statistics can be generated of the structure and duration of each transaction as desired.[1]

SIMSCRIPT

Within two years of GPSS, Harry Markowitz and associates at Rand developed SIMSCRIPT. Events in SIMSCRIPT are of two kinds: *endogenous,* which are internal to the system, and *exogenous,* which are external to the system.

Simulation comprising only the former category are closed simulations, and simulations including the latter are open simulations. The key elements in SIM-SCRIPT are (1) entities (e.g., customers), (2) attributes (e.g., dairy, fruit, and meat, which are associated with the entities—the supermarket customers), (3) sets (e.g., groups of customers), (4) state (e.g., customers in the supermarket in different phases of shopping activity), and (5) events (e.g., customers checking out at the checkout counter).[2]

CONCLUDING OBSERVATIONS

A model is an appropriate and adequate representation of reality—appropriate to the subject matter, and adequate for the decision-making purposes at hand. Dynamic models represent changes over time, as well as environments (e.g., wind pressure on aircraft wings), that are critical to decision-making. Although "average" wing surface can withstand "average" wind pressure, high values of variable 1 combined with low values of variable 2 will cause cracks. How often that will occur is found out by wind tunnel testing.

Reality can be replicated without destructive testing à la the wind tunnel. Circumstances like atomic bomb blast do not lend themselves to experimental data collection. The profile of the blast and its radiation are described by a number of variables. The probability distribution of each critical variable has to be specified based on tight reasoning of applicable physical laws.

However, no analytic solution is possible because the analytic solution provides the expected values, while the outcome is produced by combinations of high and low values of the different variables. The occurrence of these values has to conform to random sample data, carefully collected, as in the case of customer arrivals and service at a gas station, and carefully generated by tight reasoning, as in the case of nonexperimentable instances.

The question faced by the gas station owner is, Should I install an additional gas pump? The answer depends on the number of customers he would lose if he did not install the additional pump versus the hours during which the pump (and the attendant) would be idle. To determine the waiting time of the customer and of the facility, a Monte Carlo simulation is performed, replicating the arrival of customers and their individual service times, to determine the two types of waiting times.

How many customer arrivals should be simulated? How many times should the simulation be performed? Useful rules of thumb have been developed. The simulation steps are identified for a perennial problem: when to hire additional professional personnel in an office.

Various activities in real life can now be computer-modeled using suitable simulation languages. Perhaps the earliest example is the GPSS to stimulate a supermarket shopper's activities, such as acquiring a basket, buying different items, and waiting in line at the checkout counter. Simulation languages such as SIMSCRIPT, which permit the replication of reality in words instead of by diagrams, continue to improve the realism and repeatability of the replication of reality.

From multiple-variable decision-making with many data points, we now turn to single- and multiple-variable decision-making with very few data points.

QUESTIONS: CONCEPTS AND COMPUTATIONS FOR COMMITMENT

Our focus is decision-making, not number-crunching. Therefore, we divide the reinforcement of the text material into six categories: (1) Concepts: Foundational, (2) Concepts: Formulational, (3) Computations, (4) Conclusions, (5) [Resource] Commitments, and (6) Caveats. See chapter 11 for answers to questions for this chapter.

Concepts: Foundational

1. Why can you not determine the interaction of two variables by "adding" their respective probability distributions?

2. "When in doubt, simulate." Do you agree? Why? Why not?

The Problem: Additional Pump for the Gas Station

3. The average service time at a gas station is five minutes. There are three gas pumps and three attendants, each working eight hours. What is the maximum number of customers that can be served in a day?

4. Then why does the gas station owner lose customers?

The Problem: Nonexperimentable Situations

5. In a nonexperimentable situation (nuclear blast), how does one develop a basis for simulation: (1) model, (2) variables, (3) values? Be specific in your variables. Give reasons for your choice.

Concepts: Formulational

The Problem: Hiring Additional Staff

6. To justify increasing your staff by 25%, the key consideration is the unacceptability to your boss of the *delay* in meeting the demand for the services of your group, such as not meeting the suspense dates of tasked reports. Classify the *delay* into the fewest categories possible based on the degree of *un*acceptability.

7. The *delay* is the result of demand and supply. In the gas station problem the delay was counted in minutes. In (6) we counted it in terms of unacceptability. Classify the *demand* into the fewest categories possible based on the resources demanded.

Computations

The Problem: Hiring Additional Staff

8. To develop the Table of Correspondence between the observed demand and supply values and the RN, we need to specify the *nonoverlapping* categories of both demand and supply. In (6) we could classify the delay consequence of demand and supply into (a) most unacceptable, (b) moderately unacceptable, and (c) least unacceptable. We could add a category between (a) and (b), definitely unacceptable. Similarly, another category could be added between (b) and (c), somewhat unacceptable, yielding (1) most unacceptable, (2) definitely unacceptable, (3) moderately unacceptable, (4) somewhat unacceptable, and (5) least unacceptable.

What should be the frequency of the unacceptable occurrences? We want to maximize (4) and (5) and minimize (1) and (2). Let the former be 60% of the time and the latter, 10%. That leaves (3) with a frequency of 30%. Because (1) carries the highest penalty, let us keep its frequency at, say, 3%, leaving 7% for (2). Because (5) carries the least penalty, let its frequency be 40%, leaving 20% for (4).

Set up the Table of Correspondence for the delay *time* (see Table 6.1, columns 3 and 4).

9. To specify the demand characteristics with the most consequence for delay, let us say that a big job delayed is worse than a small job delayed. Developing five categories as we did in (8), the demand categories by size of resources required are (1) very big, (2) big, (3) average, (4) below average, and (5) small.

Each job can be completed on time, with no delay, or completed after it is due, incurring delay. We will ignore completions ahead of schedule. Let us say that a very big job being completed on time is half as likely as an average job and one-third as likely as a small job. So if the on-time completion of the small job is 30% of the time, the on-time completion of the very big job is 10% of the time and the on-time completion of the average job is 20% of the time. If the on-time completion of the big job is one-and-a-half times as frequent as the very big job, the on-time completion of the big job is 15% of the time. The below average size job should be expected to be completed on time more frequently than the average job, say 25% of the time. Set up a Table of Correspondence for the demand (see Table 6.1, columns 3 and 4).

10. *Conduct a simulation of 20 arrivals* (see Tables 6.3, 6.4, and 6.5).

Conclusions

The Problem: Calibrating the Deficiency of Office Service

11. In the case of the gas station, the average customer waiting time was found to be 8.25 minutes in Table 6.5. The maximum number of customers waiting at

any time was three, and the attendant was idle 40 minutes in 370 minutes. Should the owner install a new pump?

The astute reader would have noticed several differences between (10) and the gas station simulation: (1) there is no time between arrivals of demand, (2) there is no service time demanded by each arrival of demand, and (3) the outcome of the simulation is not the delay experienced by the customer in getting service or the delay experienced by the facility in giving service.

To make any decision regarding the hiring of additional staff, we need to convert the two variables—size of job (demand) and degree of dissatisfaction (supply)—into quantities.

A very big job being most unacceptable would merit a 0. Because very big job is category 1 in demand and most unacceptable is category 1 in supply, (11) has a score of 0. The very big job being definitely unacceptable (12) can also be given a score of 0. We could say that (13), (14), and (15) should also be scored 0 because a very big job must be most acceptable.

How about a big job, which is category 2 in size? We could say that when it is most unacceptable (21) it can be given the low score of say, 5. A big job being definitely unacceptable (22) can be given a slightly higher score of 10. Similarly, (23) gets a score of 15, (24) a score of 20, and (25) a score of 25.

The five categories of dissatisfaction of an average job can be given scores in successive increments of 5: (31) gets a score of 30, (32) 35, (33) 40, (34) 45, and (35) 50. Similarly, a below-average job gets the following scores: (41) 55, (42) 60, (43) 65, (44) 70, and (45) 75. Finally, a small job gets the following scores: (51) 80, (52) 85, (53) 90, (54) 95, and (55) 100.

Set up a table of deficiency index of office service.

12. Using a different page from the RN table (row 5, column 3, first two digits for arrivals; row 1, column 4, first two digits for service, we obtained the total of 1,005 for the 20 arrivals (average of fifty-one for the deficiency index). *Compare with your result.*

[Resource] Commitments

13. How would you justify hiring any additional staff based on (12)? Your boss points out that 51 in (12) simply means that your section is average in meeting the different sizes of jobs, and that you do not need any additional staff.

14. You counter the argument by pointing out that the *actual,* and not the *average,* deficiency should be the basis of resource commitment. In (3) the average values tell us that ($12 \times 3 \times 8 =$) 288 customers could be served if they *arrive precisely* in 5-minute intervals, each requiring *service precisely* for 5 minutes. But customers do not come at the average rate, and they do not ask for average service.

Which dissatisfaction is most damaging to the section? Small jobs or large jobs? If we say that very big jobs and big jobs are critical to the section, then the scores 0 to 25 are the most undesirable. The next 25 points, scores 26 to 50, are definitely undesirable. The next 25 points, scores 51 to 75, are desirable. The final 25 points, scores 76 to 100, are most desirable.

The results of the simulation are: most undesirable 5, definitely undesirable 5, desirable 7, and most desirable 3. *What resource commitment would you argue for? Why?*

Caveats

The Problem: Hiring Additional Staff

15. Why can you not convince your boss that the last paragraph applies to you?
16. Based on (14), argue for additional staff for small jobs.
17. Based on (14), argue for additional staff for very big jobs.

NOTES

1. Geoffrey Gordon, "Preliminary Manual for GPSS-General Purpose Systems Simulator" (White Plains, N.Y.: IBM, 1961).
2. H. M. Markowitz, B. Hausner, and H. W. Karr, "SIMSCRIPT: A Simulation Programming Language" (Santa Monica, Calif.: Rand, RM-3310, Nov. 1962).

Part IV *Single- and Multiple-Variable Decision-Making with Very Few Data Points—Single Decision-Makers*

Part IV
Single- and Multiple-Variable Decision-Making with Very Few Data Points—Single Decision-Makers

7 Improving the Initial Guess with New Data

OVERVIEW: *In chapter 3 we stated that rows (condition) and columns (effect) are independent of each other if joint probability = product of corresponding marginal probabilities. We also noted that marginal probability = sum of joint probabilities.*

Now we introduce conditional probability = *joint/marginal. A variant of conditional probability is stated as Bayes' theorem, after Thomas Bayes, an English Presbyterian minister, who, as we said in chapter 4, was influenced by the* Doctrine of Chances *by De Moivre, the originator of the normal curve of error.*

Both De Moivre and Bayes attempt to prove the existence of God. De Moivre uses infinite trials; Bayes uses very few trials. He increases the odds in favor of stable orderliness of nature with each recurrence of an event like the sunrise.

Turning from heavenly to earthly issues, the Bayesian approach discusses the probabilities before and after new data. Should a new product be introduced? The decision is based on the sum of the expected payoffs: *each possible market share multiplied by its probability before taking a sample survey* (prior probability).

Suppose 3,000 out of the current 5,000 customers are physically and financially able to use the new product. A random sample of 20 is interviewed, and one customer says yes by placing 10% nonrefundable deposit on the new product, which costs \$3,000 per unit. The yes or no makes it a Bernoulli process whose values are given by the binomial distribution. The sample market share is 1 out of 20 ($r = 1$, $n = 20$), or 5%. How often can $n = 20$, $r = 1$ come from a population *of 2%, 4%, 6%, 8%, and 10%* (conditional probability)?

The conditional probability (the likelihood) is multiplied by the prior probability to get the joint probability, which is normalized by dividing each joint probability by their sum (posterior probability).

Applying the posteriors to the loss incurred by not pursuing the best act (conditional opportunity loss), we get the revised expected opportunity loss (EOL). Choose the act with the least EOL.

The prior dominates the likelihood in business decision-making, although the reverse is usually true of scientific inferences, as illustrated by the revision of two guesses about a physical constant in light of experimental evidence.

HEAVENLY MISSION APPLICATION 2: "RECURRENCY OR ORDER . . . IS DERIVED FROM STABLE CAUSES OR REGULATIONS IN NATURE, AND NOT FROM IRREGULARITIES OF CHANCE"

In our discussion of the normal curve in chapter 4 we cited Karl Pearson, who pointed out that the causes that led De Moivre to his "Approximation," or Bayes to his theorem, were more theological and sociological than purely mathematical. Thomas Bayes (1702–61) was an English Presbyterian minister, a mathematician, and a fellow of the prestigious Royal Society. His paper, "An Essay towards solving a Problem in the Doctrine of Chances," was read posthumously on December 23, 1763, by Richard Price, another fellow.

Bayes' Approach versus De Moivre's

Both De Moivre and Bayes were interested in proving the existence of God. De Moivre developed the relative frequency concept of probability, with p approaching a specified value as n tends to infinity (see chapter 3). Richard Price comments on De Moivre's solution:

Mr. De Moivre . . . has applied to a very important purpose . . . to shew what reason we have for believing that there are in the constitution of things *fixt laws* according to which events happen, and that, *therefore, the frame of the world* must be the effect of the wisdom and power of *an intelligent cause;* and thus to confirm the argument taken from the final causes for the existence of the Deity [emphasis added].[1]

De Moivre uses infinite trials to arrive at a probability value. Price asks: How many trials in practice make "infinity"? He finds Bayes' approach to the "converse" problem more directly applicable:

It will be easy to see that the converse problem solved in this essay is more directly applicable to this purpose [confirming the argument taken from final causes for the existence of the Deity]; for it shews us, with distinctions and precision, in every case of any particular *order or recurrency of events,* what reason there is to think that such recurrency or order is *derived from stable causes or regulations in nature,* and not from any irregularities of chance [emphasis added].[2]

Bayes' Rule

Bayes states his problem as follows: "Given the number of times in which an unknown event has happened and failed: Required the chance that the probability of its happening in a single trial lies somewhere between any two degrees of probability that can be named."[3]

He develops meticulously the expansion of the binomial series, and offers three rules that specify the range of probability as follows: "If nothing is known concerning an event but that it has happened p times and failed q in $p + q$ or n trials, and from hence I guess that the probability of its happening in a single trial lies between $p/n + z$ and $p/n - z$."[4]

Price's Application of Bayes' Rule

Price provided an appendix to Bayes' paper to show how stable and permanent laws govern nature. He considers the case of a person just brought forth into this world and left to deduce from his observations the way it functions. The sun would probably be the first object to attract his attention. After seeing it for the first time, he would not know during the long night if he would see it again:

But let him see a second appearance or one return of the Sun, and an expectation would be raised in him of a second return, and he might know that there was odds of 3 to 1 for some probability of this. . . . [After a million returns] there would be the odds of the millionth power of 2 to one that it was likely that it would return again at the end of the usual interval. . . . The probability [would be between] .5105 [and] .5352. . . .

It should be carefully remembered that these deductions suppose a previous total ignorance of nature. After having observed for some time the course of events it would be found that the operations of nature are in general regular, and the powers and laws which prevail in it are stable and parmanent (sic) [emphasis added].[5]

Bayes' Rule (Theorem), Conditional Probability

What Bayes' rule shows is that starting from ignorance about the sun the second return of the sun (given the first return) has an odds of 3 to 1. Bayes' rule (also known as Bayes' theorem) is a variant of conditional probability.

Conditional probability = joint probability/marginal probability
$P(A|B) = P(A,B) / P(B)$ $P(A|B)$ is read as probability of A given B

We will now demonstrate Bayes' theorem.

What Bayes' theorem does is to *reverse* the condition and conclusion: $P(A|B)$ is *reversed* to $P(B|A)$ and multiplied by $P(A)$.

$$P(B,A) = P(B|A).P(A)$$ Numerator

The denominator P (B) occurs as (1) P (B and A), or (2) P (B and $\bar{A}$). Therefore, adding the probability of independent events:

$$P(B) = P(B,A) + P(B,\bar{A})$$

Applying the definition of joint probability to the two elements:

$$P(B,A) = P(B|A).P(A)$$
$$P(B,\bar{A}) = P(B|\bar{A}).P(\bar{A})$$

$$P(B) = P(B|A).P(A) + P(B|\bar{A}).P(\bar{A}) \qquad \text{Denominator}$$

$$P(A|B) = \frac{\text{Joint}}{\text{Marginal}} = \frac{P(A,B)}{P(B)} = P(B,A)/P(B)$$

$$= \frac{P(B|A).P(A)}{P(B|A).P(A) + P(B|\bar{A}).P(\bar{A})}$$

Bayes' Theorem and the Existence of God

Bayes reverses (conclusion given condition) into (condition given conclusion). Instead of drawing the conclusion from the given condition, he asks, What condition will follow from this conclusion?

His contemporaries would hypothesize a creator, and look at the creation as a consequence. Instead, Bayes looked at the creation and asked about the creator it pointed to. We could paraphrase it thus:

Probability of (creation given creator) = Probability of (creator given creation) times the probability of (creation) divided by probability of (creator given creation) plus probability of (creator given no creation).

Because Bayes' paper was published posthumously, we can at best surmise his proof of the existence of God. From Price's appendix to the paper we could state the probability of (creator given creation) as the probability of (creator given "stable and parmanent" "Powers and Laws of Operations of Nature"). In other words, the crux of Bayes' argument would be stable orderliness— "recurrency of order . . . derived from stable causes or regulations in nature, and not from any of the irregularities of chance." Starting from a "previous total ignorance of nature," events such as successive sunrises would establish a stable orderliness pointing to an intelligent cause.

A PRIORI AND A POSTERIORI PROBABILITIES

Turning from heavenly to earthly issues, the Bayesian approach discusses the probabilities before and after the new data. Much controversy surrounds the development of the *prior* probabilities (*a priori* = *before* [sampling]) because it can be purely subjective.

Initial Guess and Subsequent Revision

In deciding whether or not to introduce a new product, the management could (1) offer subjective values of prior probabilities, (2) obtain data from a sample survey or experiment, and (3) revise the prior into posterior probabilities on the basis of (2).

Scientific Inference versus Business Decision-Making

In the case of *scientific inference,* the prior is based on scientific theory, which explicates the differences in approach. Experimental data can significantly revise the priors, as we will see below.

However, there is little theoretical basis that can be invoked in *business decision-making* based on one's estimate of how a brand new product will do in the market. One's "gut feeling," being personal, cannot be verified; therefore, it cannot be contradicted.

Prior, Likelihood, and Posterior

The prior greatly influences the posterior. We will see how the posterior is related to prior by examining Bayes' theorem.

$$P(A|B) = \frac{P(B|A).\ P(A)}{P(B|A).\ P(A) + P(B|\bar{A}).\ P(\bar{A})}$$

The exclusive and exhaustive occurrences of B are with A or A:$P(B,A) + P(B,\bar{A})$. The sum of the probabilities of mutually exclusive and exhaustive events is 1, making the *denominator* 1. The left-hand side of the *numerator* is the *posterior* probability. The extreme right-hand side, $P(A)$ is the *prior* probability. The prior is modified by the *likelihood function* $P(B/A)$.

PHYSICAL MISSION APPLICATION 2: POSTERIOR PROBABILITIES OF A PHYSICAL CONSTANT

We will use the data from Box and Tiao on priors and posteriors.

Prior Mean and Standard Deviation

A physical constant, θ, is to be measured by well-experienced physicist A and less-experienced physicist B. Both represent their priors as normal distributions, the greater spread (standard deviation) reflecting the greater uncertainty owing to less experience:

Physicist A: mean 900, standard deviation 20
Physicist B: mean 800, standard deviation 80

Incorporating the New Experimental Data into the Prior

When new data are made available, how should the priors be modified? Box shows that if normal distribution specifies the new data, the prior means are weighted by the reciprocals of variances:

The posterior mean θ is a weighted average of the prior mean θ and the observation y, the weights being proportional to w_0 and w_1 which are, respectively, the reciprocal of the variances of the prior distribution of θ and that of the observation. This is an appealing result, since the *reciprocal of the variance is a measure of information which determines the weight to be attached to a given value*. The variances of the posterior distribution is the reciprocal of the sum of the two measures of information w_0 and w_1, reflecting the fact that the two sources of information are pooled together [emphasis added].[6]

Let the experimental measurement read 850, which is from a normal distribution with mean 850 and standard deviation 40.

Posterior Mean, Standard Deviation

We revise Physicist A's values of θ as follows:

Posterior mean = (prior mean × reciprocal of its variance) + (observed mean × reciprocal of its variance) DIVIDED BY (reciprocal of prior's variance + reciprocal of observation's variance).

For A, prior mean 900, variance 20^2; observed mean 850, variance 40^2

$$
\begin{aligned}
Posterior\ mean\colon\ & [(900 \times 1/400) + (850 \times 1/1600) / [(1/400 + 1/600)] \\
& = [900/400) + (850/1600)]/[(4 + 1)/(1600)] \\
& = [(3600 + 850)/5] \\
& = 890
\end{aligned}
$$

Sum of reciprocals of variance: $(1/400 + 1/1600) = (4 + 1/1600)$
$(1/\text{std. dev.}^2) = (5/1600)$
Standard deviation $= \sqrt{(1600/5)} = (40/\sqrt{5}) = 17.89$

Similarly, we revise Physicist B's values as follows:
For B, prior mean 800, variance 80^2; observed mean 850, variance 40^2

Posterior mean: $[(800 \times 1/6400) + (850 \times 1/1600)/[(1/6400) + (1/1600)]$
$= [800/6400) + (850/1600)]/(4 + 1/6400)]$
$= [(800 + 3400)/5]$
$= 840$

Sum of reciprocals of variance: $(1/6400 + 1/1600) = (4 + 1/6400)$
$(1/\text{std. dev.}^2) = (5/6400)$
Standard deviation $= \sqrt{(6400/5)} = (80/\sqrt{5}) = 35.77$

Different Influences of Prior and Likelihood

We see that the differences between Physicist A and Physicist B have been halved: from $(900 - 800 =)$ 100 to $(890 - 840 =)$ 50. However, A's prior was changed only 1.12%, while B's changed by *ten times* as much: 11.25%.

This greater amount of learning by B is due to the uncertainty in the prior versus the uncertainty in the experimental measurement. The variance of the experimental measurement, 1600, was much smaller than that of B's 6400, whereas 1600 was much larger than that of A's 400.

For A, the prior has a stronger influence on the posterior; for B, the likelihood has a stronger influence on the prior. Says Box:

In this example, the contribution of the prior in helping to determine the posterior distribution of the location parameter was seen to depend on its sharpness or flatness *in relation* to the sharpness or flatness of the likelihood with which it was to be combined. After a single observation, the likelihood was not sharply peaked relative to either of the prior distributions. . . . These priors were therefore influential in deciding the posterior distribution. Because of this, the two different priors, when combined with the same likelihood, produced different posterior distributions.[7]

MARKET APPLICATION 5: INTRODUCTION OF A NEW PRODUCT A PRIORI

The foregoing problem of estimating a physical constant is one of scientific inference in which most often the likelihood dominates the prior. In contrast, in problems of business decision-making, most often the prior dominates the likelihood.

Developing the Null Hypothesis

The decision whether or not to introduce a new product, X, depends on the expected payoff from the decision. The payoffs depend on the *state of nature* realized. With respect to new product X, let the states of nature be: θ_1 : high sales; θ_2 : low sales.

Which will be the "worse" consequence: introducing X when low sales is the

Table 7.1
Introduction of a New Product: Hypothesis of Adequate Break-Even Market Share

Truth / Perception	Null Hypothesis: Potential Market Share of New Product ≥ Break-Even Market Share	
	TRUE	FALSE
TRUE	OK	Type II error: False acceptance of the False as True = Lose Investment in the New Product
FALSE	Type I error: False rejection of the True as False = Lose Potential Profits	OK

truth or not introducing X when high sales is the truth? Following our procedure in Table 1.1., we generate Tables 7.1 and 7.2. If the investment in X could ruin the decision-maker if high sales are not realized, false rejection of the truth of low sales in Table 7.2 would be the appropriate null hypothesis (NH).

1. *WO*rse of the two consequences: Loss of the investment in X.
2. *TRU*th denied in (1): Potential market share too low to break even.
3. *QU*antify the essence of truth: If the break-even point is 3% market share, the potential market share of X < 3%, say 2.9%. Because the NH is a statement that something is zero, what becomes zero when the true market share is 2.9%?

NH: (Potential market share of X − 2.9% =) 0.

Determining the Break-Even Point

To calculate the break-even point, we need to know (1) total costs, (2) contribution of each unit of sale, and (3) number of customers. To simplify matters, let us say that the firm is considering introducing X to its current 5,000 customers. What fraction of the 5,000 should buy X for it to break even?

Fixed development costs	$300,000
Fixed promotional costs	$200,000
Fixed Total costs	$500,000

Selling price per unit	$3,000
Cost of sales per unit	$1,000
Net contribution per unit	$2,000

To recover $500,000 in fixed costs, 250 customers out of the 5,000 should buy X, or five percent of the current customers should buy X.

Prior Probability of Market Share

We do *not* know what *state of nature* (market share) will be realized. The decision-maker could use applicable prior experience as a logical probability or subjective probability.

Logical Probability: The (1) *logical premise* (product Y of the firm) and (2) *logical conclusion* (achieved 8% market share within three months of introduc-

Table 7.2
Introduction of a New Product: Hypothesis of Inadequate Break-Even Market Share

Truth / Perception	Null Hypothesis: Potential Market Share of New Product < Break-Even Market Share	
	TRUE	FALSE
TRUE	OK	Type II error: False acceptance of the False as True = Lose Potential Profits
FALSE	Type I error: False rejection of the True as False = Lose Investment in the New Product	OK

tion) may be applied to the (3) *empirical observation* (X is similar to Y) to draw the (4) *empirical conclusion* (X will achieve 8% market share within three months of introduction).

Subjective Probability: Given the identical three elements, (4) *empirical conclusion,* could be different from 8%. It could be 4%, 17%, or whatever, if the gut feeling of the decision-maker is strong enough to set aside the logical conclusion.

We determined that 5% of the market share is required for X to break even; or that the *state of nature* required for break even is market share .05. Can the decision-maker assign prior probabilities to other states of nature in the vicinity of .05? For example:

Market Share	Probability
.02	.10
.04	.30
.06	.30
.08	.20
.10	.10

What revenue can be expected for each market share?

Market share   .02 : (5,000 × .02 × \$2,000) = \$200,000
                .04 : (5,000 × .04 × \$2,000) = \$400,000
                .06 : (5,000 × .06 × \$2,000) = \$600,000
                .08 : (5,000 × .08 × \$2,000) = \$800,000
                .10 : (5,000 × .10 × \$2,000) = \$1,000,000

Expected Payoff of Prior Market Share

Bayesian decision-making is based on the expected payoff of available actions. The two actions are:

a_1: introduce new product X (*develop*)
a_2: do not introduce new product X (*do not develop*)

The expected payoff is calculated as if it were a mathematical expectation.

The mathematical expectation of random variable X that assumes values x_1, $x_2, \ldots, x_n$ with respective probabilities $p_1, p_2, \ldots, p_n$ is $E(X) = x_1 p_1 + x_2 p_2 + \ldots + x_n p_n$, provided the series converges absolutely.

We know that every value of a random variable has an equal chance of occurrence in every trial. Each value 1, 2, . . . , 6 on a die has an equal chance to occur (1/6). The mathematical expectation of the random variable X (die face) is $(1 \times 1/6) + (2 \times 1/6) + (3 \times 1/6) + (4 \times 1/6) + (5 \times 1/6) + (6 \times 1/6) =$

$(21 \times 1/6) = 3.5$. This holds only if the series converges absolutely. As discussed in chapter 3, it means that as the number of trials increases, the value of p gets closer and closer to a specified value, such as $1/6$ for a face of the die, or $1/2$ for heads. But *subjective and logical probability do not require convergence; n* is not infinite, but finite, and usually small. If the same decision-maker is asked, he could estimate the market share to be .6, .9, .1, and so on, the successive values *not converging* at all.

Without the two cardinal requirements of (1) infinite trials and (2) convergence, Bayesian computation of expected payoffs still uses identical algebra. Market share X assumes values x_1, with probability 0.1, x_2 with probability 0.3,. . . , x_6 with probability 0.1.

Conditional Opportunity Loss, Expected Opportunity Loss

If the decision were made to develop when the market share was .02, the payoff would be $(5,000 \times 0.2 \times \$2,000 =) \$200,000$. The loss would be $(\$500,000 - \$200,000 =) \$300,000$. We can compute the outcomes below and above the break-even market share:

Conditional outcome: $\$500,000 - (5,000 \times .02 \times \$2,000) = \$300,000$
Below break even: $\$500,000 - (5,000 \times .04 \times \$2,000) = \$100,000$

Conditional outcome: $(5,000 \times .06 \times \$2,000) - \$500,000 = \$100,000$
Above break even: $(5,000 \times .08 \times \$2,000) - \$500,000 = \$300,000$
                      $(5,000 \times .10 \times \$2,000) - \$500,000 = \$500,000$

The decision *develop* brings loss of current costs, whereas the decision *do not develop* brings loss of potential profits. We define:

Conditional opportunity loss (COL) is the loss owing to failure to take the best possible action under the particular condition.

Expected opportunity loss (EOL) = COL × probability of condition

Choose the act with the lower EOL: Develop (Table 7.3).

MARKET APPLICATION 6: INTRODUCTION OF A NEW PRODUCT A POSTERIORI

Unlike in scientific inference, prior dominates in business.

Data from Survey (Experimental Data)

Our decision *develop* is based on the prior probabilities provided by the decision-maker. How will they be modified with the new data developed empirically?

Table 7.3
Conditional Opportunity Table: Prior

Condition (Market Share)	COL of Act: DEVELOP	Prob. of Condition	EOL of Act: DEVELOP	COL of Act: DO NOT DEVELOP	EOL of Act: DO NOT DEVELOP
0.02	$300,000	0.10	$30,000	$ 0	$ 0
0.04	$100,000	0.30	$30,000	0	0
0.06	0	0.30	0	$100,000	$ 30,000
008	0	0.20	0	$300,000	$ 60,000
0.10	0	0.10	0	$500,000	$ 50,000
			$60,000		$140,000

The usual mechanism to develop data in scientific inference is experimentation; the usual mechanism in business decision-making is sample survey.

Ensuring Randomness—The Characteristic of Interest

Before introducing a new product, X, that costs $3,000 per unit, it would seem reasonable to survey a random sample of the 5,000 customer population. As emphasized in chapter 3, we must ensure randomness with respect to the characteristic of interest, which in this instance is the disposition to buy the new product. Let us say that of the 5,000 current customers, 3,000 are physically and financially able to buy the new product, from which population of 3,000 a random sample of 20 is drawn.

Conditional Probabilities from Random Sample

It is not enough simply to ask the 20 if they would buy the new product. We should ensure that an affirmative answer can be counted on as a sale. For instance, a deposit of 10% of the $3,000 would indicate that the prospective customer is serious about his declaration of intent to buy X. The deposit is refundable only if the product is unsatisfactory, meaning that the 10% deposit is "cash on the barrel head." Let us say that 1 out of 20 thus says yes. Each could say yes or no. These two exclusive and exhaustive outcomes are a Bernoulli process, generating the binomial distribution. How will the priors be revised when 1 out of 20 says yes? In the binomial table we identify $n = 20$, $r = 1$ and read the entry in the column headed $p = .02$. It is .2725. What does it mean?

1. The column heading is the population market share $= .02$. The sample market share is 1 out of 20 $= .05$. Conditional probability: $P(r = 1|n = 20)$ given population $p = .02$ is .2725. In other words, 27.25% of the time a sample of 5% could come from a population of 2%.

2. The column heading is the population market share $= .04$. The sample market share is 1 out of 20 $= .05$. Conditional probability: $P(r = 1|n = 20)$ given population $p = .04$ is .3683. In other words, 36.83% of the time a sample of 5% could come from a population of 4%. Similarly, we determine $P(r = 1|n = 20)$ for $p = .06$, .08, and .10.

Posterior Probabilities

Posterior probability $=$ likelihood . prior $=$ conditional . marginal

We calculate the posterior probabilities in Table 7.4 and show the relationship between the posterior and prior probabilities in Table 7.5. We now apply the posteriors to COL to get the new EOLs.

Revised EOL

Our break-even point is 5% market share, at which point there is no profit or loss. If the decision is taken to *develop*, the COL is $0. If the market share is

Table 7.4
Calculation of Posterior Probabilities: New Product

(1) Market Share	(2) Marginal	(3) Conditional	(4) Joint (2)x(3)	(5) Posterior
.02	0.1	0.2725	0.0272	0.0797
.04	0.3	0.3683	0.1105	0.3237
.06	0.3	0.3703	0.1111	0.3254
.08	0.2	0.3282	0.0656	0.1921
.10	0.1	0.2702	0.0270	0.0791
			0.3414	1.0000

Table 7.5
Prior and Posterior Probabilities

Market Share	Prior	Posterior	Posterior Prior
.02	0.1	.0797	79.7%
.04	0.3	.3237	107.9%
.06	0.3	.3254	108.5%
.08	0.2	.1921	96.2%
.10	0.1	.0791	79.1%

10%, and if the decision made is *not to develop,* the COL is $500,000. We calculate EOLs using posterior in Table 7.6. Choose the act with the lower EOL: *develop.*

CONCLUDING OBSERVATIONS

The Rev. Thomas Bayes, a member of the prestigious Royal Society, wanted to prove the existence of God. A fellow member, Richard Price, forwarded Bayes' paper for publication. The title of the paper reflects the influence of the book by De Moivre, the inventor of the normal curve of error: "An Essay towards solving a problem in the *Doctrine of Chances.*"

De Moivre uses infinite trials; Bayes uses very few trials. He increases the odds in favor of stable order(liness) of nature with each recurrence of an event like the sunrise to establish the intelligent cause that ordained it. What Bayes' rule shows is that starting from ignorance about the sun, (the second return of the sun given the first return) has an odds of 3 to 1. Bayes' rule (also known as Bayes' theorem) is a variant of conditional probability.

The Bayesian approach to both scientific inference and business decision-making uses the revision of probabilities by new data. The probability *prior* to new data is revised by the *likelihood* of the sample data coming from *populations* of different parameters.

In the case of measurement of a physical constant, two physicists specify the

Table 7.6
Conditional Opportunity Table: Posterior

Condition (Market Share)	COL of Act: DEVELOP	Prob. of Condition	EOL of Act: DEVELOP	COL of Act: DO NOT DEVELOP	EOL of Act: DO NOT DEVELOP
0.02	$300,000	0.0797	$23,910	$ 0	$ 0
0.04	$100,000	0.3237	$32,370	0	0
0.06	0	0.3254	0	$100,000	$ 32,540
008	0	0.1921	0	$300,000	$ 57,630
0.10	0	0.0791	0	$500,000	$ 39,550
			$56280		$129,720

mean value of the physical constant and its spread (900, 20; 800, 80), the larger spread of 80 indicating the greater uncertainty of Physicist B, who is less experienced than Physicist A. The reciprocal of the variance is a measure of information that determines the weight to be attached to a given value. The experimental data (850, 40) revises the priors respectively to (890, 18) and (840, 36). Less uncertain A is influenced more by the prior; more uncertain B is influenced more by the likelihood.

In scientific inference, likelihood often dominates the prior; in business decision-making often the prior dominates the likelihood. Let us say that the firm is considering the introduction of a new product, X, to its 5,000 customers. What fraction of the 5,000 should buy X for the firm to break even? We divide the total fixed costs by the contribution per unit to determine the required fraction.

We do not know what state of nature (market share) values will be realized. The decision-maker could use prior applicable experience to assign the probability of occurrence of different market shares. The loss (profit) for given market shares multiplied by its probability gives the EOL. Choose the act with the least EOL.

Let us say that 5% of a random sample would buy X. How often can the 5% sample come from a 2%, 4%, 6%, 8%, or 10% population? Multiply this conditional probability by the prior and divide each by their total to get the posterior probability. The EOLs using posterior probability give a better basis for the business decision.

The decision-maker starts with prior probabilities on the basis of logical and subjective reasoning. We have to allow for the ambiguity in the qualitative characteristics and their occurrence. A range of values and a range of probabilities associated with each outcome make the process more diffuse—which is the domain of Fuzzy Sets, to which we turn in chapter 8.

QUESTIONS: CONCEPTS AND COMPUTATIONS FOR COMMITMENT

Our focus is decision-making, not number-crunching. Therefore, we divide the reinforcement of the text material into six categories: (1) Concepts: Foundational, (2) Concepts: Formulational, (3) Computations, (4) Conclusions, (5) [Resource] Commitments, and (6) Caveats. See chapter 11 for answers to questions for this chapter.

Concepts: Foundational

1. What is Bayes' contribution?
2. Contrast scientific inference with business decision-making.
3. What critical assumption underlying standard statistical tables is absent from subjective and logical probability?
4. In the light of (3) how do you develop a posteriori probabilities?

Concepts: Formulational

The Problem: Rain and Rain Gear

A statistics class of 20 students was asked, "Given the weather bureau probabilities of rain, how many would take raingear?" When $p = .1$, $n = 0$; $p = .2$, again $n = 0$; $p = .3$, $n = 1$; $p = .4$, $n = 1$; $p = .5$, $n = 2$; $p = .6$, $n = 2$; $p = .7$, $n = 3$; $p = .8$, $n = 8$; $p = .9$, $n = 16$.

5. What type(s) of probability is the weather bureau p?
6. What type(s) of probability is the student p'?

The Problem: Acceptance Quality Level

7. How will you use conditional probability to meet fraction defectives in the population of batch-produced items (light bulbs)?

The Problem: Revised Estimates of Market Size

8. If the cost of sampling with $n = 50$ is four times that of sampling with $n = 20$, how would you decide which sample size to choose?

Computations

The Problem: Rain and Rain Gear

9. Compute the p' values for (taking) rain gear for each p.
10. Compute the average of p and p' for the nine sets of values.

The Problem: Acceptance Quality Level

11. The vendor submits three lots of a batch product. He says that 20% of the time the fraction defective (p) will be .10, 55% of the time $p = .15$, and 25% of the time $p = .20$. The customer inspects a random sample $n = 20$ and finds $r = 1$ (one defective). What is the revised probability of defective products?

12. What is the revised probability if $r = 2$?

13. What is the revised probability if $r = 3$?

The Problem: Revised Estimates of Market Size

14. A new product requires 4% market share to break even. The chief executive officer estimates the probability of .01 market share at .05, .02 market share at .10, .03 at .15, .04 at .30, .05 at .30, .06 share at .10. In a random sample $n = 20$ of potential customers, 2 say yes ($r = 2$) to the new product. What are a posteriori probabilities?

15. Recompute the posterior probabilities with $r = 1$, $n = 20$.

Conclusions

The Problem: Rain and Rain Gear

16. Interpret the results of (9).

17. Interpret the results of (10).

The Problem: Acceptance Quality Level

18. How reliable is the vendor's estimate of the quality of his products?

The Problem: Revised Estimates of Market Size

19. Based on (14), will the market support the new product?

20. Based on (15), will the market support the new product?

21. In (15) only 5% say yes and in (13), 10%. Yet you decide not to develop the product with the higher response. Why?

[Resource] Commitments

The Problem: Revised Estimates of Market Size

22. Based on (14), should he introduce the new product if the cost of development is $500,000, the contribution of 1 unit = $2,000, and the population $N = 12,500$?

23. Should he change his decision with the results of (15)?

Caveats

24. Why are the results of (9) and (10) meaningless?

25. What is the underlying assumption of posterior calculations?

26. Why would you not introduce the new product despite the favorable revised EOLs?

NOTES

1. Thomas Bayes, "An Essay Towards Solving a Problem in the *Doctrine of Chances,*" *Philosophical Transactions of Royal Society,* 53 (1763): 370–418.

2. Ibid., pp. 373–74.

3. Ibid., p. 376.

4. Ibid., p. 400.

5. Ibid., pp. 409–10.

6. George E. P. Box and George Tao, *Bayesian Inference in Statistical Analysis* (Reading, Mass.: Addison-Wesley, 1973), p. 17.

7. Ibid., p. 19.

8 Firm Decisions on Fuzzy Foundations

OVERVIEW: In chapter 7 we discussed how to improve the initial guesses about decision variables, such as the market share of a new product, with empirical data, such as the percentage of customers in a sample survey who make down payments on the new, unseen product.

Does the likelihood always fully capture the new evidence? Shafer thinks not. He and Tversky suggest that equally, if not more, important than the evidence itself is how well we draw the analogy between the given situation and its earlier parallel, be it historic or experiential. Further, we match parts of our evidence with parts of the parallels and try to fit the parts together: construction of probability arguments.

The recently discovered authorship of George Hooper makes his the earliest paper on combining testimonies of different witnesses. Later, Laplace considered a generalization of the problem: Each witness drawing a ball from an urn, and reporting what he saw. The probability that he reports the truth = his veracity.

When the evidence pertaining to A is conflicting with evidence pertaining to B, Shafer applies Dempster's rule to show that A∩B is supported to the extent of the interaction of their support functions.

When a witness draws a red ball, we treat the outcomes as (red, not red), only one of which materializes. In real life, however, there are several shades of outcome, as when a witness describes the color of a get-away car. The imprecision inherent in reality is handled by fuzzy sets, *defined by Lotfi Zadeh in 1968.*

The proposition "John is tall" translates into a procedure that yields a possibility distribution *of the variable* height (John). *Different values of the variables (e.g., 5'0", 6'3") can assume a number in the interval [0, 1] (e.g., .00, .02, .98). Negoita offers a generalization of the definition of fuzzy sets.*

How can conflicting evidences be combined? Negoita offers certainty factor *in the interval [−1, 1] to assess the certainty with which each fact or rule is believed. This changes the expert systems approach, if A then B, to the fuzzy systems approach, if A (to degree X), then B (to degree Y).*

Using fuzzy-OR operation, if symptom A indicates 70% chance of a disease, and symptom B 40%, the likelihood is max (0.4, 0.7) = 0.7. However, the probability of either A or B (independent events) occurring is p (A or B) = p(A) + p(B) − [p(A) × p(B)] = 0.4 + 0.7 − (0.4 × 0.7) = 0.82, which shows an accumulation of evidence. This is the probability-OR (p-OR) function that Richards incorporates in his Fuzzy PROLOG program.

ARGUMENT BY ANALOGY

In chapter 7 we had a single criterion: (expected) payoff. It was obtained by multiplying the payoffs for each state of nature by the probability of its occurrence—prior and posterior.

Likelihoods Not Fully Capturing New Evidence

How valuable is the prior probability figure? How valid is the evidence that changes prior into posterior probability? We saw in chapter 7 that in scientific inference, likelihood often dominates the prior, whereas in business decisions the prior often dominates the likelihood. In both cases likelihood is central.

Shafer points out that this Bayesian procedure implies that likelihoods fully capture the new evidence. He challenges this view, and argues that Bayesian inference is an argument by analogy, and that the weight it carries depends not just on the numbers, but also on how good the analogy is:

It is often asserted that Bayes' theorem provides a recipe for dealing with new evidence: we determine the "likelihoods" associated with this evidence, and we multiply prior probabilities by these likelihoods. This means that the likelihoods fully capture the evidential import of the new evidence. . . .

Shafer and Tversky[1] suggest that . . . when we make Bayesian probability judgments, we are matching our actual problems to a scale of canonical examples from games of chance or physics . . . [with] well-defined and known [objective] probabilities. . . .

Of course, we do not match all the evidence we have about a problem to a complex canonical example in one fell swoop. Instead we *match parts of our problem or parts of our evidence* to more modest canonical examples. Then we try to *fit these partial matches together*. This process should be thought of as the *construction of an argument*, an argument that draws an analogy between our actual evidence and knowledge of objective probabilities in a complex physical experiment or game of chance [emphasis added].[2]

Combining Confirming Evidence

How credible is the declaration of a respondent in a market survey on a brand new product? A and B both respond yes to the question, Will you buy the new product at $5,000? If A is perceived to be, say, 100% dependable and B 60%, the expected revenue from the new product should be suitably modified.

The basic question is that of combining the evidence of buying intentions of A and B. Generically, the problem is one of combining different pieces of evidence. In 1699 George Hooper discussed how the credibility of reporters affected the credibility of their respective reports: The credibility of a report is weakened by the chain of reporters through whom it is transmitted, but it is stronger when the reporters concur.[3-5]

Shafer finds the best early account of the Bayesian approach in Laplace's 1814 book,[6] which discusses both a single witness and several witnesses. The witness' veracity p: the chance that he would report faithfully and accurately is explicitly incorporated. Let A be the *fact* that he reports and B the *event* that he reports it. $P(A)$ is the probability of A based on evidence other than the witness report. $P(B|A)$ is the conditional probability that the witness will report A if it is true. The witness is to find out which of the n balls in an urn represents the truth. If we designate the probability $P(A) = 1/n$,

$$P(A,B) = \frac{(1/n) \cdot p}{(1/n) \cdot p + (n - 1/n) \cdot (1 - p/n - 1)} = p.[7]$$

Assuming that each witness has veracity p, $P(A|B)$ for two witnesses works out to $p^2 + (1 - p)^2$, if $P(A) = 1/2$. With three witnesses it is $p^3 + 3p (1 - p)^2$.

Combining Conflicting Evidence

Combining conflicting evidence is as critical as it is difficult. Shafer modified Dempster's rule of combination of evidence. He shows that the combining of evidence pertaining to A with evidence pertaining to B is quite simple when $A \cap B = \emptyset$ (nonzero), but more complicated when $A \cap B = 0$:

For the two bodies of evidence are not just heterogeneous; they are conflicting, and the effect of each is diminished by the other. . . .

Suppose $A \cap B = \emptyset$, and we wish to combine S_1 and S_2, where S_1 is a simple support function focused on A, with $S_1(A) = s_1$, and S_2 is a simple support function focused on B, with $S_2(B) = s_2$. Then to what extent, exactly, does the *combined evidence provide positive support* for $A \cap B$?

Dempster's rule provides a reasonable answer: $A \cap B$ is supported *to the extent [of]* $s_1 s_2$. . . .

[In Table 8.1] the lower-left rectangle is committed to $\emptyset$. To apply Dempster's rule, we must therefore eliminate this rectangle and inflate the measure of the remaining rectangles by the factor $1/1-s_1 s_2$ [emphasis added].[8]

Table 8.1
Combining Conflicting Evidence

Bodies of Evidence / Support Functions	For A	For B
$1 - s_2$	Committed to A	Uncommitted
s_2	Committed to $\emptyset$	Committed to B
	s_1	$1-s_1$

The *interaction* of the conflict is reflected in the product $s_1 s_2$ of the belief in the proposition A and the belief in proposition B. In one numerical example where $s_1 = 1/10$ and $s_2 = 9/10$, the conflicting evidence changes the respective values to $1/91$ and $81/91$. Notice that they add up to $82/91$, which is less than the original sum of unity.

That the revised probabilities add to less than 1 is an important principle. In real-life situations of interactive variables and participants, decisions often have to be based on incomplete and contradictory evidence that is not necessarily exhaustive.

FROM PROBABILISTIC TO POSSIBILISITIC

In Laplace's generalization the witnesses were picking up one out of n balls in an urn and reporting truthfully or untruthfully what they drew. In Shafer's combination of conflicting evidence the two propositions were well identified as A and B.

Suppose that there were several red balls in the urn, and the witness was picking one up and reporting faithfully and accurately what he saw. He could say

"Deep Maroon," "Chinese Red," "Crimson Red," and so on. If two witnesses were to describe the same ball that they both drew (quite similar to their describing the same car that they both saw being driven away fast from the scene of the crime), it is unlikely that they would both use the same words to describe what they witnessed. Are they talking about the same getaway car?

Fuzzy Sets

In 1968 Lotfi Zadeh introduced the concept of fuzzy sets as a model of a vague fact to represent imprecisely defined properties or quantities, such as "a long story," "a beautiful woman," "a tall man."[9] In 1985 Constantin V. Negoita modified the definition as follows:

First, we define the Cartesian product as the set of all ordered pairs whose first elements are in the domain and whose second elements are in the codomain. This permits the fuzzy set to be defined as a triple (domain, codomain, relation), where the relation from domain to codomain is the graph of the function such that the previous condition is satisfied.[10]

Consider heights 5'0", 5'4", . . . , 7'0". "Heights" is the domain or source of "tall." We apply subjective evaluations to assign degrees of membership in the interval 0-1, each height getting one and only one value in the interval, such as 0, 0.08, 0.50, 0.98., 1.0. The relation from *domain* to *codomain* is the *graph* of the function.

"Heights" is the domain or source of "tall"; [0,1] is the codomain or target. The heights 5'0" to 7'0" can each take values in the codomain of 0.00 to 1.00 to represent its degree of membership in the domain. Thus 5'0" is 0.00 tall; 6'0" is 0.50 tall; 7'0" is 1.00 tall, making 5'4" to be 0.08 tall, 5'8" to be 0.32 tall, and so on.

Possibility Distribution

Zadeh presented in 1981 "PRUF-A Meaning Representation Language for Natural Languages."[11] PRUF stands for *possibilistic relational universal fuzzy*. It assumes that the imprecision intrinsic to natural languages is possibilistic. The *proposition* that "John is tall" translates into a *possibility distribution* of the variable height (John). Each value of the variable height (John) (e.g., 5'0" 5'2" etc.) is associated with a number in the unit interval [0,1] [e.g., 0.00, 0.08, etc.), representing the possibility that the variable could assume that value.

1. In general, a *proposition* translates into a *procedure*, which returns a *possibility distribution* representing its meaning.

Truth as Compatibility

The logic underlying PRUF is not two-valued or multivalued, but linguistic. It is of the form true, not true, very true, more or less true, and so on, as in "John is tall is not very true."

2. The truth value of a proposition is defined as its *compatibility with a reference proposition.*

This permits us, given two propositions, to compute the truth of one relative to the other.

3. Because of the *cardinality of a fuzzy set,* the linguistic quantifiers in PRUF are given a concrete interpretation.

This permits the translation into PRUF statements like "Many tall men are much taller than most men," and "All tall women are not blonde is not very true."

Conforming or Opposing Evidence

How do we combine opposing or nonconcurring evidence? Rule-based expert systems usually deal with a single correct decision. However, fuzzy sets deal with situations in which truth of facts or relations is not well established, requiring qualifiers:

Expert Systems: If A then B.

Fuzzy Systems: If A (to degree X) then B (to degree Y)

Negoita uses the interval $[-1, 1]$ to combine opposing evidence:

Because we cannot be completely certain that some facts are true or that certain relations hold, each fact and each production rule is associated with a certainty factor (CF). The CF, a number in the interval $[-1, 1]$, indicates the certainty with which each fact or rule is believed. Positive and negative CFs indicate a predominance of conforming or opposing evidence respectively. CFs of 1 or -1 indicate absolute knowledge.

1. The CF of a conjunction of several facts is taken to be the minimum of the CFs of the individual facts.
2. The CF for the conclusion produced by a rule is the CF of its premise multiplied by the CF of the rule.
3. The CF for a fact produced as the conclusion of one or more rules is the maximum of the CFs produced by the rules yielding that conclusion. [12]

Richards points out that the foregoing throws away evidence. For instance, if symptom A indicates a 70% chance of the disease, and symptom B indicates a 40% chance, max $(0.4, 0.7) = 0.7$. He says this totally disregards the accumulation of evidence; it only considers the single most important symptom.

Now let's consider a probability function. Given two independent events A and B, the probability of either occurring is $p(A \text{ or } B) = p(A) + p(B) - (p(A) \times p(B))$.

If we apply this function to the diagnosis above, we find that the likelihood of the disease is 0.4 p-OR $0.7 = 0.4 + 0.7 - (0.4 \times 0.7) = 0.82$, which does show an accumulation of evidence. This is the probability-OR (p-OR) in fuzzy logic.[13]

Richards incorporates p-OR in the Turbo PROLOG programs: FUZZY, PRO and CITY.PRO. The ADA interpreter is in the pubic domain.

CONCLUDING OBSERVATIONS

In chapter 7 we multiplied the prior probability by the likelihood to obtain the posterior probability. The likelihood was obtained by physical experimentation in the case of scientific inference, and by market survey in the case of business decision-making. Do the likelihoods fully capture the content of the new evidence? Shafer thinks not. He and Tversky suggest that we match problems to canonical examples. It is not done in one fell swoop, but in pieces, matching part of the evidence with some examples and part with other examples. Then we try to fit the parts together.

In his belief-function approach Shafer modifies Dempster's rule for combining evidence from different sources. Citing Grier's discovery of George Hooper's authorship of a 1699 paper on calculating the credibility of human testimony (predating Bayes' 1763 paper), Shafer identifies Hooper as the first exponent of belief-functions, which Laplace discussed in 1814.

Hooper calculates the credibility of a report transmitted by n reporters each with a credibility of p as p^n. Laplace obtains the conditional probability $P(B|A)$, the probability that the witness will report A if it is true $= p$, the witness's veracity. When $P(A) = 1/2$, with two witnesses, $P(A|B) = p^2 + (1 - p)^2$; and three witnesses, $p^3 + 3(1 - p)^2$.

What happens when the evidence is contradictory: evidence pertaining to proposition A and B yield $A \cap B = \emptyset$? Shafer applies Dempster's rule to show that $A \cap B$ is supported to the extent of the interaction of their respective support functions s_1 and s_2.

In Laplace's example the witness is supposed to draw a ball from an urn and report its color. In real life we have to allow for not simply "red," "not red" descriptions, but several shades of red. The inherent imprecision in reality is handled by fuzzy sets, defined in 1968 by Lotfi Zadeh. The proposition "John is tall" translates into a procedure, which returns a *possibility distribution* representing its meaning. The variable height (John) can assume different values (e.g., $5'0''$, $5'4''$), each specified by a number in the interval $[0,1]$ (e.g., 0.00, 0.02).

How can conflicting evidence be combined? Negoita offers certainty factor in $[-1, 1]$ to indicate the certainty with which each fact or rule is believed, and the rules of combining the confirming and opposing evidence. Richards points out that fuzzy operator f-OR disregards accumulations of evidence. If symptom A indicates 70% chance of disease and symptom B 40%, f-OR would find max $(0.4, 0.7) = 0.7$. If instead, probability-OR (p-OR) operator is used, $p(A \text{ or } B) = p(A) + p(B) - ((p(A) \times p(B))) = 1.0 - 0.28 = 0.82$.

Decision-making depends on outcome, as well as attitude: the preparedness to accept an (adverse) outcome. From our discussion of evidence that modifies initial guesses about outcome, we turn in chapter 9 to the significance of the outcomes to the decision-maker.

QUESTIONS: CONCEPTS AND COMPUTATIONS FOR COMMITMENT

Our focus is decision-making, not number-crunching. Therefore, we divide the reinforcement of the text material into six categories: (1) Concepts: Foundational; (2) Concepts: Formulational, (3) Computations, (4) Conclusions, (5) [Resource] Commitments, and (6) Caveats. See chapter 11 for answers to questions for this chapter.

Concepts: Foundational

1. In chapter 7 what was the role of likelihood in revising prior probabilities?
2. What is Shafer's objection to the Bayesian position in (1)?
3. What is the "construction of an argument" process?
4. What is Dempster's rule of combination of evidence?
5. What is the possibility distribution?
6. Contrast (5) with probability distribution.
7. How do you combine opposing evidence?
8. Contrast fuzzy and probability approaches to (7).

NOTES

1. Glenn Shafer and Amos Tversky, "Languages and Designs for Probability Judgment," *Cognitive Science* 9 (1985): 309–39.

2. Glenn Shafer, "The Construction of Probability Arguments." Symposium on Probability and Inference in the Law of Evidence, Boston University School of Law, April 4–6, 1986, pp. 15, 5.

3. George Hooper, "A Calculation of the Credibility of Human Testimony," *Philosophical Transactions of the Royal Society,* 21 (1699): 359–65. In 1931 this paper was referred to as "anonymous" in (4); 50 years later (5) identified the author as George Hooper.

4. Helen M. Walker, *Studies in the History of Statistical Method* (Baltimore: Williams & Wilkins, 1931), p. 30.

5. B. Grier, "George Hooper and the Early Theory of Testimony." Department of Psychology, Northern Illinois University, Dekalb, 1981.

6. P. S. Laplace, *Oeuvres de Laplace,* vol. 7 (Paris: 1886).

7. Glenn Shafer, "The Combination of Evidence," *International Journal of Intelligent Systems,* April 1986, equation 6.

8. Glenn Shafer, *A Mathematical Theory of Evidence* (Princeton, N.J.: Princeton University Press, 1976), pp. 82, 79.

9. Lotfi A. Zadeh, "Fuzzy Sets," *Information and Control,* 8 (1965): 338–53.

10. Constantin V. Negoita, *Expert Systems and Fuzzy Systems* (Menlo Park, Calif.: Benjamin/Cummings Publishing Co., 1985), p. 52.

11. Lotfi A. Zadeh, "PRUF-A Meaning Representation Language for Natural Languages," in *Fuzzy Reasoning and Its Application,* ed. E. H. Mamdani and B. R. Gaines (London: Academic Press, 1981).

12. Negoita, *Expert Systems,* pp. 27–28.

13. Bradley L. Richards, "When Facts Go Fuzzy," *Byte,* April 1988, p. 286.

Part V Single- and Multiple-Variable Decision-Making with Very Few Data Points—Multiple Decision-Makers

Part V
Single- and Multiple-Variable Decision-Making with Very Few Data Points—Multiple Decision-Makers

9 Attitude Toward Outcomes—Single and Multiple Decision-Makers

OVERVIEW: In chapters 7 and 8 our concern has been with outcome: how to decide on the basis of outcome and how to improve the expected outcomes by incorporating empirical data. Now we turn to another element of decision-making—attitude: the preparedness to accept (adverse) outcome.

The expected monetary value (EMV) of $100,000 invested in Stock A is found to be better than the investor's investment in Stock B. However, on the basis of his (her) utility function of money, he (she) decides to invest in neither. Why? The EMV of A is based on a chance of 50% gain combined with a chance of 60% loss of the $100,000 investment. The (smaller) prospects of losing $60,000 scares the investor much more than the (greater) prospects of EMV of $5,500 gain.

The investor's utility function is constructed by determining his point of indifference between different guaranteed outcomes versus a lottery of the best and worst outcomes. When not one criterion, but six attributes (criteria) generate a multiattribute utility function, the conditions of utility and preference independence have to be satisfied in order to develop an additive utility function.

The additive utility function ignores the interaction between criteria (attributes). Even if the linear structure is justifiable as a first approximation, the really serious question is, How can one criterion be traded for another? Any trade-off should be based on its impact on the higher entity whose fulfillment is measured by the traded criteria.

We define a system and develop a system performance measure, called penalty for nonfulfillment (PFN). PFN is the degradation of the system effectiveness owing to nonperformance at subsystem or lower levels. By developing horizontal scores and vertical weights for PFN, we are able to pinpoint the impairment to the system owing to nonperformance at subsystem or lower levels. Every element can be allocated a portion of the system budget in proportion to its contribution to the system objective, as measured by the ratio of the weighted PFN scores of the element to the weighted PFN score of the system.

A MATTER OF INDIFFERENCE

Decisions based on expected monetary outcome implicitly assume that only money matters. However, gains or losses have to be viewed in perspective: a $100,000 loss would mean much less damage to a $100 million corporation than to a $200,000 small business. The $100,000 loss would half ruin the latter, but leave 999 out of 1,000 of the former's funds intact.

Risk

Risk is the occurrence of an outcome other than the one specified. It is this eventuality that makes the precommitting of resources painful. To reduce the risk, we try to improve our knowledge of the future—or rather, reduce our ignorance of the future—through laboratory experiments or market research surveys. But none would reduce the risk to zero.

Utility

Decision-making depends not only on the outcome, but also on the *attitude: the preparedness to accept [adverse] outcome.* When one expects sunshine but is caught in a downpour, that is an adverse outcome. How prepared is one to accept such an outcome? On the other hand, when one expects a downpour but is surprised by sunshine instead, how prepared is one to accept that outcome, also different from the expected outcome? Usually one is happier with the latter kind of unexpected outcome than with the former.

What is the cost of surprise? If one is physically rundown, one would rather take rain gear and be inconvenienced by sunshine than not take rain gear and get drenched, and possibly catch a bad cold. If, on the other hand, one is quite healthy, one may choose to get caught in the downpour rather than be saddled with rain gear. In other words, the choice of whether or not to take rain gear will depend on the potential significance of its consequences to the subject. *Utility is the potential significance of or satisfaction from goods and services.* The potential aspect of utility must be underscored. It is what the decision-maker expects *at the time of decision-making;* not what it actually turns out to be.

Indifference between Certainty and Uncertainty (Lottery)

Turning to business decision-making, what is the utility of money to the decision-maker? We determine it by asking the decision-maker to choose between a certainty and a gamble between two outcomes with probabilities p and ($1 - p$). The certainty carries no risk: the outcome is known. The lottery or gamble, however, has two possible outcomes—a high profit or a high loss. Each outcome has an associated probability. The question is, What probability value, p, would make the decision-maker indifferent between the certainty and the uncertainty?

MARKET APPLICATION 7: UTILITY FUNCTION OF STOCK MARKET INVESTOR

Let us consider an investor who is contemplating investing $100,000 in stocks. He can invest in Stock A or Stock B, but not both. The stock prices could go up, down, or remain unchanged. Let us also say that he knows from experience that the probability of the market going up is 30%, going down is 20%, and staying the same is 50%.

Expected Payoffs

Table 9.1 presents the expected payoffs of the three decisions: (1) buy Stock A, (2) buy Stock B, and (3) do not buy A or B, corresponding to the three states of nature: (1) higher stock prices, (2) stationary stock prices, and (3) lower stock prices. Which is the best decision?

Applying the respective probabilities to the outcomes,

Buy Stock A: 0.3 ($50,000) + 0.5 ($5,000) + 0.2 (− $60,000) = $5,500

Buy Stock B: 0.3 ($20,000) + 0.5 (− $8,000) + 0.2 (− $50,000) = − $8,000

Do Not Buy: 0.3 ($0) + 0.5 ($0) + 0.2 ($0) = $0

The decision: *Buy Stock A.*

Table 9.1
Monetary Payoffs

Stock Prices / Decision	Higher	Stationary	Lower
Buy Stock A	$50,000	$5,000	-$60,000
Buy Stock B	$20,000	-$8,000	-$50,000
Do not buy	$0	$0	$0

Utility Considerations

The fact that the investor can invest only in Stock A or Stock B suggests that he is financially not too strong. If the $100,000 investment were to result in serious loss, the investor would be in great jeopardy. It is the high value of the losses, amounting to 50% (Stock B) and 60% (Stock A) of his investment that gives pause to the investor in his relatively weak financial position. Although Stock A gives the expected payoff of $5,500, the possibility of losing $60,000 would be a serious deterrent to the investment decision. Whether or not he will invest in Stock A or Stock B or neither depends on his utility for money.

Developing the Utility Function

To determine the decision-maker's attitude toward outcomes, we determine his point of indifference between certainty and uncertainty. We determine the highest and lowest outcomes. In the payoff table the highest outcome is $50,000, and the lowest is a loss of $60,000. We can assign any value to the outcomes, as long as the scale is monotonic (i.e., the higher outcome has higher utility than the lower outcome). Let us assign utility U ($50,000) = 10 and Utility U (− $60,000) = 0.

Suppose the investor is guaranteed $20,000 (Stock B's best outcome). Will he prefer that to a lottery of the best and the worst?

$50,000 with probability p, and

− $60,000 with probability $(1 - p)$

What value of p will make him indifferent between the two? Clearly, if p is very close to 1, the investor would prefer the lottery to the certain payoff of $20,000, since the lottery would virtually guarantee him $50,000. By the same token, if p is very close to 0, the investor is almost certain to lose $60,000; he would prefer the certain payoff of $20,000 to the lottery. By successive questioning of the decision-maker, let us say that we arrive at $p = .9$ as the value that will make him *indifferent* between the two choices, equating the certainty with the lottery.

$$U (\$20,000) \quad = p \cdot U (\$50,000) + (1 - p) U (- \$60,000)$$
$$= .9 (10) \qquad + (1 - p) (0)$$
$$= 9$$

The value of the utility would have been different if we assigned, say, U ($50,000) = 50 and U (− $60,000) = 5.

$$U (\$20,000) \quad = .9 (50) \qquad + (.1) (5)$$
$$= 45.5$$

If we stay with the original assignment of utility, what is the expected *monetary* value of the lottery?

$$\begin{aligned} \text{EMV} \quad &= .9\,(\$50,\!000) \quad + (.1)\,(-\,\$60,\!000) \\ &= \$45,\!000 \quad\quad + -\,\$6,\!000 \\ &= \$39,\!000 \end{aligned}$$

Although the EMV of the lottery is $39,000, the investor would prefer the guaranteed payment of $20,000 to the lottery. The 10% chance of incurring a loss of $60,000 makes him willing to give up $39,000 for $20,000, the $19,000 being his *risk premium* against losing $60,000.

Suppose the investor is guaranteed $-\,\$50,\!000$ (Stock B's worst outcome). Will he prefer that to a lottery of the best and the worst?

$50,000   with probability p and

$-\,\$60,\!000$ with probability $(1 - p)$

What value of p will make him indifferent between the two?

Arguing as before, a high value of p close to 1 would virtually guarantee $-\,\$50,\!000$, and make the investor prefer the lottery to the guaranteed loss of $50,000. We can try successive values of p. Let us say that when $p = .6$, the investor is indifferent between the two.

$$\begin{aligned} \text{U}\,(-\,\$50,\!000) &= p.\ \text{U}\,(\$50,\!000) \quad + (1 - p)\,\text{U}\,(-\,\$60,\!000) \\ &= .6\,(10) \quad\quad\quad + .4\,(0) \\ &= 6 \end{aligned}$$

What is the EMV when $p = .60$?

$$\begin{aligned} \text{EMV (lottery)} \quad &= .60\,(\$50,\!000) \quad + (.4)\,(-\,\$60,\!000) \\ &= \$30,\!000 \quad\quad + -\,\$24,\!000 \\ &= \$6,\!000 \end{aligned}$$

Although the EMV is $6,000, the investor opts for the certainty of $50,000 *loss* for fear of losing even more, $60,000.

What is the *general relationship* between (guaranteed) money outcome and utility? When we have a general relationship, we can apply that to any money outcomes without having to recompute.

$$\begin{aligned} \text{When } p &= .90,\ \text{U}\,(\$20,\!000) \quad = 9.0 \\ \text{When } p &= .60,\ \text{US}\,(-\,50,\!000) = 6.0 \end{aligned}$$

In general,

$$\begin{aligned} \text{U}\,(\text{M}) \quad &= p\,.\ \text{U}\,(\$50,\!000) + (1 - p)\,\text{U}\,(-\,\$60,\!000) \\ &= p\,(10) \quad\quad\quad + (1 - p)\,(0) \\ &= 10\,p \end{aligned}$$

Once we establish the p value for each guaranteed outcome, such as $p = .9$ for $20,000, $p = .6$ for $-50,000$, we can simply multiply p by 10 to get the corresponding utility value. The illustrative monetary values and utility values appear in Table 9.2. We can now substitute utility values for monetary values in the payoff table, as shown in Table 9.3.

The steps we used to develop the utility function are as follows:

1. Identify the attribute (e.g., income from Stock A, Stock B, or neither).
2. For each attribute, identify the best outcome ($50,000) and the worst outcome ($- $60,000).
3. Assign a value (e.g., 10) for the best outcome and a lower value (e.g., 0) for the worst outcome.
4. Determine the level of the attribute (e.g., guaranteed money outcome) that would make the decision-maker indifferent to a lottery with p for the best and $(1 - p)$ for the worst outcome.
5. Develop utility values for each outcome corresponding to the different decision alternatives.
6. Choose the decision with the highest expected utility.

Table 9.2
Utility Function of Money

Monetary Outcome	Indifference value of p	Utility Value
$50,000	Does not apply	10.00
$22,000	0.90	9.00
$10,000	0.80	8.00
-$ 5,000	0.70	7.00
-$50,000	0.20	2.00
-$60,000	Does not apply	0.00

Table 9.3
Utility of Monetary Payoffs

Stock Prices / Decision	Higher	Stationary	Lower
Buy Stock A	10.00	8.20	0.00
Buy Stock B	9.00	7.00	6.00
Do not buy	7.60	7.60	7.60

Applying the Expected Utility Criterion for Decision-Making

Now we determine the expected utility for each decision:

EU (Stock A) = .3 (10) + .5 (8.20) + .2 (0) = 7.10; (EMV = $5,500)
EU (Stock B) = .3 (9) + .5 (7.00) + .2 (6.) = 7.40; (EMV = −$8,000)
EU (neither) = .3 (7.6) + .5 (7.6) + 0.2 (7.6) = 7.6; (EMV = $0)

Table 9.4
Expected Payoffs: Monetary vs. Utility

Expected Outcome / Decision	Monetary	Utility
Buy Stock A	$5,500*	7.10
Buy Stock B	−$8,000	7.40
Do not buy	$0	7.60**

The decision: *buy neither stock*.

Although buying Stock A gives the highest EMV (marked with an asterisk in Table 9.4), the investor should not purchase it. Why? Because the 20% probability of losing $60,000 is considered too high a risk by the investor. EMV considers $5,500 in *absolute* terms; EU considers the outcome in *relative* terms: How damaging is the loss of 60% of the investment to the investor? His choice, marked by double asterisks, shows the importance of substantial potential loss to him.

Risk-Avoiding, Risk-Neutral, Risk-Accepting

Figure 9.1 presents the *utility function of money*, plotting utility against monetary value. By joining the utility for the best and the worst outcomes, we get the *risk-neutral* function. The utility function of our *risk-avoiding* investor rises above the risk-neutral line. Proceding as we did in determining the points of

Figure 9.1
Utility Function of Money

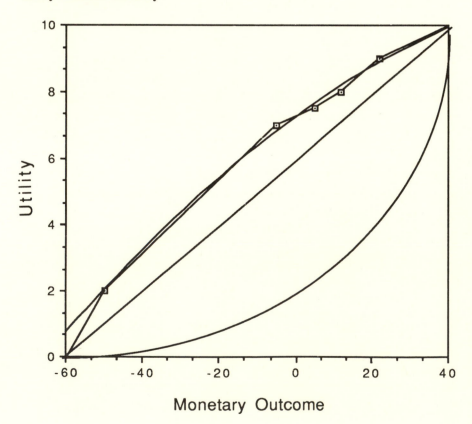

indifference between certainty and uncertainty, we can construct a *risk-accepting* function, shown in Figure 9.1.

For the no-loss ($0) outcome, the *risk-avoider* has a greater utility (7.6) than the risk-acceptor (2.5). For the risk-avoider, decreasing loss means *faster*-rising utility and increasing profits mean *slower*-rising utility function. For the *risk-acceptor*, decreasing loss means *slower*-rising utility, and increasing profits mean *faster*-rising utility function. When the decision-maker is *risk-neutral*, both EU and EMV give identical results. When the best and worst payoffs are reasonable to the decision-maker, EMV is appropriate; if not, EU is appropriate.

MARKET APPLICATION 8: MULTIATTRIBUTE UTILITY FUNCTION FOR NUCLEAR POWER PLANT SITE SELECTION

From single-person, single-criterion decision-making, we turn to *multi-criteria, multiperson decision-making*. Our stock investor had one criterion: money outcome, the attitude toward which we developed in his utility function. The decision-maker was a single person. Now we turn to a problem with many constituencies, each with several criteria.

Conflicting Objectives of Multiple-Interest Groups

The Washington Public Power Supply System (WPPSS) in the state of Washington asked a consulting company to help them select alternate nuclear power plant sites. The difficulty of the assignment is best reflected in the public's attitude: "I want nuclear power, but not in my backyard."

The WPPSS is the customer of the consulting company. To the customer, the question is not whether or not to go nuclear, but where to locate the nuclear plant(s) cost-effectively. However, to the several constituencies affected by the site decision, other criteria weigh heavily: salmon industry—don't reduce the stock of salmon; environmentalists—reduce radiation hazards, reduce to a minimum the biological impact at site, and so on.

The first job of the consulting group is to sort out the many constituencies that have a say in the nuclear plant operations. The second is to identify each group's objectives. The third is to specify a single operational measure of outcome for each group.

Multiattribute Utility Function

The consulting group selects the following six attributes of plant sites:

X_1—radiation hazard to humans

X_2—loss of salmon

X_3—biological impact at site

X_4—socioeconomic impact

X_5—length of intertie through environmentally sensitive areas

X_6—annual differential cost between sites in 1985 dollars

The *multiattribute utility function* U $(X_1, X_2, \ldots, X_6)$ can become an *additive utility function* $\Sigma k_i\, u_i\, (x_i)$, $(i = 1, 2, \ldots, n)$, where k_i, $i = 1, 2, \ldots, n$ are *scaling constants,* indicating the relative importance of changing each attribute from its least desirable to its most desirable level. As Keeney[1] puts it:

To assess these scaling constants, one generates data representing stated value judgments of the decision maker. For instance, the decision maker may be indifferent between $(x_1, \ldots, x_n)$ and $(x'_1, \ldots, x'_n)$. Then the utility of these two consequences, since they are indifferent, must be equal. They are set equal using

$$u\,(x_1, \ldots, x_n) = k_i \cdot u_i\,(x_i)\ (i = 1, 2, \ldots, n)$$

which yields an equation with the scaling factors as unknowns. Using such differences, one generates a set of n independent equations which is solved to determine values for the n unknown scaling factors. This significantly simplifies the comparison tasks required of the decision makers. More details about the assessment of utility functions can be found in Fishburn,[2] Huber,[3] Keeney and Raiffa,[4] Bell,[5] and many other sources.

Notice that the decision-maker has to find himself *indifferent* between one set of values of the attributes $(X_1, \ldots, X_n)$ and another set of values of the attributes $(X'_1, \ldots, X'_n)$, similar to the stock market investor declaring himself indifferent between one certain outcome and another uncertain outcome.

Under what conditions can a multiattribute utility function be represented by the additive utility function? (1) Utility independence—the utility attributes must be independent of each other [e.g., U (X_1) is independent of U (X_2)]. Unless each utility is independent of each other, we cannot put the $+$ sign connecting them. Only when the utility of the radiation hazard is independent of the utility of the loss of salmon can we add the effects of these two attributes. (2) Preference independence—the preference order of attribute pairs (e.g., X_1, X_2) must be independent of the *levels* of other attributes (e.g., X_3, X_4, X_5). To determine the indifference level between (a) additional plant cost, X_6, and (b) loss of salmon, X_2, we compare the different combinations, given that the other attributes were at their *best levels.* Repeat the process, given that the other attributes were at their *worst levels.* If the answer is the same in both cases, (X_6, X_2) trade-off is independent of the level of the other attributes.

Keeney and Nair provide us the values they obtained for the scaling constants.[6] How do we interpret the results? First, we need to establish a scale. A scale must have a zero point. We can use the smallest scaling constant, k_3, as zero. Second, a scale must also define the distance between zero and 1. In the present instance we can make the distance between the smallest, k_3, and the next smallest, k_5, as the scale. We find it to be $(.059 - .013 =)\ .046$. Third, we divide each k by the scale to express it in scale units:

$k_6 = .400/.046 = 8.69$ units

$k_1 = .358/.046 = 7.78$ units

$k_2 = .218/.046 = 4.74$ units

$k_4 = .104/.046 = 2.26$ units

$k_5 = .059/.046 = 1.30$ units

$k_3 = .013/.046 = 0.28$ units

The differential plant cost, k_6, is the most important factor in the nuclear plant site selection, followed by radiation hazard, k_1. The biological impact at site is the least important factor. The most important factor is 31.03 times as important as the least important.

MARKET APPLICATION 9: PENALTY FOR NONFULFILLMENT FOR NUCLEAR POWER PLANT SITE SELECTION

The Neumann-Morgenstern utility function is based on the indifference between certainty and uncertainty for the single-attribute utility function and between one set of attribute values and another. Furthermore, the conditions of utility independence and preference independence must be satisfied to convert the multiattribute utility function into additive utility function.

Indifference and Interaction Issues

We impose these conditions and ask the decision-maker to choose the level, L, of one attribute, X_2, that would make him indifferent between L and a 50:50 lottery of the best and the worst levels of another attribute, X_6. *We ignore any interaction* between X_2 and X_6.

Is it proper to ignore the interactions? Is radiation hazard to humans totally independent of the biological impact at the site? Or, is the socioeconomic impact totally independent of the loss of salmon? In imagining level L of one attribute and comparing it to a 50:50 lottery of the best and the worst outcomes of another, the decision-maker has to imagine successfully (losing 30% of the salmon, increasing the plant cost by $10 million), (losing 40% of the salmon, increasing the plant cost by $5 million), and so on. The comparison is much harder than the construction of a single-attribute utility function with a money outcome that is certain versus another that is uncertain.

Requirement of a System Performance Measure

Even after obtaining the empirical values of the different scaling constants, the question remains, How much loss of salmon can be traded for an additional cost of $10 million in nuclear plant construction? How much radiation hazard to humans can be traded for an additional cost of $30 million in nuclear plant construction?

The critical question is, What is the *performance measure of the system* of which the nuclear plant is a part? Without such a measure of the system as a whole, there is no equitable way to arbitrate between the salmon lobby, which argues for 0% loss of salmon, and the environmentalist lobby, which asks for 0% increase in radiation. We define what a system is:

A system is an entity of interacting elements functioning both individually and collectively to achieve the objectives of the entity as a whole.

We have to define what constitutes the system in terms of the performance against which the impact of salmon loss and radiation hazard can be evaluated. We can build the system from the bottom up or the top down.

Bottom-Up Hierarchy Construction of the System: Complementary Competitors

For the bottom-up approach, we need to specify the peers of the nuclear plant that (a) complement the nuclear plant in achieving the same system objective(s) and (b) compete with the nuclear plant for identical resources. These *complementing* and *competing peers* further the objectives of the same *common superior*. Because the nuclear plants produce energy, competing peers would be producers of energy from other sources, such as coal and hydroelectric. These power plants further the objective of energy production. We represent their complementarity as follows:

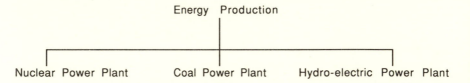

They complement each other in producing energy; by the same token they compete with each other for the resources to produce energy. The more resources allocated to nuclear energy, the less will be available for coal and hydroelectric. The resources allocated will depend on the respective contribution of nuclear, coal, and hydroelectric power plant to the objective of the common superior, energy production. Who is the energy production for? An obvious user of energy is industry; another is home; another is transportation. We can make a binary classification: industry and nonindustry.

But energy is only one of the resources that industry and nonindustry demand. Industry requires other resources, such as men, materials, machinery, money, and market. Our concern here is with the production aspects of industry, not its distribution; so we exclude market. If we concentrate on the inanimate aspects of industrial production, we exclude men. We also exclude money, as it is an inclusive surrogate of men (wages and salaries). That leaves us with materials and machinery. We thus have:

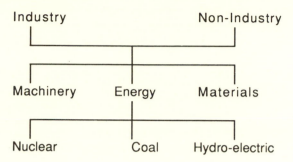

Top-Down Hierarchy Construction of the System: Complementary Competitors

We could start with the national objective of "life, liberty, and the pursuit of happiness" as the top of the hierarchy of objectives that are fulfilled in whole or in part by nuclear power plants. Ultimately the resources for nuclear power plants must compete with all other means of meeting these national objectives.

The WPPSS nuclear plant(s) contributes directly to the local community; so we should identify the community level, not the national level, of objectives. We use the phrase "quality of life" to include life, liberty, and the pursuit of happiness, making Tier 1 of the objectives hierarchy "Improve Community Quality of Life."

How can the Tier 1 objective be best pursued? By earning and enjoying. Have enough money to be comfortable, and have enough time to enjoy it. To increase earnings one must have the ability (skills) and the opportunity (jobs). The jobs can be in industry or nonindustry. The system objectives hierarchy is shown in Figure 9.2.

In Tier 4 the top-down and bottom-up constructs meet, as they should in logically consistent hierarchies. Having placed the nuclear power plant in the system perspective, the question is, How high should we go up the objectives hierarchy for resources?

Choosing the Right Hierarchical Level for Resource Allocation

Just as the nuclear power production competes with the coal and hydroelectric power production, the six attributes identified by the consulting group to WPPSS also compete with one another for resources. For instance, $5 million spent to save salmon makes $5 million less available to reduce radiation hazard to humans.

We can think of WPPSS as paying out $5 million, $40 million, and so on to the competing attributes. However, WPPSS itself must receive funding from the

Figure 9.2
Objectives Hierarchy: WPPSS

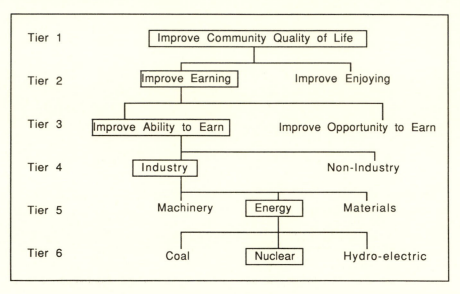

pool of energy production resources. By going one level above the immediate dispenser of funds, we have recognized the system germane to the resource allocation to the six attributes as energy: *Tiers 1 through 3 metasystem; Tiers 4 through 6 system.*

The amount of resources that should be allocated to each attribute depends on what each attribute contributes to the system objective.

Identifying Action-Level Elements as Part of the System

We find that there are different types of cost associated with the different attributes. Thus Attribute X_6, annual differential cost between sites in 1985 dollars (30-year plant life), is a *monetary cost* element. Attribute X_1, radiation hazard to humans, is measured as a *human cost*, as is Attribute X_4, socio-economic impact. Attribute X_3, biological impact at site, is an *environmental cost*, as are Attribute X_5, length of intertie through environmentally sensitive areas, and Attribute X_2, loss of salmon.

In Figure 9.3 we show all three types of costs: monetary, human, and environmental. The monetary costs should cover (1) acquisition, (2) operation and maintenance, and (3) replacement. The "30-year plant life" figure may be assumed to cover (1) and (2), so we add (3) replacement cost as a component of the monetary cost.

Figure 9.3
Action-Level Items of WPPSS Objectives Hierarchy

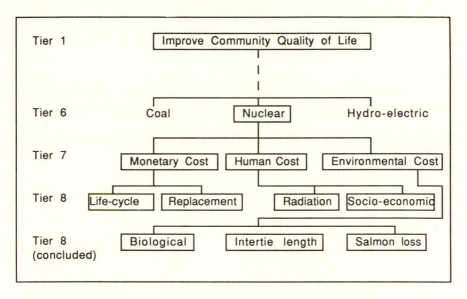

Nonfulfillment, Instead of Fulfillment, as the Criterion

Decreasing the radiation hazard to humans is a worthy goal. But how much is it worth: $5 million in additional cost of nuclear plant construction? $50 million? Although it is difficult to agree on what constitutes acceptable radiation hazard to humans, it would be much easier to reach agreement on what constitutes unacceptable radiation hazard.

A historic parallel may be drawn here with the clean air concept. When the predecessor to the current Environmental Protection Agency, called National Air Pollution Control Administration (NAPCA), was defining its objectives, it did *not* opt for clean air as an objective. How clean is clean? How many parts per million of what set of impurities? If thousands of tons of grass were planted, that should help the progress toward clean air, but tons of grass growing silently in the parks and on the sidewalks is not an exciting political event that congressmen can point to with pride and ask for appropriations.

On Thanksgiving Day, 1966, New York City experienced an atmospheric inversion, which occurs when a high-pressure system becomes almost motionless over a period of time, causing air pollutants to make a concentrated attack on the population instead of being wafted away by the wind. It particularly aggravates the illness of people who suffer from lung problems. A two-year study determined that the 1966 inversion was responsible for 180 additional deaths.[7] Such an occurrence is called an "episode." The effect of an episode is more directly visible, the 180 deaths making more direct impact on congressional decision-makers than thousands of tons of grass growing silently, making the air cleaner. No wonder NAPCA's No. 1 objective was "episode avoidance"—preventing atmospheric inversions—which is far more readily understood than clean air.

It is one thing to say that episodic avoidance is a much better understood objective than clean air. To allocate resources, we have to be able to say by how much the system objective is impaired by not having enough funds to ensure episodic avoidance. Our measure is PFN, which we define as follows:

PFN is the degradation of the system effectiveness owing to nonperformance at subsystem or lower levels.

PFN: Horizontal Scores

Of the *monetary cost* elements, which will have a more adverse impact on system performance: life cycle cost, or replacement cost? Obviously, the former. Let us assign it the maximum PFN of 9 on a scale of 1 to 9. Let us assign a PFN of 4 to the replacement cost.

Of the *human cost* elements, which is worse for the system objective if not performed? (Reduction of) radiation hazard to humans, or (reduction of) socioeconomic impact? Let us assign as high a PFN as possible, next to life cycle costs, to radiation hazard: 8. What should be the corresponding PFN for socioeconomic impact? Half as much? A third? Three-quarters as much? Let us assign it 6. *No two elements should have the same PFN.* We force the decision-maker to explicate his subjective estimate of every element's importance to the system unambiguously, using $>$ relationships.

Of the three *environmental cost* elements, let us say that intertie is the least critical and the loss of salmon the most critical, with the biological impact on the site falling in between. Let us give a PFN of 5 to the loss of salmon, a 3 to biological impact at site, and a 1 to length of intertie through environmentally sensitive areas.

By how much would the system performance be degraded if the two activity elements of monetary value were not performed? We add their PFNs: (from left to right: 9 + 4 =) 13. To allow for other peer elements on the same tier (Tier 8) that could have been left out, we multiply the sum of the PFNs by 1.5: (13 × 1.5 =) 19.5, rounded up to 20 for monetary cost PFN.

Similarly, we get (from left to right: 8 + 6 =) 14 for the components of the human cost. Multiply the total PFN of 14 by 1.5 to get 21 for human cost PFN. Similarly, we get (from left to right: 3 + 1 + 5 =) 9, multiplied by 1.5 = 13.5, rounded up to 14 for environmental cost PFN.

Tier 7 elements together total a PFN of (from left to right: 20 + 21 + 14 =) 55. Multiplying it by 1.5, we have 82.5, rounded up to 83 as the PFN for nuclear [power production]. We will use 84 for easier computations.

How significant is coal and hydroelectric power in terms of nuclear power? Let us say that coal is half as important, and that hydroelectric two-thirds as much, yielding PFNs, respectively, of (84 × .5 =) 42 for coal and (84 × 2/3 =) 56 for hydroelectric. The horizontal scores of Tier 6 add to (from left to right: 84 + 56 + 42 =) 182, which when multiplied by 1.5 gives 273 for Tier 5, energy production.

PFN: Vertical Weights

We know that the impairment of energy production is much worse than the impairment of one of its components, such as nuclear, coal, or hydroelectric. Further, the impairment of energy is much worse than the impairment of one of its sub-subcomponents, such as monetary cost or human cost.

The PFN for a subsystem is higher than that for its sub-subsystems, and the PFN for a system is much higher than that for a subsystem. This is reflected in the nonlinear weights for each tier.

Our system is energy production at Tier 5. Its logical components are subsystems in Tier 6, nuclear, coal, and hydroelectric plants. Its logical components are the sub-subsystems in Tier 7, monetary cost, human cost, and environmental cost. Its logical components are the sub-sub-subsystems in Tier 8, life cycle cost, replacement cost, radiation hazard to humans, and so on.

To reflect the fact that the nonperformance of monetary cost is much worse than life cycle or replacement cost, if we give a weight of 10 to Tier 8, then Tier 7 should be given a higher weight of, say, 15. Because Tier 7 is higher than Tier 8 by 5, the next higher rung (Tier 6) should have a greater difference than 5— say, 8. Thus Tier 6 has a weight of (15 + 8=) 23. Tier 5 gets a higher increase over Tier 6 than Tier 6 over Tier 5, say 12, to yield a weight of (23 + 12 =) 35, as shown in Table 9.5.

Weighted PFNs for Resource Allocation

The amount of resources that should be allocated to any one of the Tier 8 level activities depends on the impairment of the system (Tier 5) owing to nonperformance of the activity (Tier 8).

We now insert the (horizontal) scores and (vertical) weights into the objectives hierarchy in Figure 9.4. Consider the radiation hazard to humans. Its weighted score is given by (horizontal score × vertical weight) = (8 × 10) = 80. What is the significance of (not reducing) radiation hazard to humans? Divide the *activity weighted score* by the *system weighted score*. The system weighted score is (273 × 35 =) 9,555. The resource allocation to (reduce) radiation hazard to humans is given by:

Table 9.5
Nonlinear Vertical Weights of PFN

Tier	Vertical Weight	(Tier i+1 - Tier i)
Tier 5	35	
Tier 6	23	12
Tier 7	15	8
Tier 8	10	5

Figure 9.4
PFN Scores and Weights of WPPSS Objectives Hierarchy

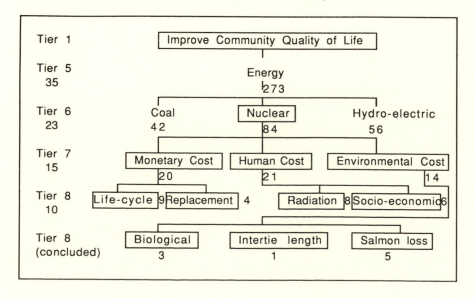

System budget (activity weighted score/system weighted score).

If energy production budget is $250 million, then radiation hazard reduction should receive ($250 million × 80/9,555 =) $2.093 million. See Chacko (1989)[8] for many applications of the method.

Meaning of PFN

This illustrative calculation does not mean that radiation hazard reduction will receive or must receive $2.093 million. What it does say is that *if* the subjective scores and subjective weights truly reflect the reality, *then* radiation hazard reduction contributes 0.83% to the system performance. Or, nonperformance of radiation hazard reduction will impair the system performance by 0.83%

Clearly, the exact percentage will change according to the weights and scores. If, for instance, it takes $10 million to do an effective reduction of radiation hazard to humans, then it has to be convincingly demonstrated to the decision-maker that radiation reduction contributes not 0.83%, but 4.0% to the system performance; or that the reduction of radiation hazard is 4.82 times as important to the system as it is now shown.

At each tier the decision-maker has to agree with the weighted scores given by different activities to themselves and to their common superior. Tiers 7, 6, and 5 decision-makers have to reconcile the different weights and scores proposed by their lower-tier components. Each would challenge their subordinates to justify the particular scheme of PFNs. The process of explicating the assumptions underlying the PFNs will make real to the entire system its interdependencies in furthering the system objective(s).

PFN versus Utility Function

Utility Function	PFN
1. Utility as a measure of significance (money) gained or gainable	1. Penalty as a measure of significance lost or losable
2. Associate probability with each outcome	2. Not applicable
3. Determine the indifference between certainty and uncertainty	3. Determine > relationship between penalties
4. Not applicable	4. Hierarchical relationships explicate component penalties

CONCLUDING OBSERVATIONS

Decision-making is based not only on outcomes, but also on attitudes. In chapter 7 we modified the initial guesses about outcomes by empirical data, such as experiment in the laboratory and market research survey in the field. In this chapter we turned to *attitude:* the preparedness to accept [adverse] outcome.

We have considered an investor contemplating $100,000 investment in Stock A, or Stock B, not both. Based on prior experience, he believes that the market will go up 30% of the time, down 20% of the time, and remain stationary 50% of the time. Corresponding to each situation, the outcomes are Stock A $50,000 gain when the market is up; $5,000 gain when the market is stationary; and − $60,000 when the market is lower. The corresponding figures for Stock B are $20,000, − $8,000, − $50,000.

Based on the expected outcome, he would buy Stock A; but based on expected utility, he would buy neither stock. Why? Primarily because the decision-maker fears the loss of 50% and 60% of his total investment more gravely than the prospect of winning $20,000 and $50,000. His utility function is constructed by eliciting the probability p of a lottery of the best and worst outcomes ($50,000 and − $60,000), which will make him indifferent to guaranteed outcomes, both positive and negative.

In the stock market investment there has been only one criterion: monetary outcome of the investment. When there are not one, but six attributes (criteria), the multidimensional function has to be reduced to a single-dimensional additive utility function by ensuring both utility and preference independence, making it possible to elicit the point of indifference between one set of values of the function and another. The scaling constants are interpreted to signify the relative importance of each attribute.

However, the utility function does not answer the question, How much resources should be allocated to a particular attribute? For instance, if it takes $10 million to effectively reduce the radiation hazard to humans, is it worthwhile to spend that money on radiation instead of, say, reducing the loss of salmon? To answer this type of question, each competing activity should be expressed as logical components of an objectives hierarchy, at the apex of which is the appropriate system.

Each activity is assigned a score to grade it horizontally with reference to complementary and competing peers, and vertically with reference to superiors. Each activity receives resources according to its contribution to the system objective.

QUESTIONS: CONCEPTS AND COMPUTATIONS FOR COMMITMENT

Our focus is decision-making, not numbering-crunching. Therefore, we divide the reinforcement of the text material into six categories: (1) Concepts: Foundational, (2) Concepts: Formulational, (3) Computations, (4) Conclusions, (5) [Resource] Commitments, and (6) Caveats. See chapter 11 for answers to questions for this chapter.

Concepts: Foundational

1. Why does the utility function override the EMV decision?
2. How are the points on the utility function determined?

3. How well can salmon fishermen specify (1) their utility of losing 30% of the salmon for an increase in the nuclear plant cost of $10 million, (2) their utility of losing 40% of the salmon at an increase in the nuclear plant cost of $5 million, and (3) the sure salmon loss S, which makes them indifferent between S and a 50-50 lottery of $40 million additional nuclear plant costs and $0 additional nuclear plant costs?

4. What does the utility function ignore?

5. How can one criterion (salmon loss) be traded for another (radiation hazard)?

6. How does the PFN recognize the interaction of conflicting criteria and claims?

7. How can the utility function help to allocate resources between conflicting objectives?

8. How can PFN help the allocation problem in (7)?

Concepts: Formulational

The Problem: System Contribution of Two Competing Projects

Identify the project most strongly favored by *your boss,* A. Identify a similar project of your *boss' peer,* B. A and B report to K, who controls their resources. K and his peers, L and M, report to T, who controls their resources.

9. Develop a bottom-up hierarchy of the appropriate system.

10. Develop a top-down hierarchy of the appropriate system.

11. Develop a system performance characteristic and operational values to judge "before" and "after" allocation of resources.

Computations

The Problem: Resources Allocation for Two Competing Projects

12. Assign, with reasoning, horizontal PFN scores.

13. Assign, with reasoning, vertical weights to the PFN scores.

14. Allocate resources to A's project.

Conclusions

The Problem: Revised Resources Allocation for Two Competing Projects

15. What does (14) signify?

16. If the resources allocated to A's project in (14) are inadequate, how would you proceed to argue A's case?

Caveats

The Problem: Multiattribute, Multiperson Decision-Making

17. What are the limitations in fulfilling the primary conditions in constructing a multiattribute, multiperson utility function?

18. What limitations of (15) are overcome by the PFN approach?

19. What are the limitations of the PFN approach?

NOTES

1. Ralph L. Keeney, "Decision Analysis: An Overview," *Operations Research,* 30 (Sept.–Oct. 1982): 816.

2. Peter C. Fishburn, "Methods of Estimating Additive Utilities," *Management Science,* 13 (1967): 433–53.

3. George P. Huber, "Methods for Quantifying Subjective Probabilities and Multi-attribute Utilities," *Decision Science,* 5 (1974): 430–58.

4. Ralph L. Keeney and Howard Raiffa, *Decisions with Multiple Objectives* (New York: Wiley, 1976).

5. David E. Bell, "Consistent Assessment Procedures using Conditional Utility Functions," *Operations Research,* 27 (1979): 1054–66.

6. Ralph L. Keeney and Kesavan Nair, "Selecting Nuclear Power Plant Sites in the Pacific Northwest using Decision Analysis," in *Conflicting Objectives in Decision,* ed. David E. Bell (New York: Wiley, 1979), p. 310.

7. Jack C. Fensterstock and Robert K. Frankhauser, "Thanksgiving 1966 Air Pollution Episode in the Eastern United States," HEW National Air Pollution Control Administration Publication No. Ap. 45, Raleigh, N.C., July 1968.

8. George K. Chacko, *The Systems Approach to Problem Solving: From Corporate Markets to National Missions* (New York: Praeger, 1989).

10 Aggregate Action-Outcome Anticipations of Multiple Decision-Makers

OVERVIEW: In chapter 9 linear utility functions were used to assess the attitude of single decision-makers and multiple decision-makers. The iterative *approach to determine the indifference between certainty and uncertainty is not a luxury allowed in choosing options in* interactive *nuclear confrontation. Using the only nuclear brink ever experienced in human history, the Cuban Missile Crisis, the presidential decision-maker's own statements during the crisis are used to develop seven major concerns in interactive decision-making.*

On the 12th day of the 13-day crisis, contradictory evidences were mounting. How would they be handled by (1) subjective probability—the utter uniqueness of nuclear confrontations makes any estimate hard to sustain; (2) Bayes' theorem—to estimate the conditional probability of strategic nuclear war, one has to already know it: a catch-22; (3) construction of probability argument—emphasis on quality of evidence is well taken, but how should the individual support functions be assessed? and (4) fuzzy sets—useful in explicating degrees of control exercised by Khrushchev, but requires a certainty factor for each piece of evidence.

A different approach is required. It should explicate the interactive *nature of alternative moves by the different parties, who themselves have to anticipate successive alternative outcomes. The anticipations have to provide plausible outcomes in not the 1st or 2nd moves, but much farther down the line, say the 10th or 15th set of moves and countermoves. In international relations, statements are designed to convey, as much as to camouflage, purposes and plans: many a war broke out because signals were misread. It is little use to assume the veracity of the opponent's statements. More often the contrary is true.*

We define bluff *as any characterization of a situation. It becomes a* threat *with an identified/implemented effective response. Notice that no requirement is made that the characterization be correct, true, or rational. The only question is, Does it cause the other party to take effective response, or seek to identify one? A's bluff, AB1, is countered by B's threat, BT1. To A, it is B's bluff, BB1, that A counters with a threat, AT1, which B responds to with BT2, and so on. The bluffs–threats (B–T) matrix explicates* interactive sequence of moves *by the parties. Of course, the B–T matrix as seen by A would probably be different from the B–T matrix as seen by B.*

The four statistical methods discussed earlier are all iterative, not interactive: their concern is on improving a single value or range of values. The scope is micro: the investor choosing a stock; the witness describing a get-away car. In international issues, however, the scope is macro. Enumerating the probability of outcome of every single micro move would be hardly useful even if it were possible.

We divide every possible action in international relations into four macro categories: (1) commercial, (2) diplomatic, (3) political, and (4) military. If A's commercial action is responded to in kind by B, it is commercial-commercial (C-C). If the commercial action is responded to by the other macros we have C-D, C-P, and C-M.

The purpose of these four aggregate actions *is to calibrate how the situation can be aggravated or ameliorated. In the hypothetical instance discussed, a Polish ham imports embargo by the United States could elicit a C-C, such as a Polish embargo on U.S. potato imports. It could also conceivably lead to C-D (recall of the Polish ambassador to the United States), C-P (Polish subversion to destabilize the United States), or even C-D (Polish declaration of war on the United States).*

The purpose of the B–T matrix is to determine the number of steps in which the initial action could lead to the highest military conflict, strategic nuclear war. At the Cuban Missile Crisis, President Kennedy's embargo around Cuba was a premilitary move. If Khrushchev interpreted it as an M, he could respond with an M-unconventional, conventional, tactical nuclear, strategic nuclear war (SNW). The number of steps from the Cuban embargo to SNW was clearly far fewer than those from the embargo on Polish ham to SNW.

To determine the number of steps separating any action from Armageddon, we need to determine the probability of response in kind (CC, DD, PP, MM). Expert opinion can be elicited; it has to be explicated. The response not-in-kind should also be ascertained. These probabilities can be applied successively to determine the sequence of steps required to reach a specified probability, say 5%, of SNW. Choose the sequence that will take the larger number of steps to reach SNW.

In the case of a real-life military situation, the author briefed at the Pentagon a group of senior military officers chosen from each armed service, and asked them to suggest the wildest characterization they could of the given situation. What was the situation? What would they do? Their analysis and recommendations were explicated by their choice of the B–T matrix cell to represent their perception of the situation and the recommended course of action. When the individual B–T matrices were placed physically on top of each other, the chosen cells were found to cluster together in a very small area. Despite their deliberate efforts to exaggerate their differences, the macro moves of B–T matrix clarified their fundamental agreement on the course of action.

MILITARY MISSION APPLICATION 3: THE ODDS THAT THE SOVIETS WOULD GO ALL THE WAY TO WAR, [JOHN F. KENNEDY] LATER SAID, SEEMED TO HIM THEN "SOMEWHERE BETWEEN ONE OUT OF THREE AND EVEN"

The Cuban Missile Crisis, the single nuclear brink ever experienced in human history, provides us with a unique instance of global survival hanging in the balance of multivariable decision-making by multiple decision-makers, operating with very few data points. What moves and countermoves did the principals themselves anticipate as they had to make real-time decisions?

"This Would Mean War"

"This would mean war" was Robert Kennedy's somber assessment based on Edgar Hoover's information the night before "that certain Soviet personnel were apparently preparing to destroy all sensitive documents on the basis that the U.S. would probably be taking military action against Cuba or Soviet ships and *this would mean war*" (emphasis added).[1]

We discussed at length in chapter 2 the logical probability considerations that could have weighed on Robert Kennedy's mind in support of the conclusion "This would mean war"; and we identified the type of subjective probability reasoning that led him to reject the compelling evidence pointing to the conclusion. Robert Kennedy was certainly very close to the decision-maker. In fact, it was his recommendation to ignore the second letter from Khrushchev that John Kennedy accepted, and that turned the tide.

Point of Escalation; Point of De-Escalation

The letter was drafted by Robert Kennedy and Ted Sorensen, special counsel to the president. What the president did with the letter suggests his estimate of nuclear war at 50:50 probability.

At the private request of the President, a copy of the letter was delivered to the Soviet Ambassador by Robert Kennedy with a strong verbal message: *The point of escalation was at hand;* the United States could proceed toward *peace and disarmament,* or as the Attorney General later described it, we could take *"strong and overwhelming retaliatory action . . .* unless [the president] received immediate notice that the missiles would be withdrawn" [emphasis added].[2]

It is quite interesting that the president conveyed to Moscow that the point of escalation was at hand: even at the 12th day of the 13-day crisis, things could go either way—which means even odds on war. As a matter of fact, Sorensen quotes President Kennedy on what he felt were the odds at the time: "The odds that the Soviets would go all the way to war, he later said, seemed to him then, 'somewhere between *one out of three and even*' " (emphasis added).[3]

Although we do not know *when* Kennedy thought the probability of nuclear war was 33%, we can infer that it was 50% on Day 12 when Robert Kennedy transmitted the verbal message. Admittedly, we recognize that John Kennedy's reflecting on what he thought during the Cuban Missile Crisis as narrated later, does not suggest strict numerical precision. The question is not whether the probability was 32.6% or 33.3%, but rather the order of magnitude. A value higher than 50% means that he, the decision-maker on the U.S. side, felt that the outcome was in question: outbreak of nuclear war was inevitable.

Escalation Calibration Approach 1: Subjective Probability

If the initial guess of the outcome was 33%, how did it rise to 50%? What new data did he use? How did he use them? In chapter 2 we explored the new evidence that appeared to raise the logical probability of war to 1. We also saw that Robert Kennedy overruled the logical probability. We know *what* happened; we will try to reason *how*.

Savage, whose interpretation of Bayes in *The Foundations of Statistics*[4] has gained wide acceptance, considers Bayesian probability as a particular person's opinion deducible from his behavior when he chooses among bets or other acts with uncertain outcome. Following Savage, Bender and Nack[5] hold that Bayes' theorem can help judges and jurors combine evidence.

It may appear that Bayesian probabilities are ready-made, waiting to be elicited. In Savage's last paper he says that an idealized real person may be induced "to reveal his opinions as expressed by the probabilities that he associates with events, or more generally, his personal expectation of random quantities."[6]

Savage suggests that probability is a price, a marginal rate of substitution. This is an expectation $E(I_A)$, where $I_A = 1$ if A occurs and 0 if it does not. The rate of substitution $E(V)$ is the person's expectation of the unknown, or random quantity V:

There is reason to postulate that an ideally coherent person has a rate of substitution $P(A)$ for money contingent on the event A. When q is not too large, he is indifferent to buying or selling q dollars contingent on A for qP dollars overnight, and $P(A)$ is defined as the probability of A for that person.[7,8]

A probability $P(A)$ is itself plainly an expectation. . . . It is meaningful and convenient to write $P(A) = E(A)$.[9]

Savage points out that the person's utility function is implied to be *linear* in money, an assumption that he says is not unreasonable if only moderate sums of money are involved. We have already examined the linear utility function in chapter 9. But it is a long way from "moderate sums of money" to global annihilation. Savage bases his definition of probability as a rate of substitution on Bayes' concept of commodity: "Money payable subject to a contingency, such as the accidental burning of a house or the outcome of a race can be regarded as a commodity."[10] Facing the very first nuclear war, no such "commodity" is available.

Escalation Calibration Approach 2: Bayes' Theorem

Setting aside the empirical problems of assessing subjective (prior) probabilities in nuclear confrontation, let us consider if Bayes' theorem applies to unknown events (e.g., strategic nuclear war). In chapter 7 we said that Bayes reverses (conclusion given condition) into (condition given conclusion). The question he asks is, What condition will follow from this conclusion?

We can say that SNW does not appear clear out of the blue, with no prior signs. Significant conflicts of a global nature (e.g., conventional war [CW] are an indispensable precondition. What is the conditional probability of SNW given CW?

$$P\,(\text{SNW}|\text{CW}) = \frac{P\,(\text{CW}|\text{SNW})\,.\,P\,(\text{SNW})}{P\,(\text{CW}|\text{SNW})\,.\,P\,(\text{SNW}) + P\,(\text{CW}|\overline{\text{SNW}})\,.\,P\,(\overline{\text{SNW}})}$$

It is a catch-22! We need to know already as a given the probability of SNW, which is what we are looking for! Further, there is a real problem of meaning for the transition from SNW to CW.

We see that Bayes' theorem does not apply to truly unknown/unknowable situations. Its contribution is in converting an unknown situation into exclusive and exhaustive components that are experimentally or empirically known or knowable, which SNW is not. In addition, the illogic of (CW|SNW) rules out using Bayes' theorem.

Escalation Calibration Approach 3: Construction of Probability Arguments

We saw in chapter 8 that Shafer questions the Bayesian practice of determining the "likelihoods" associated with evidence, without reference to its quality. In the Cuban Missile Crisis the quality of evidence was crucial. Was the conciliatory Khrushchev of Letter 1 really in control (A); or was the confrontary Khrushchev of Letter 2 in control (B)?

The Dempster-Shafer procedure requires two support functions $s_1(A) = s_1$, and $s_2(B) = s_2$. In the simplest instance we could say that s_1 (in favor of conciliatory Khrushchev) $= s_2$ (in favor of confrontary Khrushchev). If both are equally likely, $s_1 = s_2 = .5$ and $s_1 s_2 = .25$, Robert Kennedy would see that the combined evidence provides positive support for A∩B of .25.

How would we physically interpret A∩B: Khrushchev is in control and he is not in control? If we mean that half the time Khrushchev could be overruled, the support for that view is 25%.

Let us say that Letter 1 was consistent with all the evidence up to Letter 2, making s_1, say, .8 (corresponding s_2 being $1 - .8 = .2$). Then the proposition that Khrushchev would be overruled half the time is supported $(0.8 \times 0.2 =)$ 16% of the time.

The highest value of $s_1 = .99$ makes the support for Khrushchev being overruled 50% of the time given by $(s_1 . s_2 = .99 \times .01 = .0099)$. The range of support for Khrushchev being overruled is thus 1% to 25%.

Escalation Calibration Approach 4: Fuzzy Sets

The support functions throw into relief the inexactness in reality itself. We saw in chapter 8 that the proposition that "John is tall" translates into a possibility distribution of the variable height (John). Each value of the variable height (John) (e.g., 5'0", 6'7", etc.) is associated with a number in the unit interval [0,1] (e.g., 0.00, 0.08, etc.) representing the possibility of the variable assuming that value.

Apropos the Cuban Missile Crisis, "Khrushchev is in control" is the variable. The values of the variable could be (0.00, 0.35, . . . 1.00). [control (Khrushchev, 0.00)] could have the possibility 0.01, 0.02, . . . , 1.00. Similarly, [control (Khrushchev, 0.53)], [control (Khrushchev, 0.89)], and so on could have similar possibilities.

Let us say that Letter 1 gives 70% chance for Khrushchev to be in control and Letter 2, 40% chance. The fuzzy operator f-OR disregards the accumulation of evidence and takes the max $(0.4, 0.7) = 0.7$. If instead probability -OR (p-OR) operator is used, $p(A \text{ or } B) = p(A) + p(B) - (p(A) \times p(B)) = .7 + .4 - .28 = 0.82$. The increase of 0.12 indicates the accumulation of evidence.

Inadequacies of the Four Escalation Calibration Approaches

The four escalation calibration approaches differ in their emphasis, but they all deal with uncertainty.

Subjective Probability. Apropos the Cuban Missile Crisis, we found that Savage's prior probability assessment requires a tangible commodity as the outcome, against which the decision-maker assesses his preferences. Such a concrete outcome is inappropriate and unavailable for unique events of cataclysmic proportions.

Bayes' Theorem. It was found that the conditional probability of SNW given CW requires us to already know the probability of SNW—a catch-22 situation. Further, one of the components, P (CW|SNW), is meaningless.

Construction of Probability Argument. Although the emphasis on the quality of evidence is well taken, the support functions for each proposition, A and B, has to be determined, and their interaction measures for the support of A∩B.

Fuzzy Sets. The question confronting Robert Kennedy was not an either-or proposition, Khrushchev was in control or not in control. Rather, Khrushchev was somewhat fully in control, something that fuzzy sets can formulate. But to combine conflicting evidence we need a certainty factor for each piece of evidence.

The fundamental question that remains is, How should the decision-maker evaluate the evidence? We develop Bluffs–Threats Interactive System (BTIS) as an analytical framework of reasoning in problems with interactive participants and interactive variables.

BLUFFS–THREATS INTERACTIVE SYSTEM

What are the principal presidential concerns?

"It isn't the first step that concerns me."

It is important that the elegance of analysis should pass the test of relevance of solution. At the height of the unprecedented crisis, with no prior applicable parallels, what was it that concerned the decision-maker the most? He had to act; and he had to do so in the face of overwhelming evidence in support of an imminent Soviet attack. Consider the chronology (time approximate).

Fri. Oct. 26, 1962: 6 P.M. Letter 1—Conciliatory

Sat. Oct. 27, 1962: 6 A.M. Letter 2—Confrontational

> 10:00 A.M. Edgar Hoover—Senior Soviet consular personnel in New York preparing to destroy all sensitive material
>
> 10:30 A.M. Robert McNamara—Russians and Cubans are working round the clock at the missile sites in Cuba
>
> 10:45 A.M. Joint Chiefs of Staff recommend air strike Monday, to be followed shortly by invasion of Cuba
>
> 11:00 A.M. U.S. Air Force Major Anderson's U-2 plane was reported hit by a surface-to-air missile (SAM) in Cuba; his plane crashed, and he was killed

What questions does the president want answered? We hear his concerns as recorded by his closest confidant and adviser:

"How can we send any more U-2 pilots into this area tomorrow unless we take out all of the SAM sites?" the President asked. *"We are now in an entirely new ball game."*

At first, there was almost unanimous agreement that we had to *attack early next morning [Sunday]* with bombers and fighters and destroy the SAM sites. But again the President pulled everyone back. "It isn't the first step that concerns me," he said, but *both sides escalating to the fourth and fifth step*—and we don't go to the sixth because there is no one around to do so. . . .

He asked for *absolute verification* that the U-2 was shot down and did not crash accidentally. . . . Again and again he emphasized that we must understand the implications of *every step. What response could we anticipate?* . . .

His mind went to other areas of the world. What was going to occur in Berlin, in Turkey? If we attacked Cuba and the Russians reciprocated with an attack on Turkey, would or should the Turkish missiles be fired? He ordered preparations taken to defuse missiles with atomic warheads, so that *he personally would have to give permission before they were used.* What role should Turkey and the rest of NATO have in determining our response? . . .

While the letter [Robert Kennedy-Ted Sorensen reply to the first Khrushchev letter, as modified by the President] was being typed and prepared for transmission, I sat in his office. . . . He talked about the miscalculations that lead to war. War is rarely intentional. The Russians don't wish to fight any more than we do. They do not want war with us nor we with them. . . .

He wanted to make sure that he had done everything in his power, everything conceivable, to prevent such a catastrophe. Every *opportunity was to be given to the Russians to find a peaceful settlement* which would not diminish their national security or be a *public humiliation.* . . .

Later, he was to say in his speech at American University in June of 1963: "Above all, while defending our own vital interests, nuclear powers must avert those confrontations which bring an adversary to the choice of either a humiliating defeat or a nuclear war" [Emphasis added; we could paraphrase the last thought as "humiliation or holocaust"].[11]

International Interactive System Desiderata*

We can identify seven primary presidential concerns from the words of President Kennedy and/or reports of Robert Kennedy, particularly during the 11th hour (12th day of the 13-day crisis). In fact, they can be considered the essential features of the *p*residential foreign policy *d*ecision *s*upport *s*ystem (PDSS).

1. Anticipated response at each step   (Anticipations)
2. Identification of allies at trigger points of war   (Allies)
3. Alternative scenarios of mutual escalation to
   the fourth and fifth steps   (Alternatives)
4. Ample opportunity for the adversary to avoid
   humiliation   (Avoidance)
5. Steps of de-escalation firmly in the president's
   hands   (Authority)
6. Full preparedness for appropriate escalation   (Arms)
7. Absolute verification of apparent provocations   (Absolute)

BTIS Feature 1: Comprehensive Classification of Every Conceivable Situation

Policy is multidimensional. Therefore, a PDSS should allow for explicit considerations of all possible dimensions of any word or deed anywhere in the international arena.

*Plural of desideratum—something needed and wanted.

Bluff in International Relations

We define bluff as *any characterization of a situation*. Notice that no reference is made to the truth or rationality or other quality of the content; "any characterization" means that deliberate misstatements, outright falsehood, and absolute truth are all bluffs. Words, which are the premier coin of the international realm, are used to communicate as well as to camouflage. Therefore, more than an hour before transmitting the reply to Moscow, Robert Kennedy was sent to meet with Ambassador Dobrynin at 7:45 P.M., Saturday, when Robert Kennedy engaged in some blunt talk:

> The Soviet Union had secretly established missile bases in Cuba while at the same time *proclaiming privately and publicly that this would never be done*. We had to have a commitment by tomorrow that these bases would be removed. I was not giving them an ultimatum but a statement of fact. He should understand that *if they did not remove those bases, we would remove them* [emphasis added].[12]

Notice that public and private proclamations were used by the Soviets to deceive the United States. The gravity of the deceit is illustrated by President Kennedy's calling the Soviets liars in his October 22 television address:

> This action also contradicts the repeated assurances of Soviet spokesmen, both publicly and privately delivered, that the arms build-up in Cuba would retain its original defensive character. [Referring to the public statement by the Soviet government on September 11] *That statement was false.*
>
> Only last Thursday, . . . Soviet Foreign Minister Gromyko told me in my office that he was instructed to make it clear once again, as he said his Government had already done, that Soviet assistance to Cuba, and I quote, "pursued solely for the purpose of contributing to the defense capabilities of Cuba." . . . *That statement also was false* [emphasis added].[13]

Threats in International Relations

In Washington, D.C., it is said, "Nobody believes anything in Washington until it is denied." The point underscores the more predominant role of camouflage than communication in political pronouncements, domestic and/or foreign. In the Cuban Missile Crisis, Kennedy already had incontrovertible proof of the Soviet missile sites being constructed in Cuba when he let Gromyko blatantly deny the fact to his face.

The content becomes important only in the context. If Kennedy had chosen to ignore the emplacement of Soviet missiles in Cuba, the content of the Soviet government statement on military buildup in Cuba, as well as the *content* of the message delivered in person by Gromyko, would have been treated at face value. However, in the *context* of the vigorous buildup of missile sites unmistakably photographed by American U-2 reconnaissance flights, the Soviet intent to tilt the nuclear balance decisively against the United States by shortening the distance that their missiles would have to travel from 5,000 miles to 90 miles, Kennedy called the *content* into question. It is interesting to note that the everyday expression Kennedy "called Khrushchev's bluff" is particularly appropriate here. The expression comes from bridge, in which the players are expected to bluff, make statements to camouflage their true hand.

In our definition any characterization of a situation is a bluff, so that the intrinsic veracity is immaterial. What is material is the *response*. Khrushchev's statement that the Soviet buildup in Cuba is purely to bolster Cuban domestic defense capabilities (implying that there were no intercontinental missiles involved) remained a bluff until Kennedy made a response best represented in Robert Kennedy's telling Anatoly Dobrynin, "If you don't remove the missile bases, we will remove them."

The response converted the bluff into a threat. *Threat is the identification/implementation of an effective response to the bluff.* When someone shouts, "There is a bomb in the building," if someone on the sixth floor as much as looked at the nearest window, the bluff has thereby become a threat to him. If, however, the hearer ignored the bluff, it remains a bluff. For our purposes, the inadequacy of the identified response is immaterial: He may not be able to get out through the window, which is wall to wall and made of shatter-proof glass. Nevertheless, his having eyed the window on hearing that there was a bomb in the building converted the bluff into a threat.

Comprehensive Classification

We classify all actions that can be taken in international relations into four macro categories: (1) commercial, (2) diplomatic, (3) political, and (4) military.

Commercial moves are the activities undertaken by one country that affect the allocation by another of scarce resources for economic results. Diplomatic moves are the activities undertaken by one country to communicate, clarify, and/or camouflage its position through the resident foreign representatives of another country or their surrogates. Political moves are the activities undertaken by one country to influence the internal political process of another. Military moves are the activities undertaken by one country using military and paramilitary forces, equipment, and supplies, covering the spectrum from low-intensity conflicts through SNW, to protect its vital interests.

These four are *macro-content* categories. An action could fall into one or all of the four categories (*"bluffs of initiation"*) of Country A, which would be responded to by *"threats of resolution"* by Country B, also in one or more of these categories.

BTIS Feature 2: Comprehensive Classification of Sequence of Interactive Steps

When a country makes a primarily commercial move—for example, if the United States bans imports of Polish ham into the United States, (American bluff 1: AB 1)—what would be the Polish response (Polish threat 1: PT 1)? Would the commercial bluff be responded to by a commercial threat? Or, would the commercial bluff bring a Polish diplomatic threat, such as the Polish expulsion of U.S. diplomats?

We define a *"step"* as *one set of bluff–threat, or move–countermove sequence* (e.g., AB 1–PT 1). It comprises two possible sequences: (1) C-C or (2) C-D. Treating PT 1 as PB 1, will the United States respond (AT 1) with something graver, say D-P, countering with a United States effort to destabilize the Polish government? Would it bring a response in kind, P-P, with the Polish government trying to destabilize the United States government, or even something graver, say P-M, the Polish government declaring conventional war (CW) on the United States? Would the United States then respond in kind, say M-M, escalating CW into SNW?

The purpose of this highly hypothetical and highly melodramatic scenario is to highlight that *a bluff becomes a threat only when a response is made, either in kind* (e.g., C-C) *or not in kind* (e.g., C-D, C-P, C-M). The response can utilize all the four categories *equally,* say, C-C 25%, C-D 25%, C-P 25%, and C-M 25% or *unequally,* say, C-C 10%, C-D 30%, C-P 50%, and C-M 10%. In the former we say that a C is responded to by a move that is 25% C, 25% D, 25% P, and 25% M; in the latter a C is responded to by a move that is 10% C, 30% D, 50% P, and 10% M.

BTIS Feature 3: Imbedding Each Participant
in a Macro Category

"What role should Turkey and the rest of the North Atlantic Treaty Organization have in determining our response?" is a question that President Kennedy raised during the Cuban Missile Crisis. BTIS provides for the classification of each country into four categories: (1) superpowers (2) primary allies, (3) secondary allies, and (4) non-allies.

Under commercial we can have (1) expansion (of trade) or (2) embargo.

01. Commercial expansion, non-allies
02. Commercial expansion, secondary allies
03. Commercial expansion, primary allies
04. Commercial expansion, superpowers
05. Commercial embargo, non-allies
06. Commercial embargo, secondary allies
07. Commercial embargo, primary allies
08. Commercial embargo, superpowers

Under diplomatic we have three alternatives: (1) expansion, (2) embargo, and (3) ambivalence.

09. Diplomatic expansion, non-allies

10. Diplomatic expansion, secondary allies

11. Diplomatic expansion, primary allies

12. Diplomatic expansion, superpowers

13. Diplomatic embargo, non-allies

14. Diplomatic embargo, secondary allies

15. Diplomatic embargo, primary allies

16. Diplomatic embargo, superpowers

17. Diplomatic ambivalence (DA), disputed rights of unspecified third parties

18. DA, disputed rights of specified third parties

19. DA, disputed treaty of unspecified third parties

20. DA, disputed treaty of specified third parties

21. DA, disputed territory of unspecified third parties

22. DA, disputed territory of specified third parties

Similarly, each country group is identified with respect to classes of problems in political and military categories.

BTIS Feature 4: Aggregate Action-Outcome in the Bluffs–Threats Micro Matrix Interaction

We now expand the 4×4 B–T matrix into 20×20.

We present in Table 10.1 general strategies of bluffs of initiation and threats of resolution. In the rows we show only 2 moves under commercial, 3 under diplomatic, 1 under political, and 14 under military, for a total of 20. Each bluff is responded to by a threat. Thus there are 20 rows (bluffs) and 20 columns (threats).

BTIS Feature 5: Aggregate Action-Outcome in the Bluffs–Threats Mini Matrix Interaction

From the 20×20 matrix we proceed to develop the full 110×90 B–T matrix in Table 10.2.

BTIS Feature 6: Expert Estimates of Only One Transition Probability

How can we use the B–T matrix to develop what would happen at the fourth or fifth step and beyond? The United States (USSR) can make its first move either completely C, D, P, or M, or 100% C, D, P, or M. (*pure strategies*). Or, it can use 0% to 99% of each variable (*mixed strategies*),as shown in Figure 10.1.

As we saw in our discussion of the Polish ham embargo, C can elicit a C response or a non-C response. Similarly, D, P, and M can elicit a response in kind or not in kind. We present in Figure 10.2 an illustrative interactive sequence of *mixed strategies,* opening with the USSR making a political move, eliciting a U.S. diplomatic response. Both the United States and the USSR respond with *mixed strategies,* selecting responses with fractions of C, D, P, and M.

We find that the key probability is just one: *probability of response in kind*— CC, DD, PP, MM. The experience and wisdom of the experts in many disciplines and fields of endeavor can be crystallized in their estimate of the probability of a response in kind by the other nation when the United States makes a move.

BTIS Feature 7: Unequal Number of Steps to Armageddon

In the 110 × 90 B–T matrix the U.S. embargo on Polish ham would be at the northwest corner, and SNW at the southeast corner. The objective of preventing SNW could be translated as *increasing the number of steps* between any action and the, say, 5% probability of the outbreak of SNW. How can we increase the number of intervening steps?

What the probability of response in kind enables us to do is to compute the probability of response not in kind as its complement. The four *initial* states of C, D, P, and M each can change to (transition) four *eventual* states C, D, P, and M. The 16 transitions can be computed by the United States as shown in Table 10.3, and by the USSR as shown in Table 10.4. We postulate that the SNW will occur only after MM.

Using the B–T transition matrix, we can find the number of steps it will take to reach 5% probability of SNW from any initial move. Given two sequences of steps, choose the one with the larger number of steps to SNW.

CONCLUDING OBSERVATIONS

In this concluding chapter we considered multiple-variable decision-making with multiple decision-makers. The Cuban Missile Crisis, the only nuclear brink experienced in human history, provided the empirical framework.

On the 12th day of the 13-day crisis a second letter was received from Khrushchev, reversing the conciliatory stance of the first letter. Overwhelming evidence was rapidly being built up to suggest that the Soviets were going to war.

We discussed four statistical approaches to assess the dramatic change: (1) subjective probability requires a commodity like money, unavailable for unique events of cataclysmic proportions; (2) Bayes' theorem leads to a catch-22 situation, the probability of SNW having already to be known to estimate it conditionally; (3) construction of probability argument requires the determination of support functions for competing propositions; and (4) fuzzy sets require that each piece of evidence have a certainty factor.

Table 10.1
General Strategies of Bluffs of Initiation and Threats of Resolution

	THREATS OF RESOLUTION (COLUMNS)

COMMERCIAL RESOLUTION

01. Commercial Expansion
02. Commercial Embargo

DIPLOMATIC RESOLUTION

03. Diplomatic Expansion
04. Diplomatic Embargo
05. Diplomatic Specification

POLITICAL RESOLUTION

06. Political Negotiation
07. Political Arbitration
08. Political Settlement

MILITARY RESOLUTION -PREPARATION

09. Nonuse of Military Power
10. Use of Military Preparation
11. Military Expansion
12. Military Embargo
13. Increased Effectiveness of Power
14. Intensification of Permissible Tests
15. Preparation for Test Resumption
16. Resumption of Banned Tests
17. Initiation of Space Tests

MILITARY RESOLUTION - ENGAGEMENT

18. Military Encounter Inititation
19. Military Encounter Escalation
20. Military Encounter Consummation

Table 10.1—Continued

THREATS OF RESOLUTION (COLUMNS)
BLUFFS OF INITIATION (ROWS)

COMMERCIAL INITIATION

01. Commercial Expansion
02. Commercial Embargo

DIPLOMATIC INITIATION

03. Diplomatic Expansion
04. Diplomatic Embargo
05. Diplomatic Ambivalence

POLITICAL INITIATION

06. Global Moral Imperative

MILITARY INITIATION

07. Nonuse of Military Power
08. Military Expansion
09. Military Embargo
10. Nuclear Capability Attainment Plans
11. Nuclear Detonation Bluff
12. Nuclear Detonation Initiative

13. Opponent's Bluff of Increased Capability
14. Intelligence of Opponent's Increased Capability
15. Detection of Opponent's Increased Capability
16. Opponent's Power Effectiveness Anticipation
17. Opponent's Power Effectiveness Accomplished

18. Military Encounter Inititation
19. Military Encounter Escalation
20. Military Encounter Consummation

THREATS OF RESOLUTION

(COLUMNS)

COMMERCIAL RESOLUTION

01. Commercial Expansion, non-allies
02. Commercial Expansion, secondary allies
03. Commercial Expansion, primary allies
04. Commercial Expansion, superpowers

05. Commercial Embargo, non-allies
06. Commercial Embargo, secondary allies
07. Commercial Embargo, primary allies
08. Commercial Embargo, superpowers

DIPLOMATIC RESOLUTION

09. Diplomatic Expansion, non-allies
10. Diplomatic Expansion, secondary allies
11. Diplomatic Expansion, primary allies
12. Diplomatic Expansion, superpowers

13. Diplomatic Embargo, non-allies
14. Diplomatic Embargo, secondary allies
15. Diplomatic Embargo, primary allies
16. Diplomatic Embargo, superpowers

17. Diplomatic Specification (DS), Identity of Third Party (WHO?)
18. DS, Identity of Area of Third Party Encounter (WHERE?)
19. DS, Identity of Aegis of Third Party Encounter (HOW?)
20. DS, Identity of Timing of Third Party Encounter (WHEN?)

POLITICAL RESOLUTION
* * * * * *

MILITARY RESOLUTION -PREPARATION
* * * * * *

MILITARY RESOLUTION - ENGAGEMENT

90. Military Consummation, Specified Unlimited

Table 10.2—Continued

```
┌──────────────────────────────────────────────────────────┐
│                  THREATS OF RESOLUTION                   │
│                                    (COLUMNS)             │
│                                                          │
│   BLUFFS OF INITIATION   (ROWS)                          │
├──────────────────────────────────────────────────────────┤
```

COMMERCIAL INITIATION
01. Commercial Expansion, non-allies
02. Commercial Expansion, secondary allies
03. Commercial Expansion, primary allies
04. Commerical Expansion, superpowers

05. Commercial Embargo, nonallies
06. Commercial Embargo, secondary allies
07. Commercial Embargo, primary allies
08. Commercial Embargo, superpowers

DIPLOMATIC INITIATION

09. Diplomatic Expansion, non-allies
10. Diplomatic Expansion, secondary allies
11. Diplomatic Expansion, primary allies
12. Diplomatic Expansion, superpowers

13. Diplomatic Embargo, non-allies
14. Diplomatic Embargo, secondary allies
15. Diplomatic Embargo, primary allies
16. Diplomatic Embargo, superpowers

17. Diplomatic Ambivalence, Disputed Rights of Unspecified Third Parties
18. Diplomatic Ambivalence, Disputed Rights of Specified Third Parties
19. Diplomatic Ambivalence, Disputed Treaty of Unspecified Third Parties
20. Diplomatic Ambivalence, Disputed Treaty of Specified Third Parties
21. Diplomatic Ambivalence, Disputed Territory of Unspecified 3rd Party
22. Diplomatic Ambivalence, Disputed Territory of Specified Third Parties

POLITICAL INITIATION
* * * * * * *

MILITARY INITIATION
* * * * * * *

110. Military Consummation, Specified Unlimited

Figure 10.1
Overview of Escalation of Encounter Variables

INITIAL CONDITIONS OF OPERATIONAL VARIABLES	Historic Data
TRANSITION PROBABILITIES	Historic Data; Hypothetical
EFFORT VARIABLES, ENCOUNTER SCENARIO	Analytic

THE U.S./ THE U.S.S.R CHOOSES (Initiates/Responds)

Commercial	0%, 1%,..., 100%
Diplomatic	0%, 1%,..., 100%
Political	0%, 1%,..., 100%
Military	0%, 1%,..., 100%

Each policy choice is a vector (C,D,P,M), each element of which may have values (0%,1%...,100%) at each move and counter-move. The mix of (Commercial, Diplomatic, Political, and Military) efforts makes the policy problem one of MIXED STRATEGIES

However, the fundamental question remains: How should the decision-maker evaluate the evidence? We offered BTIS as an analytical framework.

Based on President Kennedy's direct statements, and those he made to Robert Kennedy, seven major presidential concerns have been identified. The principal concern is to know the fourth and fifth interactive sequence of steps. Any characterization of any situation is defined as bluff. It becomes a threat only when an effective response is identified/implemented. All actions can be classified into four: (1) commercial, (2) diplomatic, (3) political, and (4) military.

Given a hypothetical embargo on Polish ham imports into the United States, a commercial move, what would be the response: CC (Polish embargo on U.S. potatoes) or CD (expulsion of U.S. representatives in Poland)? If the probability

Figure 10.2
Illustrative Interactive Sequence

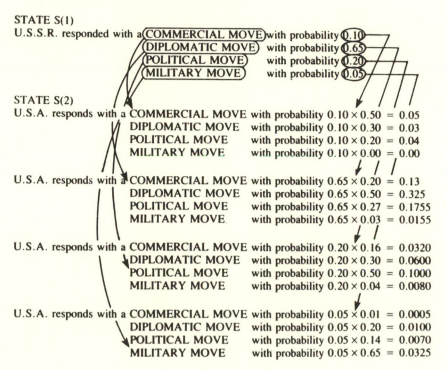

STATE S(0)
U.S.S.R. made a POLITICAL MOVE
U.S.A. responded with a DIPLOMATIC MOVE

STATE S(1)
U.S.S.R. responded with a COMMERCIAL MOVE with probability 0.10
DIPLOMATIC MOVE with probability 0.65
POLITICAL MOVE with probability 0.20
MILITARY MOVE with probability 0.05

STATE S(2)
U.S.A. responds with a COMMERCIAL MOVE with probability $0.10 \times 0.50 = 0.05$
DIPLOMATIC MOVE with probability $0.10 \times 0.30 = 0.03$
POLITICAL MOVE with probability $0.10 \times 0.20 = 0.04$
MILITARY MOVE with probability $0.10 \times 0.00 = 0.00$

U.S.A. responds with a COMMERCIAL MOVE with probability $0.65 \times 0.20 = 0.13$
DIPLOMATIC MOVE with probability $0.65 \times 0.50 = 0.325$
POLITICAL MOVE with probability $0.65 \times 0.27 = 0.1755$
MILITARY MOVE with probability $0.65 \times 0.03 = 0.0155$

U.S.A. responds with a COMMERCIAL MOVE with probability $0.20 \times 0.16 = 0.0320$
DIPLOMATIC MOVE with probability $0.20 \times 0.30 = 0.0600$
POLITICAL MOVE with probability $0.20 \times 0.50 = 0.1000$
MILITARY MOVE with probability $0.20 \times 0.04 = 0.0080$

U.S.A. responds with a COMMERCIAL MOVE with probability $0.05 \times 0.01 = 0.0005$
DIPLOMATIC MOVE with probability $0.05 \times 0.20 = 0.0100$
POLITICAL MOVE with probability $0.05 \times 0.14 = 0.0070$
MILITARY MOVE with probability $0.05 \times 0.65 = 0.0325$

in kind (CC, DD, PP, MM) can be specified, the probability not in kind can be determined as its complement. The transition from an initial state to an eventual state is determined using the transition probability. Given two alternate sequences of actions, choose the one that will take a larger number of steps to reach 5% probability of SNW. BTIS provides a comprehensive classification of all conceivable moves and countermoves to identify and evaluate alternate sequences of choices by multiple decision-makers dealing with multiple variables.

QUESTIONS: CONCEPTS AND COMPUTATIONS
FOR COMMITMENT

Our focus is decision-making, not number-crunching. Therefore, we divide the reinforcement of the text material into six categories: (1) Concepts: Foundational, (2) Concepts: Formulational, (3) Computations, (4) Conclusions, (5)

Table 10.3
U.S. Transition Matrix: Illustrative

Threat / Bluff	CC 1	CD 2	CP 3	CM 4	DC 5	DD 6	DP 7	DM 8	PC 9	PD 10	PP 11	PM 12	MC 13	MD 14	MP 15	MM 16
1.CC	0.5	0.4	0.1													
2.CD	0.0				.46	.50	.03	.01								
3.CP	0.0								.18	.30	.50	.02				
4.CM	0.0												.01	.30	.19	.50
5.DC	0.5	0.3	0.2													
6.DD	0.0				.20	.50	.27	.03								
7.DP	0.0								.16	.30	.50	.04				
8.DM	0.0												.01	.30	.19	.50
9. PC	0.5	0.2	0.3													
10.PD	0.0				.15	.50	.30	.05								
11.PP	0.0								.19	.25	.50	.06				
12.PM	0.0												.01	.19	.30	.50
13.MC	.01	.25	.19	.55												
14.MD	0.0				.01	.25	.19	.55								
15.MP	0.0								.01	.25	.19	.55				
16.MM	0.0												.01	.25	.04	.65
17.SNW	0.0															

P(MM-SNW) = P(16,17) = 0.05
P(SNW-SNW) = P(17,17) = 1.00

[Resource] Commitments, and (6) Caveats. See chapter 11 for answers to questions for this chapter.

Concepts: Foundational

The Problem: Cuban Missile Crisis

FBI Director Hoover's information (1) that certain Soviet personnel were apparently preparing to destroy all sensitive documents on the basis (2) that the United States would probably be taking military action against Cuba or (3) Soviet

Table 10.4
USSR Transition Matrix: Illustrative

Threat / Bluff	CC 1	CD 2	CP 3	CM 4	DC 5	DD 6	DP 7	DM 8	PC 9	PD 10	PP 11	PM 12	MC 13	MD 14	MP 15	MM 16
1.CC	.65	.25	0.1													
2.CD	0.0				.25	.65	.09	.01								
3.CP	0.0								.08	.25	.65	.02				
4.CM	0.0												.01	.25	.09	.65
5.DC	.65	0.2	.15													
6.DD	0.0				.08	.65	.24	.03								
7.DP	0.0								.11	.20	.65	.04				
8.DM	0.0												.01	.20	.14	.65
9. PC	.65	.15	0.2													
10.PD	0.0				.10	.65	.20	.05								
11.PP	0.0								.10	.19	.65	.06				
12.PM	0.0												.01	.14	.20	.65
13.MC	.01	.25	.09	.65												
14.MD	0.0				.01	.20	.14	.65								
15.MP	0.0								.01	.20	.14	.65				
16.MM	0.0												.01	15	.04	.75
17.SNW	0.0															.

P(MM-SNW) = P(16,17) = 0.05
P(SNW-SNW) = P(17,17) = 1.00

ships was evaluated by Robert Kennedy: "*and this would mean War*" (emphasis added.)

1. Why would Bayes' theorem be *in*applicable to the situation?

2. What support functions should be developed under the construction of probability arguments?

3. What possibilistic distribution of outcomes would you construct?

4. Give three reasons to *overrule* the overwhelming evidence in support of the Soviets' immediately going to war.

5. What is the limitation common to (1) through (4)?

6. Contrast interactive with iterative approach to escalation.

7. Briefly explain the seven features of the BTIS matrix.

Concepts: Formulational

The Problem: DEFCON 5

8. Formulate the NORAD computers flashing "It is 99.9 percent certain that you are under ICBM attack!" using BTIS matrix.

9. What fundamental premise of BTIS was unfulfilled?

10. Incorporate into BTIS the two factors discussed in chapter 1 as leading to the NORAD deputy commander's rejecting DEFCON 5.

The Problem: Beijing Confrontation

The military massacre of pro-democracy demonstrators in Tiananmen Square would be a political move in the B–T matrix. However, it had profound impact on diplomatic and commercial fronts.

Diplomatic. France, the Netherlands, and Sweden "cut all links short of diplomatic relations with China."

Commercial. President George Bush at his press conference on June 5, 1989, suspended "all government-to-government sales and commercial export of weapons." The sanctions cover $600 million in military sales.

Further Steps. "Bush also held out the possibility of taking further steps to isolate China if the violence continued. . . . Vote against loans to China in the World Bank, Asian development bank. . . . Deny insurance to U.S. investors under the Overseas Private Investment Corp. programme" (*Far Eastern Economic Review*, June 15, 1989, p. 11).

11. Formulate the macro B–T matrix elements as of June 5, 1989.

12. Formulate the macro B–T matrix scenario of escalation.

13. Formulate the macro B–T matrix scenario of de-escalation.

Computations

The Problem: Beijing Confrontation

14. Construct with reasoning, three steps of China–U.S. escalation.

15. Construct, with reasoning, three steps of China–U.S. de-escalation.

Conclusions

The Problem: Beijing Confrontation

16. Do you consider (14) or (15) more likely? Why?

17. What is the probability of a Beijing response in kind to a U.S. move that you have assumed in (14) or (15)? Why?

[Resource] Commitments

The Problem: Beijing Confrontation

18. Recommend a strategy (sequence of three steps) to President Bush.
19. How would you modify (19) if the Deng Xiaoping regime is toppled?

Caveats

20. Which experts are you using to arrive at the probability of response in kind? What are their limitations?
21. How would (19) change if the Soviet Union sends back to the Chinese border Russian troops stationed there until Gorbachev visits Beijing?
22. How would you translate into the B–T matrix President Bush's policy statement on June 5 that the U.S. move was not an emotional response but "a reasoned, careful action that takes into account both our long-term interests and recognition of a complex internal situation in China."

NOTES

1. Robert F. Kennedy, *Thirteen Days: A Memoir of the Cuban Missile Crisis* (New York: New American Library, 1969), p. 93.
2. Theodore C. Sorenson, *Kennedy* (New York: Harper & Row, 1965), p. 715.
3. Ibid., p. 705.
4. Leonnard J. Savage, *The Foundations of Statistics* (New York: Wiley, 1954).
5. Rolf Bender and Armin Nack, *Taatsachenfeststellung vor Gericht*, vol. 1 (C. H. Beck'sche Verlagsbuchhandlung: 1981).
6. Leonard J. Savage, "Elicitation of Personal Probabilities and Expectation," in *Studies in Bayesian Econometrics and Statistics*, ed. S. N. Feinberg and A. Zellner (Amsterdam: North-Holland, 1975), p. 111.
7. Bruno de Finetii, "La prevision: ses lois logiques, ses sources subjectives," *Annales de l' Institute Henri Poincaré*, 76 (1937): 1–68 (English translation appears in note 8).
8. Henry E. Kyburg, Jr., and Howard E. Smokler, *Studies in Subjective Probability* (New York: Wiley, 1964).
9. Savage, "Elicitation of Personal Probabilities and Expectations," pp. 113–14.
10. Thomas Bayes, "Essay Towards Solving a Problem in the *Doctrine of Chances,*" *Philosophical Transactions of the Royal Society*, 1763, reprinted in Biometrika, 45 (Dec. 1958): 293–315.
11. Kennedy, *Thirteen Days*, pp. 98–99, 105–6, 126.
12. Ibid., p. 108.
13. Ibid., pp. 132–33.

Part VI   Answers to Questions

11 Development and Discussion of Process and Products

The intent of the Answers to Questions is not to provide full-blown answers, but to indicate what appear to be the most important elements in discussing the questions. It is hoped that the reader will use them as helpful points of departure, and not as "the" Answers.

CHAPTER 1

Concepts: Foundational

1. Mr. Decision-maker, please identify (1) what type of facts on (2) what variables and (3) what participants do you consider critical to your decisions? Further, (4) what type of interactions among (2) and (5) what type of interactions among (3) are most critical to your decisions? The errors in which of the five types of facts would damage your decision most? It is *not* "*all* the facts," but *some* of the facts on *some* of the variables, participants, and interactions that are critical to the decision.

2. Forecasts. Fore (front); cast (throw)—throw the past into the future. What will *probably, possibly, most likely happen* at the earliest future instant t when today's resource commitment can yield results? What are the future forecast of results $r_{t'}$ *without* the resources and r_t *with* the resources? Compare with the actuals.

The Problem: Ammunition Acceptance

3. The only way you can be sure that the ammunition is good is to destructive test by firing it. Even if 100% inspection were carried out, the inspection would measure *external* characteristics, such as weight, but not the *internal* charac-

teristics, such as combustibility. With hundreds of thousands of ammunition rounds pouring out of the factories, only a small fraction can be inspected. That fraction can be so chosen that we can be sure 99.999% of the time that the ammunition would work, but not 100% because the small fraction is considered to come from *infinite* rounds of ammunition. Like infinity, 100% certainty can never be reached, but only approached *asymptotically*—getting ever closer but never reaching.

Concepts: Formulational

The Problem: Nuclear Freeze

4. Underlying one's stand on something involving another party is the (ours/theirs) or (O/T) ratio. In this instance, if (our nuclear capability for *delivered destruction*/their nuclear capability for *delivered destruction*) >1, then I want to freeze the U.S. position of advantage (as would the USSR with an (O/T) > 1). To construct a null hypothesis (NH), something has to be zero. Let us choose an operational value of the (O/T) > 1 as, say, 1.5. As a senator voting for nuclear freeze, my NH is (ours/theirs) delivered destruction ratio $- 1.5 = 0$.

5. (Ours/theirs) delivered destruction ratio $- .8 = 0$.

6. Mr. Senator, you believe that our capability for delivered destruction is greater than that of our adversary. In which arena—air, land, sea—do you think we are ahead? Okay, you think we are ahead at sea. Which particular weapon system are we ahead in? Okay, you think we are ahead in the Trident submarine system. If we give you a top-secret-restricted-data-eyes-only briefing with our highly classified data on Trident versus equivalent Soviet class submarines, and if we can convince you that the ratio is < 1, would you promise to vote nay on the nuclear freeze resolution?

The Problem: Reinstatement of the Death Penalty

7. The purpose of the death penalty is to punish and to deter. Deter the would-be criminals from what? Capital offenses and other major crimes. If the death penalty deterred major would-be offenders, the major crimes per 100,000 population (*after* the reinstatement/*before* the reinstatement) <1, say, .8. The NH is:

Major crimes per 100,000 population (after reinstatement of the death penalty/before reinstatement of the death penalty) $- .8 = 0$.

8. Against reinstatement: ("after" reinstatement/"before") $- 1.25 = 0$.

Computations

The Problem: Reinstatement of the Death Penalty

9. Major crimes per 100,000 population during the decade *before* the abolition to *after* the abolition of the death penalty is the criterion. If the ratio is 0.8 or

lower, reinstate the death penalty. Even with a 1.05 ratio, I would still reinstate the death penalty, considering the 5% as fluctuations.

Conclusions

The Problem: DEFCON 5

10. Sir, the computer calculations of DEFCON showed an excessively large number of Soviet missiles launched against unknown targets. (1) The number of missiles far exceeded our best intelligence, making the data highly doubtful. Two vital pieces of data were missing: (2) the point of impact and (3) the estimated time of impact. Absent those two, we had to seriously question if what were being tracked were indeed Soviet missiles. *Fundamental factual errors* made DEFCON 3 *invalid.* (4) Khrushchev was then at the United Nations in New York. Without him personally in command, an ICBM launch would be inconceivable. (5) Intelligence reported no preparations for any launch anywhere. The *violations* required of *basic policy and procedure* made DEFCON 3 *implausible.*

The Problem: Anti-Recidivism

11. The key variable is *repeat* criminal behavior. The candidate for district attorney is running on the platform of a mandatory long prison term for the *third-time* offender. If first offense gets 5 years and the second 10, make it twenty-five for the third offense to reduce recidivism.

[Resource] Commitments

The Problem: Hanging an Innocent Person

12. Human life is priceless. To wrongly hang an innocent person is an extreme crime that society can commit against humanity. So, the frequency of wrong hanging should be set extremely small.

13. Setting a frequency of 1 in 100,000 means that as many as 99,999 first-degree murderers could be walking the streets, making life incredibly unsafe for law-abiding citizens. While 1 person wrongly hanged is 1 too many, 1 in 100,000 makes it as safe as consistent with the obligation to the rest of society as possible.

Caveats

The Problem: DEFCON 5

14. See the text.

The Problem: Reinstatement of the Death Penalty

15. It is to institutionalize review by a power above the judiciary as the very last effort to avoid overlooking "reasonable doubt." The power to commute the

death sentence is to exercise "clemency" for special mitigating circumstances *above and beyond what judiciary can consider*. In both staying the execution and commuting the death sentence, society institutionalizes its determination to make minimum its type I errors.

CHAPTER 2

Concepts: Foundational

1.   Logical probability − propositions → unique conclusion
         Subjective probability − propositions → nonunique conclusion

2. The common characteristics of interest as defined by the use(r).

The Problem: DEFCON 5

3. Yes. Because subjective probability means that different conclusions are drawn from identical data by different *people,* or the same person at different *times.*

4. For instance, DEFCON 5 during Khrushchev's absence from Moscow could mean a military coup to annihilate Khrushchev and the United States. Request presidential authority for retaliatory strike.

Concepts: Formulational

The Problem: Cuban Missile Crisis

5. The Joint Chiefs of Staff (JCS) recommended an air strike on Monday, followed shortly afterward by an invasion. Their *logical* premise was that the Soviet Union would understand only *significant* military steps. Their *empirical* premise was air strike, followed by invasion, the two together constituting a *significant* military step. Applying the logical conclusion to the empirical premise, JCS concluded that the Soviet Union would respond to *significant* U.S. military force applications.

The Problem: Spouse Selection

6. Logical probability would place the probability of failure rather high, say .8, since the spouse already had two failures of marriage, probability 1. Given two such failures, the *logical* probability for failure of the third marriage: 1. How would one set aside such a high logical probability? One could say that the two-time divorcee entering into a third marriage is more alert to ruinous mistakes and would be extra careful. Because it is my second marriage, I will be more sensitive to signs of trouble myself. There has to be compelling personal chemistry between the divorcee and myself that gives a strong "gut feeling" that this time it will work out.

7. (1) Employer with high *reputation,* (2) job that *uses* one's technical *know-how* and offers opportunity to develop other skills, (3) periodic presentation of one's work to the *upper echelons* above immediate superior.

1. *Relative frequency*—repeated surveys of job satisfaction rank the reputation of the employer as a primary, if not the primary, factor.

2. *Logical probability*—one's technical background is a principal asset one brings to the job; therefore, the more it is used, the better for the employee (morale) and the employer (returns on investment). Human skills become more important than technical skills as one ascends the career ladder; therefore, the more the opportunity to develop human skills, the better for the employee (capabilities enhancement) and the employer (future managers).

3. *Logical probability*—companies with outstanding reputation make the direct access of the employee to the superior two or more levels above him (her) a standard practice. The first-line manager himself (herself) is encouraged to take pride in touting the accomplishments of his (her) staff before the second-line manager. Because upward mobility is a professional career aim, the periodic exposure to upper echelon thinking and encouragement is most essential. In order of importance, the criteria and critical values are:

$$\text{Employer reputation} > \text{job content} > \text{upper echelon access}$$
$$p > .8 \qquad p > .7 \qquad p > .6$$

Computations

The Problem: Cuban Missile Crisis

8. Kennedy Reasoning on Berlin, Cuba War Probabilities

1. In the Berlin Wall crisis the Soviets were in their own "backyard." For the Soviets to operate *5,000 miles away* from home base and point missiles at the United States only *90 miles away* required that the Soviets be eager to go to war over Cuba.

2. The Berlin Wall was to keep East Germans in. Such an "internal" matter of a Soviet ally could not provoke the United States to war. But introducing missiles into Cuba *upset the nuclear power balance.*

3. Because the United States did not tear down the Berlin Wall, the Soviets could have thought that they could argue that Cuban missiles were an "internal" matter of a Soviet ally; and if the United States did not "buy" the argument, the missiles launched from only 90 miles distance (instead of 5,000 miles) *could not fail* to hit the United States.

The Problem: Spouse Selection

9. Deny logical probability because of (1) *inapplicability* of the *premise* and/or (2) *inadequacy* of the premises.

LOGICAL PROBABILITY OVERRIDE BECAUSE OF INAPPROPRIATE PREMISES

1. "Close friends from grade school through college" would suggest that the educational background is similar. But if my value system is quite different from my friends'

(limiting thereby the extent of the "close" friendship), then their logic is inappropriate for my case.

2. My *spouse may be totally unlike* the wives of my three friends, thereby making their sequence inappropriate for us.

3. The *interaction between my spouse and me* is different from the three failed marriages, making their experience inappropriate for us.

LOGICAL PROBABILITY OVERRIDE BECAUSE OF INADEQUATE PREMISES

1. What happened after college? My career has been highly professional and satisfying, while that of my three friends has been miserable.

2. Again, while all four of us are from the same neighborhood, there had been no divorce in our family for five generations, while the families of my three friends have tradition of divorces for three generations.

Inapplicability of Premises

My value system $p > .8$

My spouse $p > .8$; our interaction $p > .7$

Inadequacy of Premises

My career $p > .9$

My family $p > .9$

Conclusions

The Problem: Cuban Missile Crisis

10. Reasons to Reject Overwhelming Evidence

1. In the first letter Khrushchev did offer to withdraw or destroy Cuban missiles. Although the second letter was confrontary, there was no intelligence that Khrushchev had been *overthrown.*

2. *Unorthodox communication* through ABC newsman John Scali that the Soviets would remove the missiles under U.N. supervision.

3. The 5,000-mile long Moscow-Havana line of supply would make war doubtful and gains dubious. What would *Khrushchev gain?*

11. See answer to (9).

[Resource] Commitments

The Problem: Crisis Communication

12. Under extreme pressure of the threat of imminent Soviet-U.S. nuclear war, the nuances of the decision-maker's words would be equally, if not more, important than the words themselves. For instance, the U.S. president asks: "What does he mean it is *unacceptable?*" Although the presidential translator should not put words in the Soviet president's mouth, he could suggest from knowing the past how serious the Soviets were when they used the phrase last time. Or report that the phrase was never used before.

The presidential translator can aggravate or ameliorate by the content and context of the communication. If the hot line were available during the Cuban Missile Crisis, the presidential translator could have helped *diffuse* the enormous *50% escalation*—from a third to half—of the probability of nuclear war if, for instance, he could from the context and usage interpret the Soviets to mean, "We will remove our missiles from Cuba [as] you [will] remove yours from Turkey." Or "[if] you [later] remove your missiles."

Such a hypothetical scenario illustrates how the translator could diffuse a nuclear crisis. To do his job, he needs to continually know the temper and tenor of both the person whom he is translating and the person to whom he is translating. If we assign, say, .125% of the prevention of nuclear war to the correct translation, and if we compute the destruction of a war to be just one year's gross national product (GNP) at the current rate, and if we say that the probability of occurrence of such a crucial translation is 0.00001, the presidential translator is worth $4,500 \times 10^9$ .00125 $\times$ .00001 = \$56,250.

The Problem: Premarital Counseling

13. One cannot put a price on the devastating effect of a divorce on the spouses and children and the families of the spouses any more than one can put a price on the devastation of a nuclear holocaust. Yet we have to pay people to help prevent the nuclear holocaust; and we used illustrative figures to indicate the economic damage in terms of lost GNP in Question 12.

If we take the median family income as \$28,000 and assign a cost of 50% of the income for ten years as the economic damage of a marriage, the prevention of a divorce would save \$140,000. A premarital counselor cannot prevent a divorce; he (she) can only help decrease its chances. If we assign .5% of the prevention of divorce to the counselor, the economic worth of the premarital counseling would be \$700.

Caveats

The Problem: Applicable Marriage Parallel

14. Rationale for Parallelism

1. *Families of origin of the spouses:* (a) Our parents have had an excellent marriage for 30 years; we are very much like them. (b) Both of our families are broken; we are very much *un*like them.

2. *Personal development and outlook:* (a) Both of us have worked hard and steady at our goals in school, college, and careers. (b) Neither of us has worked hard and steady, but now that we have found each other we have a strong motivation to do so.

3. *Peer experience:* (a) All our five close friends are married to their first spouses after five years. We are very much like them. (b) All our five close friends have divorced within five years of marriage. We are scared. We are talking to our parents, our peers, and are seeing a marriage counselor for the next six months.

The Problem: Cuban Missile Crisis

15. Consult chapter 10 for further discussion of the problem. Robert Kennedy recounts the real-time concerns and constructs by President Kennedy, which we may group into three types of criteria.

1. *Other party intention:* "The Russians don't wish to fight any more than we do. They do not want to war with us nor we with them."

2. *Saving other party's "face":* "Every opportunity was to be given to the Russians to find a peaceful settlement which would not diminish their national security or be a public humiliation."

3. *Avoiding open-ended escalation:* Even when the ExComm agreed early the next morning (Sunday) that the Cuban sites had to be taken out, President Kennedy pulled every one back: "It isn't the first step that concerns me," he said, "but both sides escalating to the fourth and fifth step—and we don't go to the sixth because there is no one around to do so."

CHAPTER 3

Concepts: Foundational

1. A function of (observed-expected) frequencies is zero. (Reason: Rows and columns are independent of each other.)

2. The guarantee with a specified level of confidence that the random sample comes from a population with specified characteristics.

3. Alternative Probabilistic Statements on Sunrise

Logical probability: p (sunrise tomorrow morning) $= 1$

Subjective probability: p (sunrise tomorrow morning) $= 1$

Relative frequency: p (sunrise tomorrow morning) $\rightarrow 1$ as $n \rightarrow \infty$

Logical and subjective frequencies are based on *finite* observations, whereas relative frequency is based on *infinite* observations. Because we never reach infinity, the p only tends to, but never reaches, 1. Even with the evidence of 1,825 billion sunrises since the birth of the planet Earth, we can only say that relative frequency p (sunrise tomorrow morning) $= .999999$ . . . I will use the logical probability of 1 because the logical premise that without the sun (and the sunrise) there will be no earth tomorrow is sufficient reasoning for me to accept the logical $p = 1$ for sunrise tomorrow.

4. Relative frequency concept of probability underlies the overwhelming majority of statistical statements. Even as the 1,825 billion sunrises are nowhere near infinity, any number of observations we can make is still nowhere near infinity; so we *cannot prove*. Therefore, we state the opposite of what we would like to "prove" and *disprove* it with as high as 99.99999% confidence.

Concepts: Formulational

The Problem: High School Taxes

5. There is no statistically significant difference between the sexes in their attitude toward higher school taxes.

6. The rows are the *sexes:* male, female. The columns are the attitude toward higher school *taxes:* for, against, no opinion. The rule of *statistical indepen-dence:* rows (sexes) and columns (taxes) are independent of each other; or *tax* (attitude) is *independent* of *sex.*

The Problem: Tax Support for Nursery Schools

7. There are no statistically significant differences between the sexes in their attitude on tax support for nursery schools.

8. Tax (attitude vis-a-vis nursery school) is *independent* of sex.

Computations

The Problem: Higher School Taxes

9. See Table 11.1.
10. See Table 11.2.
11–14. See Table 11.3.

The Problem: Tax Support for Nursery Schools

15–20. See (9)-(14); only the numbers change. Chi-Squared = 4.1.

Conclusions

The Problem: Higher School Taxes

21.

1. The conclusion: There is no relationship between sex and tax attitude.
2. The cancellation: There is (no) (some) relationship between sex and tax attitude.
3. The frequency of error: 1 in 120 times; 1 in 100 times.

22. Follow (21) format.

23. The conclusion that there is some relationship between sex and tax attitude may be wrong 1 in 100 times; 1 in 1,000 times. *Interpretation:* Men and women have definite differences in their attitude toward higher school taxes. The men are a third more supportive of higher school taxes than are women (Hint: Express [the percentage of men in favor] in terms of [the percentage of women in favor of higher school taxes].)

24. Follow (23) format.

Table 11.1
Higher School Taxes: Condition (Sex)

Effect / Condition	Column 1 For Tax Increase	Column 2 Against Tax Increase	Column 3 No Opinion	TOTAL
Row 1 MEN	296	228	183	707
Row 2 WOMEN	236	226	295	757
TOTAL	532	454	478	1464

Table 11.2
Tax Increase Contingency Table: Joint and Marginal Probabilities

Effect / Condition	YES Column 1	NO Column 2	DON'T KNOW Column 3	TOTAL
Row 1 MEN	Jt. prob. MY 0.175	Jt. prob. MN 0.150	Jt. prob. MD 0.158	Row 1 Marg. probability 0.483
Row 2 WOMEN	Jt. prob. WY 0.188	Jt. prob. WN 0.160	Jt. prob. WD 0.169	Row 2 Marg. probability 0.517
TOTAL	Col 1 Marg. probability 0.363	Col. 2 Marg. probability 0.310	Col. 2 Marg. probability 0.327	1.000

Table 11.3
Tax Increase: Observed and Expected Frequencies

Effect / Condition	YES	NO	DON'T KNOW
YES	Observed : 296 - Expected 257 (O-E) = 39 2 2 (O-E)/E = 39/257 =5.918	Observed : 228- Expected : 219 (O-E) = 9 2 2 (O-E)/E =9/219 =0.370	Observed: 183- Expected: 231 (O-E) = -48 2 2 (O-E)/E =-48/231 = 9.974
NO	Observed : 236 - Expected 275 (O-E) = -39 2 2 (O-E)/E= -39/275 =5.531	Observed : 226 - Expected : 235 (O-E) = 9 2 2 (O-E)/E =9/235 =0.345	Observed: 295- Expected: 247 (O-E) = -48 2 2 (O-E)/E =-48/247 =9.328

Chi-Squared = 5.918 + 0.370 + 9.974 + 5.531 + 0.345 +9.328
           =31.466
           ======
Chi-Squared DF = (rows - 1) (columns -1)
              = (2-1) (3-1)
              = (1) (2) = 2
Table Chi-Squared for 2 DF at 99.% confidence   9.210
Table Chi-Squared for 2 DF at 99.9% confidence 13.8
Computed Chi-Squared   31.466

The conclusion that there is difference between sexes on attitude toward
school tax increase may be wrong 1 in 100 times; 1 in 1,000 times

[Resource] Commitments

The Problem: School Services Versus Tax Increase

25. As chairman of the school board, I must maintain and improve the quality
of school services. Therefore, I will *increase taxes* after ensuring that the tax
dollars are now being spent efficiently. All the adults have been polled. More
than a third (36.3%) favor the tax increase. Those who do not have an opinion are
slightly under a third. Because they could be persuaded one way or the other, let
us allocate half of the "no opinion" to "favor higher school taxes." That brings
the total to 52.7%, a *bare majority*.

26. While the no vote on higher school taxes was 31.0%, the no vote is more
than double, at 65.16% on spending tax money on nursery school children under
4 1/2 years. The (chi-squared) test shows that the opposition is spread across all

age-groups. The overwhelming vote across the board would lead me not to spend tax money on nursery children under 4 1/2.

27. I would work on the "no opinion" (on higher tax) group and leave the against (tax increase) group alone. Almost as many women have "no opinion" as the men who favor higher taxes. I would recruit pairs of men and women who favor tax increase to call on the nearly two-fifth of women who have no opinion.

On the tax support for nursery school, the three age-groups are solidly opposed with respective percentages of 66.72%, 64.25%, and 64%. The possible support base is those with "no opinion." Although a third offered such a base on higher tax, only 7.51% have "no opinion" on tax support for nursery school. I will have to work on that small base, winning all of which will only yield a total of 34.8% in support. In addition, a quarter of those who are *against* the issue now have to be persuaded to switch to the opposite view.

Caveats

28. "Each of 1,464 adult residents of Pittsburgh, Pennsylvania was interviewed." Therefore, the basis was not a *sample*, but the *whole population*.

The Problem: Higher School Taxes

29. See (27).

30. *Sampling:* It is preferable to use repeated *random sampling* even when the entire population is eventually surveyed. The sample results help to identify any *bias* on the part of the interviewers. The third of the responses with "no opinion" on a pocketbook issue suggests room for improvement in the interviewing.

Change in the Values: The 50-year-old survey results were presented so that they may be compared with the *current attitudes*. Discuss similar current issues in your community.

CHAPTER 4

Concepts: Foundational

1. When the absolute *values* (e.g., mean personal income in two states) are the object of inquiry, the NH says that there is no difference in the value between two (or more) groups. The total income divided by the number of people is a meaningful entity. However, it is not the absolute value of the number of heart attacks that is of interest, but the variation in the incidence of heart attack between different groups of people. Can the variation in the incidence be explained by the variation among the people? Or is there something not so explained—which may then be attributed to other factors, such as regimen 1 versus regimen 2.

2. *t Table:* There is no difference between the (values of) two means. *F test:* There is no difference between treatments. (Or, there is no difference between the [variations due to] treatments and subjects.)

3. See chapter 3.

1. *Binomial distribution fit to coin toss data:* The conclusion that the difference between the binomial distribution and the observed distribution is zero may be wrong 1 in 1,000 times.

2. *Pearsonian fit to coin toss data:* The conclusion that the difference between the Pearsonian type I distribution and the observed distribution is zero may be wrong 1 in 1,000 times.

3. *Normal fit to coin toss data:* The conclusion that the difference between the normal distribution and the observed distribution is zero may be wrong 1 in 1,000 times.

4. Value.

The Problem: Aspirin and Heart Attacks

5. The χ^2 is particularly useful to test a small number of observations that can be classified into nonoverlapping parts, such as those who took aspirin and those who did not. When n for χ^2 with 1 DF becomes large, $\sqrt{\chi^2}$ is distributed normally. Because the $n = 22,071$ is large, the normal distribution is appropriate. We are able to reject the NH with 100,000 times as much confidence as with χ^2: Our conclusion could be wrong 1 in 100 million times. Choose the normal curve because with $n = 22,071$, it is (1) (more) *appropriate;* (2) (much more) *accurate.*

Concepts: Formulational

The Problem: "The Rich Getting Richer"

6. Choose the richest region in time 1 (1973) and the poorest. See if they retain their 1973 differences over time.

7. At least 2 different time periods need to be used to test how the rich moved over time vis-a-vis the poor.

8. There is no difference in (rich versus poor) disparity between time 1 and time 2.

The Problem: Admission Test Scores

9. Because the scores are normally distributed, special admission would seek a specific high score to select potential high scorers (e.g., top 1%).

10. Similar to (9).

The Problem: Selecting the Text

11. We have to test if there is any statistically significant difference among the grades of the students. If there is, then the text with which the students earned the highest score would be the choice.

Computations

The Problem: "The Rich Getting Richer"

12. Mid-Atlantic is the richest in 1973: per capita personal income of $5,168 (in 1972 dollars); East South Central, with $3,681, is the poorest. In 2000 East

South Central remains the poorest, with \$6,143. The richest region in 2000 is New England, with \$8,073. Mid-Atlantic, the richest region in 1973, is 97.2% of the richest region in 2000, with \$7,847.

13. We choose the richest in 2000, New England region.

Mean in 1973: \$4.62 (in '000)   Mean in 2000: \$7.47 (in '000)

s_1^2 in 1973: 0.449667 s_1^2 in 2000: 1.118667

We also choose the poorest region in 1973 and 2000: East South Central. See Table 11.4 for the computation of mean and variance.

14. t for time 1 (1973):

$(4.62 - 3.65) \sqrt{(6 + 4 + 2)} \cdot \sqrt{6 \times 4/6 + 4} / \sqrt{0.449667 + 0.78}$
$= 0.97 \times \sqrt{8} \times \sqrt{2.4} / \sqrt{1.229667}$
$= 4.2503259/1.108903$
$= 3.832962$

15. t for time 2 (2000):

$(7.47 - 6.1) \sqrt{(6 + 4 - 2)} \cdot \sqrt{6 \times 4/6 + 4}/\sqrt{1.118667 + 0.9233}$
$= 1.37 \times \sqrt{8} \times \sqrt{2.4} / \sqrt{2.041967}$
$= 6.0030376/1.428974$
$= 4.200942$

16. Table t with $(6 + 4 - 2 =)$ 8 DF at 95% level of significance: 2.306; at 99% level of significance: 3.355.

The Problem: Admission Test Scores

17. Worked out in Questions.
18. Follow (17) format.

The Problem: Selecting the Text

19. The treatment—the text; the subject—the students.
20. There is no difference in the variation owing to the texts and the variation owing to the students.
21.

1. *Identify the given data sequentially.* Textbook 1 grade 1 is 66; or (11) is 66; Textbook 1 grade 2 (12) is 88; (13) is 77; and (14) is 72. Similarly, for Textbook 2—21, 22, 23, 24, 25, 26. For Textbook 3—31, 32, 33, 34, 35. For Textbook 4—41, 42, 43, 44, 45.

2. *Identify row and column* (e.g., row 5, column 3). *Specify the order of digit(s)* (digits 1, 2) and *direction* (Down, go east up digits 3, 4 of col. 3; go east down col. 3 digit 5 and col. 4 digit 1).

3. *Select the RN and assign correspondence.*

Table 11.4
Mean and Standard Deviations of Per Capita Income, 1973 (in 1972 Dollars) and 2000: East South Central Region

	X_i 1973	X_i^2 1973	X_i 2000	X_i^2 2000
East So. Central	3.7		6.1	
Kentucky	3.8	14.44	6.3	39.69
Tennessee	3.9	15.21	6.3	39.69
Alabama	3.6	12.96	6.2	38.44
Mississippi	3.3	10.89	5.6	31.36
TOTAL	14.6	55.74	24.4	149.18
Mean X	3.65		6.1	

$$s_i^2 = N\,(X_i^2) - (X_i^2) / N(N-1)$$

$$= 4 \times 55.74 - (14.6)^2/4 \times 3$$
$$= 222.96 - 213.6 /12$$

(1973 data)
$$= 9.36/12 = 0.78$$

(2000 data)
$$= 4 \times 149.18 - (24.4)^2 / 4 \times 3$$
$$= 596.72 - 585.64 /12$$
$$= 11.08/12 = 0.9233$$

The first RN is 05; Student 05 gets the first sequential grade 11.
The second RN is 12; Student 12 gets the second sequential grade 12.
The third RN is 03; Student 03 gets the third sequential grade 13.
The fourth RN is 15; Student 15 gets the fourth sequential grade 14.
The fifth RN is 10; Student 10 gets the fifth sequential grade 21.

The sixth RN is 02; Student 02 gets the sixth sequential grade 22.

The seventh RN is 08; Student 08 gets the seventh sequential grade 23.

The eighth RN is 12; Student 12 is already assigned grade 12.

The ninth RN is 17; Student 17 gets the eighth sequential grade 24.

The tenth RN is 20; Student 20 gets the ninth sequential grade 25.

The eleventh RN is 12; Student 12 is already assigned grade 12.

The twelfth RN is 09; Student 09 gets the tenth sequential grade 26, and so on.

22. Set up a table similar to Table 4.5

23. *The Numerator:*

For Text

$$1, (83.60 - 75.75)^2 \times 4 = 246.49$$
$$2, (83.60 - 82.50)^2 \times 6 = 7.26$$
$$3, (83.60 - 91.60)^2 \times 5 = 320.00$$
$$4, (83.60 - 83.20)^2 \times 5 = \underline{0.80}$$
$$574.55$$

Because the sum is obtained over four treatments, the DF are $(4 - 1 =)$ 3.

Mean square is $574.55/3 = 191.5167$.

24. *The Denominator:*

For Text 1, $(66 - 75.75)^2 + (88 - 75.75)^2 + (77 - 75.75)^2 + (72 - 75.75)^2$ $= 95.0625 + 150.0625 + 1.5625 + 14.0625 = 260.75$.

For Text 2, $(88 - 82.50)^2 + (89 - 82.50)^2 + (80 - 82.50)^2 + (77 - 82.50)^2$ $+ (82 - 82.50)^2 + (79 - 82.50)^2 = 30.25 + 42.25 + 6.25 + 30.25 + 0.25 + 12.25 = 121.5$.

For Text 3, $(100 - 91.6)^2 + (86 - 91.60)^2 + (96 - 91.60)^2 + (81 - 91.60)^2$ $+ (95 - 91.60)^2 = 70.56 + 31.36 + 19.36 + 112.36 + 11.56 = 245.2$.

For Text 4, $(73 - 83.20)^2 + (92 - 83.20)^2 + (99 - 83.20)^2 + (85 - 83.20)^2$ $+ (67 - 83.20)^2 = 104.04 + 77.44 + 249.64 + 3.24 + 262.44 = 696.8$.

The sum of squares for the subjects is $(260.75 + 121.5 + 245.2 + 696.8 =)$ 1324.25. The DF is the total number of observations (20) minus the total number of treatments (4), or $(20 - 4 =)$ 16.

Mean square is $1324.25/16 = 82.7656$.
Numerator/denominator $= 191.5167/82.7656 = 2.3140$.

25. The table value for F (3 DF in the columns and 16 DF in the rows) is 3.24 at 95% confidence and 5.29 at 99% confidence. Because the computed value < table value, accept the NH.

Conclusions

The Problem: "The Rich Getting Richer"

26. Steps to Develop Statistical Conclusion

1. *The conclusion:* There is no difference between the mean personal income of the rich and the poor in 1973.
2. *The cancellation:* There is (some) difference between the mean personal income of the rich and the poor in 1973.
3. *The frequency of error:* 1 in 20 times; 1 in 100 times.

27. The only difference from (26) is the year 2000 instead of 1973.

28. The conclusion that there is difference in the mean personal income between the rich and the poor in 1973 may be wrong 1 in 20 times; 1 in 100 times. *Meaning:* The mean income of the rich is significantly higher than that of the poor.

29. Same as (28) except for the year 2000 in place of 1973.

The Problem: Selecting the Text

30. Steps to Develop Statistical Conclusion

1. *The conclusion:* There is no difference in the variation owing to the text and the variation owing to the students.
2. *The cancellation:* There is (some) difference in the variation owing to the text and the variation owing to the students.
3. *The frequency of error:* 1 in 20 times; 1 in 100 times.

31. The conclusion that there is no difference in the variation owing to the text and the variation owing to the students may be wrong 1 in 20 times; 1 in 100 times. *Meaning:* Textbooks do not make a difference in student grades.

[Resource] Commitments

The Problem: "The Rich Getting Richer"

32. Recommendation to Reduce Gap Between States

1. Attract hi-tech industries to the East South Central States to take advantage of the inexpensive labor.
2. Subsidize selective statewide upgrading of skills in hi-tech industries.
3. Promote foreign hi-tech industries to start joint ventures in the poor states.

The Problem: Selecting the Text

33. Textbook 3, if the *F* test showed that the textbook influences grades. Choose the text with the *highest* mean grade (91.60).

Caveats

The Problem: "The Rich Getting Richer"

34. Insofar as all the states in the union were given an equal chance of being selected on the basis of per capita income, they are random.

The Problem: Admission Test Scores

35. Because the tests show that the examination scores of 447 college students are normally distributed, there is no reason to question the randomness of the scores.

The Problem: Selecting the Text

36. The data were modified from the reports of one professor who did not note the occurrence of very bright or very slow students as he tried the four texts. Therefore, the results are random.

37. To the extent that biases occur(red). Biases influence the data in one particular direction (e.g., if the professor chose a hard (easy) text, sensing that the students were bright (slow); if the admission exam was made harder (easier) for some of the 447 college students by administering different sets of exams; if certain parts of the United States were excluded in choosing the rich (poor) states.

CHAPTER 5

Concepts: Foundational

1. (1) Given a value of *X*, what is the corresponding value of *Y*? (2) Given a value each of a minimum of 2 *X*s (X_1, X_2), (no maximum e.g., X_3, X_4, . . . , X_n), what is the corresponding value of *Z*?
2. The *user*.
3. Ignores *interactions*.
4. Identifies the *separate contribution* of each variable.
5. (1) *Multiplicative* form of the equation $a \cdot x_1{}^\alpha \cdot X_2{}^\beta$. (2) Constraint that the *exponents* equal unity, so that if the empirical sum > 1 or < 1, it shows the interactive input contribution to the output.

Concepts: Formulational

The Problem: "The Females Grow Taller"

6. Match the female students in age by randomly chosen male upper-division students. Find the *rate of growth* of height per year in age of the females and of

the randomly matched males. Test the two rates of growth (b, the regression coefficient of height on age).

7. There is no sex difference in (age-height) relationship.

The Problem: Predicting Bookings by State

8. Instead of using the past bookings by state, establish by *logic* and experience a minimum number of factors to which the bookings can be related. How good a predictor were these factors in the past?

9. Use the percentage of total U.S. bookings in each state, since the "independent" variables are expressed as a percentage of the United States.

Computations

10. See Table 11.5.
11. Worked out in Questions.
12. See Table 11.6.
13. See Tables 11.5 and 11.6.
14. $t = 3 - .25 / \sqrt{.8/6 + .8/6} = 2.75/\sqrt{1.6/6} = 2.75/.5164 = 5.3253$

Table t with $(6 + 6 - 2 =)$ 10 DF 95% confidence 2.228; 99% confidence 3.169; 99.9% confidence 4.587 computed $t >$ table t.

Reject NH. The conclusion that there is (no) sex difference in the age-height relationship may be wrong 1 in 1,000 times.

15. Repeat (10) − (14) with Section 2 female students data.

The Problem: Predicting Bookings by State

16. See Table 5.6.

Conclusions

The Problem: "Females Grow Taller"

17. Steps to Develop Statistical Conclusion

1. *The conclusion:* There is no difference in the age-height relationship between male and female upper-division students.

2. *The cancellation:* There is (no) (some) difference in the age-height relationship between male and female upper-division students.

3. *The frequency of error:* 1 in 20 times; 1 in 100 times; 1 in 1,000 times.

The Problem: Predicting Bookings by States

18. I would use the equation giving the minimum (observed − expected)^2 for each state because that is the unit the salesman is most concerned with. I would tell the Connecticut salesman that equation 2 gave the least discrepancy. (See which other salesmen should also use the same equation? There are two others.)

Table 11.5
Computational Table: Age, Height of Female Students: Section 1

No.	Name Female Students	X_i^2	X_i Age	Y_i Height	X_iY_i
73	Atherton	441	21	68	1428
74	Bowser	441	21	72	1512
75	Ferring	361	19	62	1178
76	Janecek	400	20	67	1340
77	Mader	361	19	66	1254
78	Redholtz	400	20	63	1260
		2404	120	398	7972

$$b = 6 \times 7972 - 120 \times 398 / 6 \times 2404 - 120^2$$
$$= 47{,}832 \quad - \quad 47{,}760 \quad / \; 14{,}424 \; - \; 14{,}400$$
$$= \quad 72/24$$
$$= 3$$

$$a = 398 - 3 \times 120 / \; 6$$
$$= 398 - 360 / 6$$
$$= 38/6$$
$$= 6.3333$$

$$s^2 = 6 \times 2404 - 120^2 / 6 \times 5$$
$$= 14{,}424 \quad -14{,}400 / 30$$
$$= \quad 24 / 30$$
$$= 0.8$$
$$s = 0.89$$

Which state should use Equation 1? Rhode Island and Pennsylvania should use equation 3. Similarly for region 2, where equation 1 fits four states closest, equation 3 fits three states closest. Taking the two regions together, out of 14 states, equation 1 fits five states closest, equation 2 also five states, and equation 3 fits four states closest.

Table 11.6
Computational Table: Age, Height of Matching Male Students: Section 1

No.	Name Male Students	X^2_i	X_i Age	Y_i Height	X_iY_i
09	Blanchard	400	20	70	1400
67	Wells	441	21	70	1470
15	Daniels	400	20	67	1340
56	Shirk	441	21	73	1533
26	Gonnor	361	19	71	1349
46	Morrison	361	19	71	1349
		2404	120	422	8441

$$b = 6 \times 8441 - 120 \times 422 \ / \ 6 \times 2404 - 120^2$$
$$= 50{,}646 - 50{,}640 \ / \ 14{,}424 - 14{,}400$$
$$= 6 \ / 24$$
$$= 0.25$$

$$a = 422 - .25 \times 120/6$$
$$= 392/6$$
$$= 65.3333$$

$$s^2 = 6 \times 2404 - 120^2 \ / \ 6 \times 5$$
$$= 14{,}424 - 14{,}400 \ / \ 30$$
$$= 24/30$$
$$= 0.8$$
$$s = 0.89$$

[Resource] Commitments

The Problem: Predicting Bookings by States

19. The partial correlation in Table 5.6 shows that *retail volume* explains 68% of the bookings when effective buying income is held constant, but when things are reversed, buying income explains nothing of the bookings. If similar results

hold for *commissions* (explains 94% of bookings when advertising is held constant), increase the commissions, setting quotas using retail volume.

Caveats

The Problem: "Females Grow Taller"

20. The assumption about (age, height) variables is that they are *independent, normal, random variables*. Because of the upper-division status at a major university, the students were not a random sample of the U.S. population. The $n = 6$ makes the result questionable.

The Problem: Predicting Bookings by State

21. Under the linearity assumption, the investment by the company to increase bookings through advertising is independent of the investment in higher commissions. The advertising makes the company and its products gain better recognition, which certainly would help the salesmen in selling. That vital interaction is ignored in the linearity assumption. Further, the effect of retail sales volume in the state is similarly considered an independent input to bookings. The net result would be that higher bookings may be expected than is warranted.

CHAPTER 6

Concepts: Foundational

1. The probability distributions are statements about group behavior. To say that 1 bulb out of 1,000 would burn out in no way indicates which bulb. Similarly about the particular switch. We cannot "add" parts of the respective distributions because the *areas* under the distributions represent *group behavior as* n *tends toward infinity;* and they cannot speak about the behavior of 1 bulb, B, and 1 switch, S.

2. No. To simulate, one has to *know* the probability distributions of the *component elements of the systems,* such as the probability distribution of the life of the bulbs and, separately, the probability distribution of the life of the switches. When data are unavailable, as in the case of nuclear radiation, depend on *sound logical constructs* to identify the critical components and their respective distributions.

The Problem: Additional Pump for the Gas Station

3. $12 \times 3 \times 8 = 288$.

4. (1) One customer does *not* come just when another is leaving. (2) Although the average services time is five minutes, there are above average and below average requirements for service. (3) During the rush hours in the morning and

evening the customers crowd and during the rest of the day they tend to be sparse.

The Problem: Nonexperimentable Situations

5. Steps for Simulation

1. *Model:* Should be correct, comprehensive, and concise. Subject matter *expertise on key interactions* is critical. Because radiation is the most devastating effect, the radiation model should specify (a) the generation of the radiation, (b) the transmission of the radiation, and (c) the termination of the radiation. At least two viable alternative formulations should be tried. The Manhattan Project tried five methods to produce larger quantities of fissionable material, lest the survival race for development of the atomic bomb be lost by even a month.

2. *Variables:* Minimum of *two-interacting variables* are required for simulation. Which effects, if overlooked, can be most detrimental? What *minimum number* of variables can explain the maximum of those effects? (a) Radiation waves from ground zero and (b) wind velocity are critical to nuclear blast model.

3. *Values:* What are the *physical limits* of the values of each variable? What are two alternative *probability distributions* most appropriate to the key values of the variables? High radiation coupled with high winds would set the *upper limit,* while low radiation with low winds would set the *lower limit.* Are they likely to be uniformly distributed over time and space? Or are they likely to be most intense at ground zero and decrease rapidly toward the periphery? Two Pearsonian distributions can be chosen, and their parameters selected for simulation.

Concepts: Formulational

The Problem: Hiring Additional Staff

6. Most unacceptable delay, moderately unacceptable delay, least unacceptable delay.

7. Very big demand on resources, moderate demand on resources, little demand on resources.

8. *Unacceptability of job completion by category:* most unacceptable 3%; definitely unacceptable 7%; moderately unacceptable 30%; somewhat unacceptable 20%; least unacceptable 40%. RN 1-3, most unacceptable; RN 4-10, definitely unacceptable; RN 11-40, moderately unacceptable; RN 41-60, somewhat unacceptable; RN 61-00, least unacceptable.

9. *On-time completion of jobs by size:* very big job 10% of the time; big job 15%; average(-size) job 20%; below-average(-size) job 25%; small(-size) job 30%. RN 1-10, very big job; RN 11-25, big job; RN 26-45, average(-size) job; RN 46-70, below-average(-size) job; RN 71-00, small job.

10. Follow the format of Table 6.5.

Conclusions

The Problem: Calibrating the Deficiency of Office Service

11.

	Very Big Job (1)	Big Job (2)	Avg. Job (3)
Most unacceptable	(1) 11-0	21-5	31-30
Definitely unacceptable	(2) 12-0	22-10	32-35
Moderately unacceptable	(3) 13-0	23-15	33-40
Somewhat unacceptable	(4) 14-0	24-20	34-45
Least unacceptable	(5) 15-0	25-25	35-50
and so on through 55-100			

12. Is your simulation result > or < our result of 51?

[Resource] Commitments

The Problem: Hiring Additional Staff

13. What matters is the frequency of the deficiency index scores 0 to 25: very big jobs and big jobs unsatisfactorily accomplished. How many in the two categories would he consider tolerable?

14. Our simulation shows 5 out of the 20 (25%) are most undesirable and an additional 25% are definitely undesirable. Because the very big jobs are not being satisfactorily accomplished, I need additional staff to handle the very big jobs (next, the big jobs) in the required skills category demanded by those jobs.

Caveats

The Problem: Hiring Additional Staff

15. The simulation was based on logical reasoning universally applicable to all situations. To convince my boss, I need to collect the empirical data as specified in chapter 6 and then conduct the simulation.

16. The simulation shows that the least unacceptable jobs are only 3 out of 20, or 15%. They can be, say, doubled, with little additional staff (even overtime, part-time personnel to demonstrate the large contribution the small jobs' completion can make).

17. Any very big job is far too important for the section to be completed unsatisfactorily. Investment in additional personnel will be more expensive and more extensive, but the investment will pay off in the long run in section reputation.

CHAPTER 7

Concepts: Foundational

1. Bayes' contribution is in breaking up an unknown/unknowable situation

into exclusive and exhaustive outcomes that can be experimentally and/or experientially known.

2. In scientific inference, most often the likelihood dominates the prior; in business decision-making most often the prior dominates the likelihood.

3. Convergence (see Table 3.3).

4. The nonrepeatable, nonrandom values of subjective probabilities are treated as though they were random variables that assume values closer and closer to specified values with increasing number of observations.

Concepts: Formulational

The Problem: Rain and Rain Gear

5. Relative Frequency Probability.
6. Subjective Probability.

The Problem: Acceptance Quality Level

7. Assume that the batch-produced items come from a binomial distribution that allows two mutually exclusive and exhaustive outcomes (defective, and not-defective). The manufacturer supplies a lot that is supposed to have fraction defective of, say, .03. We inspect a random sample $n = 50$ out of the 10,000 bulbs and find $r = 1$ defective. The binomial table shows the probability of obtaining 1 out of 50, or 2% defective from a population of 3% defective.

The Problem: Revised Estimates of Market Size

8. Depends on the penalty of wrong decision. When the decision is to introduce a new product that costs $500,000 to develop, $n = 20$ may be a reasonable risk; but if it costs, say, $1 million to develop, $n = 50$ may well be worth the extra cost of sampling.

Computations

The Problem: Rain and Rain Gear

9. $p = .10, p' = .0; p = .20, p' = .0; p = .30, p' = .05; p = .40, p' = .05; p = .50, p' = .10; p = .60, p' = .10; p = .70, p' = .30; p = .80, p' = .40; p = .90, p' = .80.$

10. .05; .10; .18; .23; .30; .35; .50; .60; .85.

The Problem: Acceptance Quality Level

11. See Table 11.7.
12. See Table 11.8.
13. See Table 11.9.

Table 11.7
Calculation of Posterior Probabilities: Batch Product I

(1) % Defective	(2) Marginal	(3) Conditional	(4) Joint (2)x(3)	(5) Posterior
.10	0.20	0. 2702	0.02702	0.45750
.15	0.55	0. 1368	0.02052	0.34744
.20	0.25	0. 0576	0.01152	0.19506
			0.05906	1.00000

The Problem: Revised Estimates of Market Share

14. See Table 11.10.
15. See Table 11.11.

Conclusions

The Problem: Rain and Rain Gear

16. We computed the percentage of those who said they would take rain gear on that particular occasion. Given the same weather bureau probabilities, the

Table 11.8
Calculation of Posterior Probabilities: Batch Product II

(1) % Defective	(2) Marginal	(3) Conditional	(4) Joint (2)x(3)	(5) Posterior
.10	0.20	0. 2852	0.02852	0.31584
.15	0.55	0. 2293	0.03440	0.38095
.20	0.25	0. 1369	0.02738	0.30321
			0.09030	1.00000

Table 11.9
Calculation of Posterior Probabilities: Batch Product III

(1) % Defective	(2) Marginal	(3) Conditional	(4) Joint (2)x(3)	(5) Posterior
.10	0.20	0. 1901	0.01901	0.19697
.15	0.55	0. 2428	0.03642	0.37737
.20	0.25	0. 2054	0.04108	0.42566
			0.09651	1.00000

same group may well express themselves differently, the $n \to \infty$ *not* making the probability of taking rain gear converge, so that the p' in (9) can only apply to that experiment.

17. Garbage! The weather bureau probabilities p are based on relative frequency probability, which requires *convergence* of the random variable, while the p'

Table 11.10
Calculation of Posterior Probabilities: New Product I

(1) Market Share	(2) Marginal	(3) Conditional	(4) Joint (2)x(3)	(5) Posterior
.01	0.05	0.0159	0.00079	0.00430
.02	0.10	0.0528	0.00528	0.02872
.03	0.15	0.0988	0.11482	0.62450
.04	0.30	0.1458	0.04374	0.23790
.05	0.30	0.1887	0.01698	0.09235
.06	0.10	0.2246	0.00225	0.01223
			0.18386	1.00000

Table 11.11
Calculation of Posterior Probabilities: New Product II

(1) Market Share	(2) Marginal	(3) Conditional	(4) Joint (2)x(3)	(5) Posterior
.01	0.05	0.1652	0.00826	0.02382
.02	0.10	0.2725	0.02725	0.07860
.03	0.15	0.3364	0.05046	0.14554
.04	0.30	0.3683	0.11049	0.31868
.05	0.30	0.3774	0.11322	0.32655
.06	0.10	0.3703	0.03703	0.10681
			0.34671	1.00000

are *not* based on random values that *converge*. Combining the two produces garbage.

The Problem: Acceptance Quality Level

18. With only 1 defective in the sample of 20, the *best products* ($p = .1$) occur nearly two and one-third times as often as what the vendor estimated. With three defectives, his estimate is just met by the postsample probability. With only 1 defective in the sample of 20, the *worst products* ($p = .2$) occurs just 3% less than the vendor estimates. With three defectives, the worst product occurs 70% more than what the vendor estimated. The occurrence of the *average products* remains at about two-thirds of what the vendor estimated. The vendor *underestimates* most the occurrence of his best products, *overestimates* the occurrence of his average products, and *underestimates* the occurrence of his worst products.

The Problem: Revised Estimates of Market

19. *No.* The posterior probabilities for (break even or better) is .342.
20. *Yes.* The posterior probabilities for (break even or better) is .752.
21. Although the percentage of positive responses is twice as much at 10%, the probabilities of their *occurrences* are much *lower*. For instance, when the market share is .01, an $r = 2$ occurs only 1.59% (or .0159) of the time, while an $r = 1$ occurs more than ten times as often, 16.52% (or .1652). This lower

conditional probability results in *lower posteriors*. An $r = 1$, $n = 20$ is close to the break even point, 4%. But if the break even is close to 10%, the probability of its occurrence as $r = 2$, $n = 20$ is much smaller, *reversing the decision* to introduce the new product.

[Resource] Commitments

The Problem: Revised Estimates of Market Size

22. The 250 buyers out of 12,500 work out to a market share of .02. *Yes*, the posterior probabilities of (break even or better) is .976.

23. *No*. The posterior probabilities of (break even or better) is .996.

Caveats

24. See (15) and (16).

25. That the subjective prior probabilities can be multiplied by *relative frequency likelihoods* from the binomial (and other appropriate) distribution as though both were relative frequencies.

26. The EOLs are a *long-term tendency,* not the next-time actuality. If I do not have *infinite funds* to enjoy the expected opportunity loss over infinite trials, I would not invest. Further, although the EOL may be favorable, the probability of *loss of a significant part of my resources* would give me pause.

CHAPTER 8

1–8. See chapter 8.

CHAPTER 9

Concepts: Foundational

1. Attitude: The preparedness to accept (adverse) outcome is what the utility function presents. The prospect of losing, say, 60% of one's resources may scare the investor more than the lure of a 5.5% gain.

2. By determining the *point of indifference* between guaranteed outcomes versus a lottery of the best and the worst outcomes.

3. Probably very poorly. The fisherman knows directly the utility of losing 30% to 40% of his catch (and that of other fishermen). He has little feel for the $10 million additional cost of the nuclear plant or $40 million—which may be as remote as the national debt of $3,000 billion. Unless he can translate the additional nuclear plant construction costs into $x\%$ increase in his electric bill, he is likely to reach for some figures between which he is indifferent.

4. The *interaction* of the components of the system. Nuclear energy is a

common concern of the salmon fisherman, the environmentalists, the employees of the nuclear industry, and all others who are part of the system of future users of electric energy from the nuclear plant.

5. Only by showing both the salmon loss and the radiation hazard as *part of a single system* of which both are constituents.

6. PFN is the *impairment of the system* owing to the nonperformance at the subsystem or lower levels. PFN says by how much the system will be impaired each by radiation, by salmon loss, and by other concerns, and further says how much graver to the system it will be not to reduce each impairment. By making each concern a subsystem- or lower-level entity, PFN recognizes their interactions.

7. If the multiattribute utility function can be represented by the additive utility function, and if we construct a scale with the lowest-ranking factor (concern) as the zero point, we can assess the relative importance of the factors as expressed by people like the salmon fisherman, who has little feel for the additional nuclear plant construction costs, if we give equal weight to each such expression. Over and above the thorny questions of preference independence and utility independence, there is the absence of the *recognition of interaction* among the various subsystems, making the utility function unsuitable for resource allocation.

8. The ratio of the weighted PFN scores of *subsystems* to the system determines the allocation of the system budget.

9–16. Follow chapter 9 format.

17. The utility function is based on (1) the *indifference* between *certainty and uncertainty* for the single-attribute utility function and (2) the indifference between one set of *attribute values* and another. Further, (3) the condition of *utility independence* must be satisfied, and (4) the condition of *preference independence*. We impose these conditions and ask the decision-maker to choose level L of one attribute, X_1, that would make him indifferent between L and a 50:50 lottery of the best and worst of another attribute, X_6. The utility of X_1, $U(X_1)$, must be independent of $U(X_6)$; or, to the salmon fisherman, the utility of loss of salmon must be *totally unrelated* to, say, the radiation hazard or the added nuclear plant construction cost. Further, the preference between two attributes must be *the same* when the other several attributes are at their best level and when they are at their worst level. As pointed out in (3), the salmon fisherman has little feel for even the *most concrete* values and levels of other attributes, such as $5 million, $40 million, let alone the *more abstract* values and levels of other attributes, such as radiation hazard and length of intertie.

18. The salmon fisherman has to assign PFN scores 1 to 9 to his attribute, as well as to all other attributes that constitute the system, based on a > relationship to the *impairment to the system* objective. He knows that his scores will be challenged by his peers. The final scores will be the result of negotiations between peers and arbitration by superiors, recognizing concretely the interactions. The only abstraction that the salmon fisherman had to deal with is what the system objective is.

19. The validity of the PFN scores and weights depends on the intelligent and active negotiations between peers and superiors. The salmon fisherman does not need to concern himself with the vertical weights that would be quite abstract for him. However, his "boss" in the system hierarchy would have to negotiate on the proper vertical weights for his level. Tier 1 objective is always abstract, such as "Improve community quality of life." Who sets that objective? The mayor of the city? The county executive? The governor of the state? The system objective has to be the direct responsibility of a person(s). Unless such a person(s) is found and he is convinced of the objectives hierarchy, the salmon fisherman would not be able to express his concerns and fight for them as part of a system.

CHAPTER 10

Concepts: Foundational

1. To estimate the probability of war, you should already know the probability of Soviet destruction of sensitive materials given war, a catch-22.

2. Two opposing support functions would be (1) Soviet attack is imminent; (2) it is not. The range for support of (1) is 1% to 25%.

3. Soviet attack imminence is (1) most unlikely, (2) definitely unlikely, (3) unlikely, (4) definitely likely, (5) most likely.

4. (1) Hoover had no evidence of actual destruction of sensitive materials by the Soviets, (2) unorthodox Soviet offer through ABC newsman Scali to remove missiles under U.N. supervision, (3) no intelligence of Khrushchev overthrow by Kremlin hawks.

5. One-sided, iterative approach.

6. (1) Interactive approach is far more *realistic* because every action does have a reaction, perhaps a reaction in several dimensions. (2) Interactive approach is *anticipatory*, considering a sequence of action and counteraction (3) that makes it possible to select *alternative strategies* to reduce the conflict, (4) explicitly recognizing that one party *does not control* all the variables or all the values of the variables. Iterative approach, on the other hand, ignores the other party(ies) and their control of the variables and their values.

7. See the text.

Concepts: Formulational

The Problem: DEFCON 5

8, 9. On the face of it, the NORAD commander was faced with row 110: military consummation, specified, unlimited. If he were to accept that bluff, the logical answer would be column 90: military consummation, specified, unlimited. However, the fundamental premise of BTIS is that nuclear war does not start without prior military encounter, which seems to have gone through the

NORAD commander's mind as well. BTIS requires one to *see an action or an event as part of a sequence—which was unfulfilled in DEFCON 5*. What would be the next step in the sequence except certain and full retaliation by the United States? For the Soviets to threaten to use "First Strike" would gain far more ground than actually striking first.

10. The first factor is the indispensability of Khrushchev to order the nuclear strike; the second is the indispensability of "knee-bends" to physical launch. The indispensable *command* and the indispensable *control* (of the launch) will interpose at least two steps between row 109 and row 110, even if the decision were already made by the Soviets to go to row 110.

The Problem: Beijing Confrontation

11. While Beijing would want to consider its suppression of prodemocracy movement political—100%, we should view it as a mixed strategy.

Macro BTIS Elements

Commercial—30%: Vast exodus of foreign businessmen, uncertain future.

Diplomatic—25%: France (De Gaulle), the earliest champion of Beijing, cut diplomatic ties; United States keeps them open; Beijing appeals to fellow Communists that the suppression was a blow for communism everywhere.

Political—40%: Directly affecting how a people decide their destiny.

Military—5%: Suspension of $600 million in military sales by the United States.

12. Macro BTIS Elements

Political: Arrest of the leaders of the dissent—*public executions.*

Diplomatic: Britain hints at suspension of the handover of Hong Kong; United States and Britain *reducing diplomatic presence* in Mainland China; European embassies leave Beijing.

Commercial: Remaining foreign businessmen leave Beijing; United States *reduces trade* with Beijing as does Britain and the European community.

Military: United States freezes supplies of parts of weapons already supplied; *freezes all military contacts* for an indefinite period.

13. Macro BTIS Elements

Political: Reduce the noise level on arrests; no public executions; statements supporting reform; campaign against corruption.

Diplomatic: No harassment of foreign diplomats; "secret" visit of Beijing with key Hong Kong leaders for discussion of the future leaked later to the British press; reception for diplomats by new Chinese premier.

Commercial: Reception by the Chinese commerce minister for returning foreign businessmen; easing of red tape in trade.

Military: Unfreezing of official U.S. military contacts; statements about future military supplies for defensive purpose.

Computations

The Problem: Beijing Confrontation

14. From the four macro elements we turn to the micro elements. Under "Diplomatic" the three alternatives are (1) expansion, (2) embargo, and (3) ambivalence. The cutting of "all links short of diplomatic relations" is one step short of the worst activity under "diplomatic embargo." Escalation would mean the *breaking of diplomatic relations.* Under "commercial embargo" would be the United States vote against loans to China in the Asian Development Bank, World Bank, and so on. Under "political," "global moral imperative" is what got Beijing into trouble with the rest of the free world. Beijing can ignore the world opinion on "global moral imperative," conduct public executions of dissenters, dramatize seizing dissenters who fled China, pursue collectivization, and eliminate private enterprise. Under "military," Beijing could seek "military expansion" by acquiring weaponry from the Soviet Union and other sources to replace the United States.

15. *Diplomatic expansion* would be the opposite of diplomatic embargo. For France to restore diplomatic relations, some significant changes in the political profile of Beijing would be crucial, such as the quieting down of the furor over dissenters and the massive hunt for their arrest, maybe followed by some kind of amnesty. For Britain there needs to be the show of Beijing assurances about the rights of Hong Kong citizens after the colonial days are over. The United States has announced that it is not contemplating further actions unless things got worse. So it would behoove Beijing to make it possible for the United States to be the middleman to mediate the re-establishment of diplomatic and commercial ties with other countries. Unfreezing of formal military contacts by the United States would signal an improvement in the Chinese military expansion.

Conclusions

The Problem: Beijing Confrontation

16. (15). Beijing would be cutting its nose to spite its face if it destroys all the goodwill it had built up during the past decade. The Communist Party has already established its control, and the leading dissenters have gone into hiding. Even small gestures on China's part would be welcomed somewhat eagerly by the world.

17. If Beijing further clamps down on its people, the move will be political. The U.S. response would not be in kind because the United States would not

want to interfere in the internal affairs of China. However, the United States would respond by voting against loans to China by the World Bank. If Beijing made a diplomatic move by reducing the mental wariness of the U.S. representation in Beijing, the United States would reciprocate in kind by perhaps letting the word around the embassy circuit that China is coming around. The probability of a Chinese response in kind is .8 to .9.

[Resource] Commitments

The Problem: Beijing Confrontation

18. (1) Present a united front with Britain, France, and Germany on steps vis-a-vis Beijing; (2) respond in kind to diplomatic and commercial overtures by Beijing; (3) respond not-in-kind to political escalation, using commercial and military responses.

19. Quite probably it would create a leadership vacuum, which would be filled in by a sort of triumvirate, each watching the other fiercely. The leadership of dissent would slowly return to the Mainland. The United States could help bring stability fast by recognizing without delay even the interim triumvirate, so that a speedier transition can be engineered.

Caveats

20. "China Hands" from government (James Lily, ambassador who previously served in Taiwan), from academia (John Fairbanks of Harvard). I would use some "China Hands" who have seen the "cultural revolution" firsthand. The limitation would be their trying to cast tomorrow in the shape of yesterday. But they could rise above their own subjectivity.

21. That would possibly make Beijing want to have the United States resume promptly to be a source of military sales. The reverse of the "China Card" of Nixon would be appropriate, the "Soviet Card." The United States can demand good evidence of Beijing's improved response to the prodemocracy movement, such as a general amnesty, as a condition for considering the resumption of defensive weapons sales.

22. "Our long-term interests" would be the "global moral imperative" of economic and political freedom for a billion persons. The "recognition of a complex internal situation in China" emphasizes the positive contributions of Deng Xiaoping in liberalizing Chinese political and economic life during the past decade, only to be marred by the dramatic turnabout, which may have, in some measure, been forced on him. The principal B–T matrix elements are 02, commercial embargo; 04, diplomatic embargo; 06, global moral imperative; and 09, military embargo. How China responds to these bluffs by the United States would determine both the relative importance of the moves (*structure*) and the progression of responses (*sequence*).

Appendix: Standard Statistical Tables

Table A.1
Chi-Squared Table

df	$\chi^2_{.01}$	$\chi^2_{.02}$	$\chi^2_{.05}$	$\chi^2_{.10}$	$\chi^2_{.25}$	$\chi^2_{.50}$	$\chi^2_{.90}$	$\chi^2_{.95}$	$\chi^2_{.98}$	$\chi^2_{.99}$	$\chi^2_{.999}$	df
1	—	—	—	.02	.10	.46	2.7	3.8	5.4	6.6	10.8	1
2	.02	.04	.10	.21	.58	1.4	4.6	6.0	7.8	9.2	13.8	2
3	.11	.18	.35	.58	1.21	2.4	6.3	7.8	9.8	11.3	16.3	3
4	.30	.43	.71	1.1	1.92	3.4	7.8	9.5	11.7	13.3	18.5	4
5	.55	.75	1.1	1.6	2.7	4.4	9.2	11.1	13.4	15.1	20.5	5
6	.87	1.13	1.6	2.2	3.5	5.4	10.6	12.6	15.0	16.8	22.5	6
7	1.24	1.56	2.2	2.8	4.3	6.4	12.0	14.1	16.6	18.5	24.3	7
8	1.65	2.03	2.7	3.5	5.1	7.3	13.4	15.5	18.2	20.1	26.1	8
9	2.09	2.53	3.3	4.2	5.9	8.3	14.7	16.9	19.7	21.7	27.9	9
10	2.55	3.06	3.9	4.9	6.7	9.3	16.0	18.3	21.2	23.2	29.6	10
11	3.05	3.61	4.6	5.6	7.6	10.3	17.3	19.7	22.6	24.7	31.3	11
12	3.57	4.18	5.2	6.3	8.4	11.3	18.5	21.0	24.1	26.2	32.9	12
13	4.11	4.76	5.9	7.0	9.3	12.3	19.8	22.4	25.5	27.7	34.5	13
14	4.66	5.37	6.6	7.8	10.2	13.3	21.1	23.7	26.9	29.1	36.1	14
15	5.23	5.98	7.3	8.5	11.0	14.3	22.3	25.0	28.3	30.6	37.7	15
16	5.81	6.61	8.0	9.3	11.9	15.3	23.5	26.3	29.6	32.0	39.3	16
17	6.41	7.26	8.7	10.1	12.8	16.3	24.8	27.6	31.0	33.4	40.8	17
18	7.02	7.91	9.4	10.9	13.7	17.3	26.0	28.9	32.3	34.8	42.3	18
19	7.63	8.57	10.1	11.7	14.6	18.3	27.2	30.1	33.7	36.2	43.8	19
20	8.26	9.24	10.9	12.4	15.5	19.3	28.4	31.4	35.0	37.6	45.3	20
21	8.9	9.9	11.6	13.2	16.3	20.3	29.6	32.7	36.3	38.9	46.8	21
22	9.5	10.6	12.3	14.0	17.2	21.3	30.8	33.9	37.7	40.3	48.3	22
23	10.2	11.3	13.1	14.8	18.1	22.3	32.0	35.2	39.0	41.6	49.7	23
24	10.9	12.0	13.8	15.7	19.0	23.3	33.2	36.4	40.3	43.0	51.2	24
25	11.5	12.7	14.6	16.5	19.9	24.3	34.4	37.7	41.6	44.3	52.6	25
26	12.2	13.4	15.4	17.3	20.8	25.3	35.6	38.9	42.9	45.6	54.0	26
27	12.9	14.1	16.2	18.1	21.7	26.3	36.7	40.1	44.1	47.0	55.5	27
28	13.6	14.8	16.9	18.9	22.7	27.3	37.9	41.3	45.4	48.3	56.9	28
29	14.3	15.6	17.7	19.8	23.6	28.3	39.1	42.6	46.7	49.6	58.3	29
30	15.0	16.3	18.5	20.6	24.5	29.3	40.3	43.8	48.0	50.9	59.7	30
40	22.2	23.8	26.5	29.1	33.7	39.3	51.8	55.8	60.4	63.7	73.5	40
60	37.5	39.7	43.2	46.5	52.3	59.3	74.4	79.1	84.6	88.4	99.7	60
100	70.0	73.1	77.9	82.4	90.1	99.3	118.5	124.3	131.1	135.8	149.5	100

Source: From Table IV of Ronald A. Fisher and Frank Yates, *Statistical Tables for Biological, Agricultural and Medical Research,* published by Longman Group UK Ltd., London (previously published by Oliver and Boyd Ltd., Edinburgh) and by permission of the authors and publishers.

Table A.2
Partial _t_ Table

t 95%	t 97.5%	t 98%	t 99%	t 99.5%	t 99.9%	DF
12.706	25.452	31.821	63.657	127.32	636.619	1
4.303	6.205	6.965	9.925	14.089	31.598	2
3.182	4.176	4.541	5.841	7.453	12.941	3
2.776	3.495	3.747	4.604	5.598	8.610	4
2.571	3.163	3.365	4.032	4.773	6.859	5
2.447	2.969	3.143	3.707	4.317	5.959	6
2.365	2.841	2.998	3.499	4.029	5.405	7
2.306	2.752	2.896	3.355	3.832	5.041	8
2.262	2.685	2.821	3.250	3.690	4.781	9
2.228	2.634	2.764	3.169	3.581	4.587	10
2.201	2.593	2.718	3.106	3.497	4.437	11
2.179	2.560	2.681	3.055	3.428	4.318	12
2.160	2.533	2.650	3.012	3.372	4.221	13
2.145	2.510	2.624	2.977	3.326	4.140	14
2.131	2.490	2.602	2.947	3.286	4.073	15
2.120	2.473	2.583	2.921	3.252	4.015	16
2.110	2.458	2.567	2.898	3.222	3.965	17
2.101	2.445	2.552	2.878	3.197	3.922	18
2.093	2.433	2.539	2.861	3.174	3.883	19
2.086	2.423	2.528	2.845	3.153	3.850	20
2.080	2.414	2.518	2.831	3.135	3.819	21
2.074	2.406	2.508	2.819	3.119	3.792	22
2.069	2.398	2.500	2.807	3.104	3.767	23
2.064	2.391	2.492	2.797	3.090	3.745	24
2.060	2.385	2.485	2.787	3.078	3.725	25
2.056	2.379	2.479	2.779	3.067	3.707	26
2.052	2.373	2.473	2.771	3.056	3.690	27
2.048	2.368	2.467	2.763	3.047	3.674	28
2.045	2.364	2.462	2.756	3.038	3.659	29
2.042	2.360	2.457	2.750	3.030	3.646	30
2.021	2.329	2.423	2.704	2.971	3.551	40
2.000	2.299	2.390	2.660	2.915	3.460	60
1.980	2.270	2.358	2.617	2.860	3.373	120
1.960	2.241	2.326	2.576	2.807	3.291	∞

Source: From Table III of Ronald A. Fisher and Frank Yates, _Statistical Tables for Biological, Agricultural and Medical Research,_ published by Longman Group UK Ltd., London (previously published by Oliver and Boyd, Ltd., Edinburgh) and by permission of the authors and publishers.

Table A.3
Areas of the Standardized Normal Probability Distribution

This table shows the dark area:

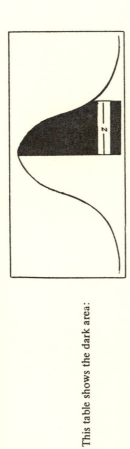

$z = \dfrac{x - \mu}{\sigma}$	.00	.01	.02	.03	.04	.05	.06	.07	.08	.09
0.0	.0000	.0040	.0080	.0120	.0160	.0199	.0239	.0279	.0319	.0359
0.1	.0398	.0438	.0478	.0517	.0557	.0596	.0636	.0675	.0714	.0753
0.2	.0793	.0832	.0871	.0910	.0948	.0987	.1026	.1064	.1103	.1141
0.3	.1179	.1217	.1255	.1293	.1331	.1368	.1406	.1443	.1480	.1517
0.4	.1554	.1591	.1628	.1664	.1700	.1736	.1772	.1808	.1844	.1879
0.5	.1915	.1950	.1985	.2019	.2054	.2088	.2123	.2157	.2190	.2224
0.6	.2257	.2291	.2324	.2357	.2389	.2422	.2454	.2486	.2518	.2549
0.7	.2580	.2612	.2642	.2673	.2704	.2734	.2764	.2794	.2823	.2852
0.8	.2881	.2910	.2939	.2967	.2995	.3023	.3051	.3078	.3106	.3133
0.9	.3159	.3186	.3212	.3238	.3264	.3289	.3315	.3340	.3365	.3389
1.0	.3413	.3438	.3461	.3485	.3508	.3531	.3554	.3577	.3599	.3621
1.1	.3643	.3665	.3686	.3708	.3729	.3749	.3770	.3790	.3810	.3830
1.2	.3849	.3869	.3888	.3907	.3925	.3944	.3962	.3980	.3997	.4015
1.3	.4032	.4049	.4066	.4082	.4099	.4115	.4131	.4147	.4162	.4177
1.4	.4192	.4207	.4222	.4236	.4251	.4265	.4279	.4292	.4306	.4319

z										
1.5	.4332	.4345	.4357	.4370	.4382	.4394	.4406	.4418	.4429	.4441
1.6	.4452	.4463	.4474	.4484	.4495	.4505	.4515	.4525	.4535	.4545
1.7	.4554	.4564	.4573	.4582	.4591	.4599	.4608	.4616	.4625	.4633
1.8	.4641	.4649	.4656	.4664	.4671	.4678	.4686	.4693	.4699	.4706
1.9	.4713	.4719	.4726	.4732	.4738	.4744	.4750	.4756	.4761.	.4767
2.0	.4772	.4778	.4783	.4788	.4793	.4798	.4803	.4808	.4812	.4817
2.1	.4821	.4826	.4830	.4834	.4838	.4842	.4846	.4850	.4854	.4857
2.2	.4861	.4864	.4868	.4871	.4875	.4878	.4881	.4884	.4887	.4890
2.3	.4893	.4896	.4898	.4901	.4904	.4906	.4909	.4911	.4913	.4916
2.4	.4918	.4920	.4922	.4925	.4927	.4929	.4931	.4932	.4934	.4936
2.5	.4938	.4940	.4941	.4943	.4945	.4946	.4948	.4949	.4951	.4952
2.6	.4953	.4955	.4956	.4957	.4959	.4960	.4961	.4962	.4963	.4964
2.7	.4965	.4966	.4967	.4968	.4969	.4970	.4971	.4972	.4973	.4974
2.8	.4974	.4975	.4976	.4977	.4977	.4978	.4979	.4979	.4980	.4981
2.9	.4981	.4982	.4982	.4983	.4984	.4984	.4985	.4985	.4986	.4986
3.0	.49865	.4987	.4987	.4988	.4988	.4989	.4989	.4989	.4990	.4990
3.1	.49903	.4991	.4991	.4991	.4992	.4992	.4992	.4992	.4993	.4993
3.2	.4993129									
5.0	.4999997133									

Table A.4

F Values: 95%, 99%

δ_1: DF for Treatment (numerator) in columns

δ_2: DF for Subjects (denominator) in rows

δ_2 \ δ_1	1	2	3	4	5	6	7	8	9	10	12	15	20	24	30	40	60	120	∞
1	161·4	199·5	215·7	224·6	230·2	234·0	236·8	238·9	240·5	241·9	243·9	245·9	248·0	249·1	250·1	251·1	252·2	253·3	254·3
2	18·51	19·00	19·16	19·25	19·30	19·33	19·35	19·37	19·38	19·40	19·41	19·43	19·45	19·45	19·46	19·47	19·48	19·49	19·50
3	10·13	9·55	9·28	9·12	9·01	8·94	8·89	8·85	8·81	8·79	8·74	8·70	8·66	8·64	8·62	8·59	8·57	8·55	8·53
4	7·71	6·94	6·59	6·39	6·26	6·16	6·09	6·04	6·00	5·96	5·91	5·86	5·80	5·77	5·75	5·72	5·69	5·66	5·63
5	6·61	5·79	5·41	5·19	5·05	4·95	4·88	4·82	4·77	4·74	4·68	4·62	4·56	4·53	4·50	4·46	4·43	4·40	4·36
6	5·99	5·14	4·76	4·53	4·39	4·28	4·21	4·15	4·10	4·06	4·00	3·94	3·87	3·84	3·81	3·77	3·74	3·70	3·67
7	5·59	4·74	4·35	4·12	3·97	3·87	3·79	3·73	3·68	3·64	3·57	3·51	3·44	3·41	3·38	3·34	3·30	3·27	3·23
8	5·32	4·46	4·07	3·84	3·69	3·58	3·50	3·44	3·39	3·35	3·28	3·22	3·15	3·12	3·08	3·04	3·01	2·97	2·93
9	5·12	4·26	3·86	3·63	3·48	3·37	3·29	3·23	3·18	3·14	3·07	3·01	2·94	2·90	2·86	2·83	2·79	2·75	2·71
10	4·96	4·10	3·71	3·48	3·33	3·22	3·14	3·07	3·02	2·98	2·91	2·85	2·77	2·74	2·70	2·66	2·62	2·58	2·54
11	4·84	3·98	3·59	3·36	3·20	3·09	3·01	2·95	2·90	2·85	2·79	2·72	2·65	2·61	2·57	2·53	2·49	2·45	2·40
12	4·75	3·89	3·49	3·26	3·11	3·00	2·91	2·85	2·80	2·75	2·69	2·62	2·54	2·51	2·47	2·43	2·38	2·34	2·30
13	4·67	3·81	3·41	3·18	3·03	2·92	2·83	2·77	2·71	2·67	2·60	2·53	2·46	2·42	2·38	2·34	2·30	2·25	2·21
14	4·60	3·74	3·34	3·11	2·96	2·85	2·76	2·70	2·65	2·60	2·53	2·46	2·39	2·35	2·31	2·27	2·22	2·18	2·13
15	4·54	3·68	3·29	3·06	2·90	2·79	2·71	2·64	2·59	2·54	2·48	2·40	2·33	2·29	2·25	2·20	2·16	2·11	2·07
16	4·49	3·63	3·24	3·01	2·85	2·74	2·66	2·59	2·54	2·49	2·42	2·35	2·28	2·24	2·19	2·15	2·11	2·06	2·01
17	4·45	3·59	3·20	2·96	2·81	2·70	2·61	2·55	2·49	2·45	2·38	2·31	2·23	2·19	2·15	2·10	2·06	2·01	1·96
18	4·41	3·55	3·16	2·93	2·77	2·66	2·58	2·51	2·46	2·41	2·34	2·27	2·19	2·15	2·11	2·06	2·02	1·97	1·92
19	4·38	3·52	3·13	2·90	2·74	2·63	2·54	2·48	2·42	2·38	2·31	2·23	2·16	2·11	2·07	2·03	1·98	1·93	1·88
20	4·35	3·49	3·10	2·87	2·71	2·60	2·51	2·45	2·39	2·35	2·28	2·20	2·12	2·08	2·04	1·99	1·95	1·90	1·84
21	4·32	3·47	3·07	2·84	2·68	2·57	2·49	2·42	2·37	2·32	2·25	2·18	2·10	2·05	2·01	1·96	1·92	1·87	1·81
22	4·30	3·44	3·05	2·82	2·66	2·55	2·46	2·40	2·34	2·30	2·23	2·15	2·07	2·03	1·98	1·94	1·89	1·84	1·78
23	4·28	3·42	3·03	2·80	2·64	2·53	2·44	2·37	2·32	2·27	2·20	2·13	2·05	2·01	1·96	1·91	1·86	1·81	1·76
24	4·26	3·40	3·01	2·78	2·62	2·51	2·42	2·36	2·30	2·25	2·18	2·11	2·03	1·98	1·94	1·89	1·84	1·79	1·73
25	4·24	3·39	2·99	2·76	2·60	2·49	2·40	2·34	2·28	2·24	2·16	2·09	2·01	1·96	1·92	1·87	1·82	1·77	1·71
26	4·23	3·37	2·98	2·74	2·59	2·47	2·39	2·32	2·27	2·22	2·15	2·07	1·99	1·95	1·90	1·85	1·80	1·75	1·69
27	4·21	3·35	2·96	2·73	2·57	2·46	2·37	2·31	2·25	2·20	2·13	2·06	1·97	1·93	1·88	1·84	1·79	1·73	1·67
28	4·20	3·34	2·95	2·71	2·56	2·45	2·36	2·29	2·24	2·19	2·12	2·04	1·96	1·91	1·87	1·82	1·77	1·71	1·65
29	4·18	3·33	2·93	2·70	2·55	2·43	2·35	2·28	2·22	2·18	2·10	2·03	1·94	1·90	1·85	1·81	1·75	1·70	1·64
30	4·17	3·32	2·92	2·69	2·53	2·42	2·33	2·27	2·21	2·16	2·09	2·01	1·93	1·89	1·84	1·79	1·74	1·68	1·62
40	4·08	3·23	2·84	2·61	2·45	2·34	2·25	2·18	2·12	2·08	2·00	1·92	1·84	1·79	1·74	1·69	1·64	1·58	1·51
60	4·00	3·15	2·76	2·53	2·37	2·25	2·17	2·10	2·04	1·99	1·92	1·84	1·75	1·70	1·65	1·59	1·53	1·47	1·39
120	3·92	3·07	2·68	2·45	2·29	2·17	2·09	2·02	1·96	1·91	1·83	1·75	1·66	1·61	1·55	1·50	1·43	1·35	1·25
∞	3·84	3·00	2·60	2·37	2·21	2·10	2·01	1·94	1·88	1·83	1·75	1·67	1·57	1·52	1·46	1·39	1·32	1·22	1·00

n_2 \ n_1	1	2	3	4	5	6	7	8	9	10	12	15	20	24	30	40	60	120	∞
1	4052	4999·5	5403	5625	5764	5859	5928	5982	6022	6056	6106	6157	6209	6235	6261	6287	6313	6339	6366
2	98·50	99·00	99·17	99·25	99·30	99·33	99·36	99·37	99·39	99·40	99·42	99·43	99·45	99·46	99·47	99·47	99·48	99·49	99·50
3	34·12	30·82	29·46	28·71	28·24	27·91	27·67	27·49	27·35	27·23	27·05	26·87	26·69	26·60	26·50	26·41	26·32	26·22	26·13
4	21·20	18·00	16·69	15·98	15·52	15·21	14·98	14·80	14·66	14·55	14·37	14·20	14·02	13·93	13·84	13·75	13·65	13·56	13·46
5	16·26	13·27	12·06	11·39	10·97	10·67	10·46	10·29	10·16	10·05	9·89	9·72	9·55	9·47	9·38	9·29	9·20	9·11	9·02
6	13·75	10·92	9·78	9·15	8·75	8·47	8·26	8·10	7·98	7·87	7·72	7·56	7·40	7·31	7·23	7·14	7·06	6·97	6·88
7	12·25	9·55	8·45	7·85	7·46	7·19	6·99	6·84	6·72	6·62	6·47	6·31	6·16	6·07	5·99	5·91	5·82	5·74	5·65
8	11·26	8·65	7·59	7·01	6·63	6·37	6·18	6·03	5·91	5·81	5·67	5·52	5·36	5·28	5·20	5·12	5·03	4·95	4·86
9	10·56	8·02	6·99	6·42	6·06	5·80	5·61	5·47	5·35	5·26	5·11	4·96	4·81	4·73	4·65	4·57	4·48	4·40	4·31
10	10·04	7·56	6·55	5·99	5·64	5·39	5·20	5·06	4·94	4·85	4·71	4·56	4·41	4·33	4·25	4·17	4·08	4·00	3·91
11	9·65	7·21	6·22	5·67	5·32	5·07	4·89	4·74	4·63	4·54	4·40	4·25	4·10	4·02	3·94	3·86	3·78	3·69	3·60
12	9·33	6·93	5·95	5·41	5·06	4·82	4·64	4·50	4·39	4·30	4·16	4·01	3·86	3·78	3·70	3·62	3·54	3·45	3·36
13	9·07	6·70	5·74	5·21	4·86	4·62	4·44	4·30	4·19	4·10	3·96	3·82	3·66	3·59	3·51	3·43	3·34	3·25	3·17
14	8·86	6·51	5·56	5·04	4·69	4·46	4·28	4·14	4·03	3·94	3·80	3·66	3·51	3·43	3·35	3·27	3·18	3·09	3·00
15	8·68	6·36	5·42	4·89	4·56	4·32	4·14	4·00	3·89	3·80	3·67	3·52	3·37	3·29	3·21	3·13	3·05	2·96	2·87
16	8·53	6·23	5·29	4·77	4·44	4·20	4·03	3·89	3·78	3·69	3·55	3·41	3·26	3·18	3·10	3·02	2·93	2·84	2·75
17	8·40	6·11	5·18	4·67	4·34	4·10	3·93	3·79	3·68	3·59	3·46	3·31	3·16	3·08	3·00	2·92	2·83	2·75	2·65
18	8·29	6·01	5·09	4·58	4·25	4·01	3·84	3·71	3·60	3·51	3·37	3·23	3·08	3·00	2·92	2·84	2·75	2·66	2·57
19	8·18	5·93	5·01	4·50	4·17	3·94	3·77	3·63	3·52	3·43	3·30	3·15	3·00	2·92	2·84	2·76	2·67	2·58	2·49
20	8·10	5·85	4·94	4·43	4·10	3·87	3·70	3·56	3·46	3·37	3·23	3·09	2·94	2·86	2·78	2·69	2·61	2·52	2·42
21	8·02	5·78	4·87	4·37	4·04	3·81	3·64	3·51	3·40	3·31	3·17	3·03	2·88	2·80	2·72	2·64	2·55	2·46	2·36
22	7·95	5·72	4·82	4·31	3·99	3·76	3·59	3·45	3·35	3·26	3·12	2·98	2·83	2·75	2·67	2·58	2·50	2·40	2·31
23	7·88	5·66	4·76	4·26	3·94	3·71	3·54	3·41	3·30	3·21	3·07	2·93	2·78	2·70	2·62	2·54	2·45	2·35	2·26
24	7·82	5·61	4·72	4·22	3·90	3·67	3·50	3·36	3·26	3·17	3·03	2·89	2·74	2·66	2·58	2·49	2·40	2·31	2·21
25	7·77	5·57	4·68	4·18	3·85	3·63	3·46	3·32	3·22	3·13	2·99	2·85	2·70	2·62	2·54	2·45	2·36	2·27	2·17
26	7·72	5·53	4·64	4·14	3·82	3·59	3·42	3·29	3·18	3·09	2·96	2·81	2·66	2·58	2·50	2·42	2·33	2·23	2·13
27	7·68	5·49	4·60	4·11	3·78	3·56	3·39	3·26	3·15	3·06	2·93	2·78	2·63	2·55	2·47	2·38	2·29	2·20	2·10
28	7·64	5·45	4·57	4·07	3·75	3·53	3·36	3·23	3·12	3·03	2·90	2·75	2·60	2·52	2·44	2·35	2·26	2·17	2·06
29	7·60	5·42	4·54	4·04	3·73	3·50	3·33	3·20	3·09	3·00	2·87	2·73	2·57	2·49	2·41	2·33	2·23	2·14	2·03
30	7·56	5·39	4·51	4·02	3·70	3·47	3·30	3·17	3·07	2·98	2·84	2·70	2·55	2·47	2·39	2·30	2·21	2·11	2·01
40	7·31	5·18	4·31	3·83	3·51	3·29	3·12	2·99	2·89	2·80	2·66	2·52	2·37	2·29	2·20	2·11	2·02	1·92	1·80
60	7·08	4·98	4·13	3·65	3·34	3·12	2·95	2·82	2·72	2·63	2·50	2·35	2·20	2·12	2·03	1·94	1·84	1·73	1·60
120	6·85	4·79	3·95	3·48	3·17	2·96	2·79	2·66	2·56	2·47	2·34	2·19	2·03	1·95	1·86	1·76	1·66	1·53	1·38
∞	6·63	4·61	3·78	3·32	3·02	2·80	2·64	2·51	2·41	2·32	2·18	2·04	1·88	1·79	1·70	1·59	1·47	1·32	1·00

Source: Table 18 from E. S. Pearson and H. O. Hartley, eds., *Biometrika Tables for Statisticians*, vol. 1, 3rd ed. (London: Imperial College of Science and Technology, Trustees of *Biometrika*, 1966).

Table A.5
Partial Binomial Table

n = 20

r	p	.01	.02	.03	.04	.05	.06	.07	.08	.09	.10		
0		.8179	.6676	.5438	.4420	.3585	.2901	.2342	.1887	.1516	.1216	20	
1		.1652	.2725	.3364	.3683	.3774	.3703	.3526	.3282	.3000	.2702	19	
2		.0159	.0528	.0988	.1458	.1887	.2246	.2521	.2711	.2818	.2852	18	
3		.0010	.0065	.0183	.0364	.0596	.0860	.1139	.1414	.1672	.1901	17	
4		.0000	.0006	.0024	.0065	.0133	.0233	.0364	.0523	.0703	.0898	16	
5		.0000	.0000	.0002	.0009	.0022	.0048	.0088	.0145	.0222	.0319	15	
6		.0000	.0000	.0000	.0001	.0003	.0008	.0017	.0032	.0055	.0089	14	
7		.0000	.0000	.0000	.0000	.0000	.0001	.0002	.0005	.0011	.0020	13	
8		.0000	.0000	.0000	.0000	.0000	.0000	.0000	.0001	.0002	.0004	12	
9		.0000	.0000	.0000	.0000	.0000	.0000	.0000	.0000	.0000	.0001	11	
		99	98	97	96	95	94	93	92	91	90	p	r

r	p	.11	.12	.13	.14	.15	.16	.17	.18	.19	.20		
0		.0972	.0776	.0617	.0490	.0388	.0306	.0241	.0189	.0148	.0115	20	
1		.2403	.2115	.1844	.1595	.1368	.1165	.0986	.0829	.0693	.0576	19	
2		.2822	.2740	.2618	.2466	.2293	.2109	.1919	.1730	.1545	.1369	18	
3		.2093	.2242	.2347	.2409	.2428	.2410	.2358	.2278	.2175	.2054	17	
4		.1099	.1299	.1491	.1666	.1821	.1951	.2053	.2125	.2168	.2182	16	
5		.0435	.0567	.0713	.0868	.1028	.1189	.1345	.1493	.1627	.1746	15	
6		.0134	.0193	.0266	.0353	.0454	.0566	.0689	.0819	.0954	.1091	14	
7		.0033	.0053	.0080	.0115	.0160	.0216	.0282	.0360	.0448	.0545	13	
8		.0007	.0012	.0019	.0030	.0046	.0067	.0094	.0128	.0171	.0222	12	
9		.0001	.0002	.0004	.0007	.0011	.0017	.0026	.0038	.0053	.0074	11	
10		.0000	.0000	.0001	.0001	.0002	.0004	.0006	.0009	.0014	.0020	10	
11		.0000	.0000	.0000	.0000	.0000	.0001	.0001	.0002	.0003	.0005	9	
12		.0000	.0000	.0000	.0000	.0000	.0000	.0000	.0000	.0001	.0001	8	
		.89	.88	.87	.86	.85	.84	.83	.82	.81	.80	p	r

r	p	.21	.22	.23	.24	.25	.26	.27	.28	.29	.30		
0		.0090	.0069	.0054	.0041	.0032	.0024	.0018	.0014	.0011	.0008	20	
1		.0477	.0392	.0321	.0261	.0211	.0170	.0137	.0109	.0087	.0068	19	
2		.1204	.1050	.0910	.0783	.0669	.0569	.0480	.0403	.0336	.0278	18	
3		.1920	.1777	.1631	.1484	.1339	.1199	.1065	.0940	.0823	.0716	17	
4		.2169	.2131	.2070	.1991	.1897	.1790	.1675	.1553	.1429	.1304	16	
5		.1845	.1923	.1979	.2012	.2023	.2013	.1982	.1933	.1868	.1789	15	
6		.1226	.1356	.1478	.1589	.1686	.1768	.1833	.1879	.1907	.1916	14	
7		.0652	.0765	.0883	.1003	.1124	.1242	.1356	.1462	.1558	.1643	13	
8		.0282	.0351	.0429	.0515	.0609	.0709	.0815	.0924	.1034	.1144	12	
9		.0100	.0132	.0171	.0217	.0271	.0332	.0402	.0479	.0563	.0654	11	
10		.0029	.0041	.0056	.0075	.0099	.0128	.0163	.0205	.0253	.0308	10	
11		.0007	.0010	.0015	.0022	.0030	.0041	.0055	.0072	.0094	.0120	9	
12		.0001	.0002	.0003	.0005	.0008	.0011	.0015	.0021	.0029	.0039	8	
13		.0000	.0000	.0001	.0001	.0002	.0002	.0003	.0005	.0007	.0010	7	
14		.0000	.0000	.0000	.0000	.0000	.0000	.0001	.0001	.0001	.0002	6	
		.79	.78	.77	.76	.75	.74	.73	.72	.71	.70	p	r

Use the value of r at the left with the values of p at the top of the section, and the values of r at the right with the values of p at the bottom of the section.

Example: $P(r = 3 \mid n = 20, p = .31) = .0619$

$\qquad P(r = 4 \mid n = 20, p = .62) = .0001$

r	p	.31	.32	.33	.34	.35	.36	.37	.38	.39	.40	
0		.0006	.0004	.0003	.0002	.0002	.0001	.0001	.0001	.0001	.0000	20
1		.0054	.0042	.0033	.0025	.0020	.0015	.0011	.0009	.0007	.0005	19
2		.0229	.0188	.0153	.0124	.0100	.0080	.0064	.0050	.0040	.0031	18
3		.0619	.0531	.0453	.0383	.0323	.0270	.0224	.0185	.0152	.0123	17
4		.1181	.1062	.0947	.0839	.0738	.0645	.0559	.0482	.0412	.0350	16
5		.1698	.1599	.1493	.1384	.1272	.1161	.1051	.0945	.0843	.0746	15
6		.1907	.1881	.1839	.1782	.1712	.1632	.1543	.1447	.1347	.1244	14
7		.1714	.1770	.1811	.1836	.1844	.1836	.1812	.1774	.1722	.1659	13
8		.1251	.1354	.1450	.1537	.1614	.1678	.1730	.1767	.1790	.1797	12
9		.0750	.0849	.0952	.1056	.1158	.1259	.1354	.1444	.1526	.1597	11
10		.0370	.0440	.0516	.0598	.0686	.0779	.0875	.0974	.1073	.1171	10
11		.0151	.0188	.0231	.0280	.0336	.0398	.0467	.0542	.0624	.0710	9
12		.0051	.0066	.0085	.0108	.0136	.0168	.0206	.0249	.0299	.0355	8
13		.0014	.0019	.0026	.0034	.0045	.0058	.0074	.0094	.0118	.0146	7
14		.0003	.0005	.0006	.0009	.0012	.0016	.0022	.0029	.0038	.0049	6
15		.0001	.0001	.0001	.0002	.0003	.0004	.0005	.0007	.0010	.0013	5
16		.0000	.0000	.0000	.0000	.0000	.0001	.0001	.0001	.0002	.0003	4
		.69	.68	.67	.66	.65	.64	.63	.62	.61	.60 p	r

r	p	.41	.42	.43	.44	.45	.46	.47	.48	.49	.50	
1		.0004	.0003	.0002	.0001	.0001	.0001	.0001	.0000	.0000	.0000	19
2		.0024	.0018	.0014	.0011	.0008	.0006	.0005	.0003	.0002	.0002	18
3		.0100	.0080	.0064	.0051	.0040	.0031	.0024	.0019	.0014	.0011	17
4		.0295	.0247	.0206	.0170	.0139	.0113	.0092	.0074	.0059	.0046	16
5		.0656	.0573	.0496	.0427	.0365	.0309	.0260	.0217	.0180	.0148	15
6		.1140	.1037	.0936	.0839	.0746	.0658	.0577	.0501	.0432	.0370	14
7		.1585	.1502	.1413	.1318	.1221	.1122	.1023	.0925	.0830	.0739	13
8		.1790	.1768	.1732	.1683	.1623	.1553	.1474	.1388	.1296	.1201	12
9		.1658	.1707	.1742	.1763	.1771	.1763	.1742	.1708	.1661	.1602	11
10		.1268	.1359	.1446	.1524	.1593	.1652	.1700	.1734	.1755	.1762	10
11		.0801	.0895	.0991	.1089	.1185	.1280	.1370	.1455	.1533	.1602	9
12		.0417	.0486	.0561	.0642	.0727	.0818	.0911	.1007	.1105	.1201	8
13		.0178	.0217	.0260	.0310	.0366	.0429	.0497	.0572	.0653	.0739	7
14		.0062	.0078	.0098	.0122	.0150	.0183	.0221	.0264	.0314	.0370	6
15		.0017	.0023	.0030	.0038	.0049	.0062	.0078	.0098	.0121	.0148	5
16		.0004	.0005	.0007	.0009	.0013	.0017	.0022	.0028	.0036	.0046	4
17		.0001	.0001	.0001	.0002	.0002	.0003	.0005	.0006	.0008	.0011	3
18		.0000	.0000	.0000	.0000	.0000	.0000	.0001	.0001	.0001	.0002	2
		.59	.58	.57	.56	.55	.54	.53	.52	.51	.50 p	r

Source: From Pratt, Raiffa, and Schlaifer, *Introduction to Statistical Decision Theory* (New York: McGraw-Hill, 1965).

Table A.6
Random Numbers

63271	59986	71744	51102	15141	80714	58683	93108	13554	79945
88547	09896	95436	79115	08303	01041	20030	63754	08459	28364
55957	57243	83865	09911	19761	66535	40102	26646	60147	15702
46276	87453	44790	67122	45573	84358	21625	16999	13385	22782
55363	07449	34835	15290	76616	67191	12777	21861	68689	03263
69393	92785	49902	58447	42048	30378	87618	26933	40640	16281
13186	29431	88190	04588	38733	81290	89541	70290	40113	08243
17726	28652	56836	78351	47327	18518	92222	55201	27340	10493
36520	64465	05550	30157	82242	29520	69753	72602	23756	54935
81628	36100	39254	56835	37636	02421	98063	89641	64953	99337
84649	48968	75215	75498	49539	74240	03466	49292	36401	45525
63291	11618	12613	75055	43915	26488	41116	64531	56827	30825
70502	53225	03655	05915	37140	57051	48393	91322	25653	06543
06426	24771	59935	49801	11082	66762	94477	02494	88215	27191
20711	55609	29430	70165	45406	78484	31639	52009	18873	96927
41990	70538	77191	25860	55204	73417	83920	69468	74972	38712
72452	36618	76298	26678	89334	33938	95567	29380	75906	91807
37042	40318	57099	10528	09925	89773	41335	96244	29002	46453
53766	52875	15987	46962	67342	77592	57651	95508	80033	69828
90585	58955	53122	16025	84299	53310	67380	84249	25348	04332
32001	96293	37203	64516	51530	37069	40261	61374	05815	06714
62606	64324	46354	72157	67248	20135	49804	09226	64419	29457
10078	28073	85389	50324	14500	15562	64165	06125	71353	77669
91561	46145	24177	15294	10061	98124	75732	00815	83452	97355
13091	98112	53959	79607	52244	63303	10413	63839	74762	50289
73864	83014	72457	22682	03033	61714	88173	90835	00634	85169
66668	25467	48894	51043	02365	91726	09365	63167	95264	45643
84745	41042	29493	01836	09044	51926	43630	63470	76508	14194
48068	26805	94595	47907	13357	38412	33318	26098	82782	42851
54310	96175	97594	88616	42035	38093	36745	56702	40644	83514
14877	33095	10924	58013	61439	21882	42059	24177	58739	60170
78295	23179	02771	43464	59061	71411	05697	67194	30495	21157
67524	02865	39593	54278	04237	92441	26602	63835	38032	94770
58268	57219	68124	73455	83236	08710	04284	55005	84171	42596
97158	28672	50685	01181	24262	19427	52106	34308	73685	74246
04230	16831	69085	30802	65559	09205	71829	06489	85650	38707
94879	56606	30401	02602	57658	70091	54986	41394	60437	03195
71446	15232	66715	26385	91518	70566	02888	79941	39684	54315
32886	05644	79316	09819	00813	88407	17461	73925	53037	91904
62048	33711	25290	21526	02223	75947	66466	06232	10913	75336

Source: Reprinted from Rand Corporation, *A Million Random Digits with 100,000 Normal Deviates* (New York: The Free Press, 1955).

Bibliography

Bayes, Thomas. "An Essay towards Solving a Problem in the *Doctrine of Chances.*" *Philosophical Transactions of the Royal Society* 53 (1763). Reprinted in *Biometrika* 45 (December 1958).

Bell, David E. "Consistent Assessment Procedures Using Conditional Utility Functions." *Operations Research* 27 (1979).

——— (ed.). *Conflicting Objectives in Decisions.* New York: Wiley, 1979.

Bender, Rolf, and Armin Nack. *Tatsachenfeststellung vor Gericht,* Vol. 1. C. H. Beck'sche Verlagsbuchhandlung, 1981.

Bernoulli, Jacques. *Ars Conjectandi.* Basel: 1713.

Box, George E. P., and George C. Tiao. *Bayesian Inference in Statistical Analysis.* Reading, Mass.: Addison-Wesley, 1973.

Box, George E. P., William G. Hunter, and J. Stuart Hunter. *Statistics for Experimenters.* New York: Wiley, 1978.

Chacko, George K. *Applied Statistics in Decision-making.* New York: Elsevier, 1971.

———. *The Systems Approach to Problem-Solving: From Corporate Markets to National Missions.* New York: Praeger, 1989.

Cobb, C. W. See Douglas, Paul H.

Copeland, A. H. "The Theory of Probability from the Point of View of Admissible Numbers." *Ann. Math. Stat.* 3 (1932).

Davis, Charles Henry (tr.). *Theoria Motus.* Washington, D.C.: U.S. Navy, 1857.

De Finetti, Bruno. "La Prevision: ses lois logiques, ses sources subjective." *Ann. Inst. Henry Poincaire* 7 (1937).

De Moivre, Abraham. *Approximatio Ad Summam Terminorum. Binomii.* London: 1733.

De Morgan, Augustus. *Formal Logic.* London: Taylor & Walton, 1847.

Douglas, Paul H., and C. W. Cobb, "A Theory of Production." *American Economic Review* 8 (1928, suppl.).

Feinberg, S. E., and A. Zellner (eds.). *Studies in Bayesian Econometrics and Statistics.* Amsterdam: North-Holland, 1975.

Fensterstock, Jack C., and Robert K. Frankhauser. "Thanksgiving 1966 Air Pollution Episode in the Eastern United States." HEW National Air Pollution Control Administration, No. Ap. 45, Raleigh, N.C., July 1968.

Fishburn, Peter C. "Methods of Estimating Additive Utilities." *Management Science* 13 (1967).

Fisher, Ronald A. "The Condition under Which χ^2 Measures the Discrepancy between Observation and Hypothesis." *J. Roy. Stat. Soc.* 87 (1924).

――――. *Statistical Methods and Scientific Inference*. New York: Hafner, 1956.

Frankhauser, Robert K. See Fensterstock, Jack C.

Gains, B. P. See Mamdani, E. H.

Galton, Francis. "Presidential Address, Anthropological Section of the British Association." Aberdeen, 1885.

――――. *Natural Inheritance*. London: 1888.

Gauss, Carl Friedrich. *Theoria Motus*. See Davis, Charles Henry.

Gordon, Geoffrey. "Preliminary Manual for GPSS—General Purpose Systems Simulator." White Plains, N.Y.: IBM, 1961.

Grier, B. "George Hooper and the Early Theory of Testimony." Department of Psychology, Northern Illinois University, De Kalb, 1981.

Halpern, Seymour. "Letter from John F. Kennedy as U.S. Senator," May 27, 1959. New York.

Hankins, F. H. *Adolphe Quetelet as Statistician*. New York: 1908.

Hausner, B. See Markowitz, H. A.

Hooper, George. "A Calculation of the Credibility of Human Testimony." *Phil. Trans.* 21 (1699).

Hubbel, J. G. "You Are Under Attack!" *Reader's Digest*, April 1961.

Huber, George P. "Methods for Quantifying Subjective Probabilities and Multiattribute Utilities." *Decision Science* 5 (1974).

Hunter, J. Stuart. See Box, George E. P.

Hunter, William G. See Box, George E. P.

Jessop, Thomas E. "Hume, David." *Encyclopedia Britannica* 11 (1960).

Keeney, Ralph. "Decision Analysis: An Overview." *Operations Research* 30 (1982).

Keeney, Ralph, and Keshavan Nair. "Selecting Nuclear Power Plant Sites in the Pacific Northwest Using Decision Analysis." See Bell, David E. (ed.).

Kennedy, Robert F. *Thirteen Days: A Memoir of the Cuban Missile Crisis*. New York: New American Library, 1969.

Kyburg, Henry E. Jr., and Howard E. Smokler. *Studies in Subjective Probability*. New York: Wiley, 1964.

LaPlace, P. S. *Oeuvres de Laplace*, Vol. 7. Paris: 1886.

――――. *A Philosophical Essay on Probability*. London: 1901.

Mamdani, E. H., and B. R. Gaines (eds.). *Fuzzy Reasoning and Its Applications*. New York: Academic Press, 1981.

Markowitz, H. M., B. Hausner, and H. W. Karr. "SIMSCRIPT: A Simulation Programming Language." Santa Monica, Calif.: Rand, RM-3310, Nov. 1962.

Nach, Armin. See Bender, Rolf.

Nair, Keshavan. See Keeney, Ralph, and Keshavan Nair.

Negoita, Constantin N. *Expert Systems and Fuzzy Systems*. Menlo Park, Calif.: Benjamin/Cummins Publishing Co., 1985.

Neyman, Jerzy. *First Course in Probability and Statistics*. New York: Holt, Rinehart & Winston, 1950.

Pearson, Karl. "On the Criterion That a Given System of Deviations from the Probable in the Case of a Correlated System of Variables Is Such That It Can Be Reasonably Supposed to Have Arisen from Random Sampling." *Phil. Mag.* 50 (1900).

————. "Communication." *Nature* 117 (April 17, 1926).

Reichenbach, Hans. *The Theory of Probability*. Berkeley: University of California Press, 1949.

Richards, Bradley L. "When Facts Get Fuzzy." *Byte,* April 1988.

Savage, Leonard J. *The Foundations of Statistics*. New York: Wiley, 1954.

————. "Elicitation of Personal Probabilities and Expectations." See Feinberg, S. E. (ed.).

Shafer, Glenn. *A Mathematical Theory of Evidence*. Princeton, N.J.: Princeton University Press, 1976.

————. "The Construction of Probability Arguments." Symposium on Probability and Inference in the Law of Evidence, Boston University School of Law, Boston, April 1986.

————. "The Combination of Evidence." *Int. J. Intell. Systems,* April 1986.

Shafer, Glenn, and Amos Tversky. "Languages and Design for Probability Judgment." *Cognitive Science* 9 (1985).

Sorenson, Theodore C. *Kennedy,* New York: Harper & Row, 1965.

Thompson, William R. "Human Behavior, Innate Factors." *Encyclopedia Britannica* 8 (1975).

Tiao, G. See Box, George E. P.

Tversky, Amos. See Shafer, Glenn, and Amos Tversky.

van Dantzig. "Statistical Priesthood (Savage on Probability)." *Statis. Neerl.* 2 (1957).

Venn, John. *The Logic of Chance*. London: 1886.

Von Mises, Richard. *Probability, Statistics and Truth*. London: Hodge, 1939.

Wald, Abraham. "Die Wiederspruchfreiheit des Kollektivbegriffes." *Actualites Sci. Indust.* 735 (1938).

Walker, Helen M. *Studies in the History of Statistical Method*. Baltimore: Williams & Wilkins, 1931.

Zadeh, Lotfi. "Fuzzy Sets." *Information and Controls* 8 (1968).

————. "PRUF-A Meaning Representation Language for Natural Language." See Mamdani, E. H., and B. R. Gates (eds.).

Zellner, A. See Feinberg, S. E.

Index

Additivity, 81, 95, 97. *See also* Interactive; Nonadditive

Advertising, 79, 93–96, 103

Age, 79, 80–82, 88–89, 91, 97

Aggregate Action-Outcome, 177–78

AMA (American Medical Association), 36, 37

Anderson, Major Rudolf, 27, 183

ANOVA (Analysis of Variance), 68, 70

Applications, 97; biological mission, 64, 67; heavenly mission, 56, 61, 126; market, 64, 92–93, 106, 114, 131, 135, 157, 163, 165; military mission, 4, 26, 179; physical, 47, 129; political mission, 18; social mission, 6, 23, 36, 59, 80–81

Aronowitz, Al, 18

Aspirin, 35, 36, 37, 38, 39, 41, 43, 44, 45, 47, 49, 50, 55, 56, 59, 61, 62, 63, 70

Attitudes, 3, 5, 6, 150, 155, 158, 163–64, 173, 177

Attributes, 155, 160, 165, 167–68

Average, 81, 103, 105–6, 108, 114–15, 117, 130

Bayes, Thomas, 61, 125–29, 134, 138, 144–45, 149, 177, 180–82, 189

Bell, David, 164

Bender, Rolf, 180

Bernoulli, Jacques, and process, 20, 125, 136

Binomial distribution, cumulative. *See* Distribution, binomial and cumulative binomial

Bluffs, 177–78, 185, 186–88, 194. *See also* Threats

BMEWS (Ballistic Missile Early Warning System), 5

Bookings, 93, 95–97. *See also* Sales

Box, George P., 129–31

BT (Bluffs-Threats) Matrix/BTIS (Bluffs-Threats Interactive System), 178–79, 183–84, 186–89, 194–95

B-T moves: commercial, 178, 186, 187, 189, 194; diplomatic, 178, 186, 187–88, 194; political, 178, 186, 189, 194; military, 178, 186, 189, 194

Carter, Jimmy, 17, 22, 29

Central value, 56. *See also* Mean

Certainty, 3, 144, 156–59, 163, 165, 177, 183, 189

CF (certainty factor), 144, 148–49

Characteristics, 19, 35, 36, 37, 38, 42, 49, 55, 56, 62, 70, 79, 103–4, 108–9, 116, 136, 140

Chi-squared, 35, 44–49, 51, 55, 59, 70

COL (conditional opportunity loss), 126, 135, 137–38

Commissions, 79, 80, 93–97, 103

Computers, 3, 5, 12, 17, 61, 92, 103, 114, 116–17

Conclusions, 21, 22, 23, 28, 30, 47, 50, 57, 61, 66–68, 108, 127–28, 133–34, 148, 179, 181

Conditions, 39, 42, 55, 59, 64, 125, 127–28, 135, 147, 181

Confidence levels, limits of, 18, 35, 37, 66

Convergence, 41, 114–15, 134–35

Copeland, A. H., 41

Correlation, 79, 80–81, 90, 91–92; multiple, 92; partial, 92, 96

Costs, 2, 115, 132–33, 135–36, 139, 156, 163–65, 168–70

Cuban Missile Crisis, 17, 26, 29, 56, 177–82, 185, 187, 189

Customer arrivals, 103–4, 106, 108–11, 114, 117

Customers, 104, 107–8, 112, 116–17, 125, 133, 136, 139, 143, 163

Data, 3, 12, 49, 50, 55, 57, 59, 64, 66, 67, 68, 77, 79–82, 89, 90–93, 97, 103, 104, 108–9, 115, 117, 123, 125, 129–30, 135–36, 138–39, 143, 153, 155, 164, 179, 180

Decisions, 1, 3, 4, 5, 6, 10, 11, 13, 17, 21, 26, 33, 35, 77, 80, 97, 103–8, 112, 114–15, 118, 123, 125–26, 129, 131–39, 143, 146, 148–50, 153, 155–58, 160–65, 170, 173–74, 177–80, 182–83, 189, 194–95

DEFCON (Defense Condition), 4, 5, 8, 11, 12, 18, 21, 22

Degree of belief (confidence), 20, 22, 28, 46, 56. *See also* Level of confidence

Demand, 103, 106–9, 112, 114–15

De Moivre, Abraham, 55, 61, 62, 70, 125–26, 138

De Morgan, Augustus, 22

Dempster's rule, 143, 145, 149, 181

DF (degrees of freedom), 45, 46, 48, 59, 66, 68, 90–91

Dickson, J.D. Hamilton, 80

Distribution, 41, 45, 48, 57, 63, 105–6, 108, 116; binomial and cumulative binomial, 35, 47, 48, 50, 55, 56, 57, 59, 61, 70, 125, 127, 136–37; continuous, 57; discrete, 57; *F*, 68, 70; multinomial, 55; normal, 35, 49, 50, 55, 56, 57, 59, 60, 61, 63, 66, 68, 70, 80–81, 96, 125–26, 129–30, 138; Pearsonian, 35, 49, 50, 56, 57; possibility, 143, 146–47, 149, 182; probability, 35, 57, 105–6, 117; *t*, 55, 63, 66, 70, 90; *z*, 63

Douglas, Paul H., 95, 97

Effects, 38, 39, 41, 42, 43, 55, 59, 64, 68, 79, 81, 93, 95, 125–26

EMV (expected monetary value), 155, 159, 162–63

EOL (expected opportunity loss), 126, 135, 137–39

Error(s), 6, 11, 55, 61, 62, 70, 79, 80, 97, 125, 138. *See also* Type I error; Type II error

Estimates, 41, 45, 89, 129, 131, 135, 188–89

Expectations, mathematical, 127, 134

Expected frequencies and values, 35, 38, 43, 44, 45, 46, 47, 48, 49, 50, 56, 57, 63, 82, 89, 108, 117, 125, 131, 134–35, 144–45, 155–57, 160–61, 174, 180

Experiments, 36, 37

Expert systems, 144, 148

F-distribution, *F*-test. *See* Distribution, *F*

Fishburn, Peter, 164

Fisher, Ronald A., 41, 45

Fuzzy sets, 140, 143–44, 147, 148–50, 177, 182–83, 189

Galton, Sir Francis, 79, 80–81, 97

Gas station, 103–4, 106–8, 110–12, 114, 116–17

Gauss, Karl Friedrich, 55, 62, 70, 80, 97

Gossett, William Sealy, 63

Gould, Lt. Col. Robert L., 4
GPSS (General Purpose Systems Simulation), 103–4, 116–17
Grier, B., 149
Groupwise togetherness, 79, 90, 97

Halpern, Seymour, 18
Heart attack, 35, 36, 37, 38, 39, 41, 42, 43, 44, 45, 46, 47, 49, 50, 55, 56, 59, 61, 62, 63, 64, 70
Height, 79, 81–82, 88–89, 91, 97, 147, 149, 182
Hooper, George, 143, 145, 149
Hoover, J. Edgar, 26, 183
Horizontal score, 155, 170. *See also* Vertical weights
Huber, George, 164
Hull, Brig. Gen. Harris B., 12
Hume, David, 20

Income, personal, 55, 56, 57, 62, 64, 66, 67, 70, 79
Independence. *See* Statistical independence
Indifference, 155–59, 163–65, 177, 180
Inference, scientific, 126, 129, 131, 135–36, 138–39, 144, 149
Infinity, 11, 30, 35, 40, 41, 56, 57, 61, 106, 114, 125–26, 135, 138
Interactions, 80–81, 95, 97, 103–6, 108, 111, 114, 116, 143, 146, 149, 155, 165–66, 177–78, 182–84, 186, 189, 194
Inter-Continental Ballistic Missiles, 3, 4, 5, 6, 11, 12, 13, 17, 19, 20, 21, 26
International Business Machines, Inc., 103

Keeney, Ralph, 164
Kennedy, John F., 17, 18, 23, 27, 29, 178–80, 184–87, 194
Kennedy, Robert F., 17, 27, 28, 29, 30, 56, 179–81, 183–86, 194
Keynes, John Maynard, 20, 27
Khrushchev, Nikita S., 12, 17, 21, 27, 28, 29, 56, 177–79, 181–84, 186, 189
Kuter, Gen. Laurence S., 12
Kyberg, Henry E., 21, 22

Laplace, Marquis de, 62, 143, 145–46, 149
Least squares, 62, 88
Legendre, Adrien-Marie, 62, 88
Level of confidence, 46, 60
Likelihood, 125–26, 129, 131, 137–39, 143–44, 149, 181
Linear, 45, 79, 80–81, 90–91, 95–97, 103, 155, 177, 180–81. *See also* Nonlinear
Logarithms, 80, 96–97, 103
Lotteries, 155–60, 165

Management, 79, 93, 95, 97, 129
Markowitz, Harry, 116
McNamara, Robert S., 27, 183
Means, sample and population, 55, 56, 57, 59, 60, 61, 63, 64, 66–68, 70, 81, 97, 105, 129–31, 139
Models, 103, 104, 105, 117
Monte Carlo simulation, 104, 115, 117
Murder, first-degree, 3, 6, 10, 11, 13, 18, 19, 29

Nack, Armin, 180
Nair, Keshavan, 164
Negoita, Constantin V., 143–44, 147–49
Neumann, John von, 115
New England Region, 55, 56, 57, 64, 66, 67
Neyman, Jerzy, 41
Nixon, Richard M., 23
Nonadditive, 95. *See also* Additivity
Nonlinear, 94–95, 171. *See also* Linear
Normal curve and distribution. *See* Distribution, normal
Normal equations I and II, 82, 85, 87
North American Air Defense (NORAD), 3, 4, 5, 6, 10, 11, 12, 13, 17, 19
Null Hypothesis (NH), 3, 4, 6, 8, 9, 10, 11, 12, 13, 44, 45, 46, 47, 50, 51, 55, 56, 59–64, 66, 70, 88, 97, 131–32

Objectives hierarchy, 167, 171. *See also* System objectives
Observed frequencies, 35, 43, 82, 87
Observed/expected frequencies, 35, 43, 44, 45, 50, 55, 62, 64, 70, 88–89

Outcomes, 3, 5, 37, 40, 41, 55, 57, 150, 155–58, 160, 162–63, 173–74, 177–78, 180–82; exclusive, 38, 40, 44, 55, 181; exhaustive, 38, 40, 44, 55, 181

Pairwise togetherness, 79, 90, 97
Parameters, 57, 63, 82, 131, 138
Payoffs, 125, 131, 134–35, 144, 157–58, 160
PDSS (Presidential Decision Support Systems), 184
Pearson, Karl, 45, 49, 90, 126. *See also* Distribution, Pearsonian
Personnel, 114–15, 117
PFN (Penalty for Nonfulfillment), 155–56, 165, 170, 171, 173
Population, 18, 19, 36, 37, 42, 45, 49, 55, 56, 57, 63, 66–68, 70, 79, 81, 88, 90–91, 97, 108, 125, 136–39, 169
Presidency, 5, 6, 17, 18, 19, 22, 26, 28, 29, 179–80, 183–84
Price, Richard, 126–28, 138
Probabilities, 17, 20, 21, 22, 23, 40, 41, 45, 47, 57, 59, 61, 62, 70, 125–29, 134, 138–40, 143–46, 149–50, 157, 159, 162, 174, 178, 180–81, 189; conditional, 61, 125, 127, 136–39, 145, 149, 177, 181–82; construction of, 143, 177, 181–82, 189; joint, 38, 42, 43, 44, 125, 127–28; logical, 4, 12, 13, 17, 18, 20, 21, 22, 23, 25, 26, 27, 28, 29, 30, 35, 56, 133–35, 139, 180; marginal, 38, 42, 43, 45, 49, 125, 127, 137; posterior, 125–26, 128, 129–31, 135, 137, 139, 144, 149; prior, 125–26, 128–31, 133–39, 144, 149, 181–82; relative frequency, 18, 29, 30, 35, 38, 39, 40, 41, 42, 56, 126; subjective, 17, 18, 22, 23, 25, 26, 28, 29, 30, 35, 56, 133–35, 140, 177, 179, 180–82, 189
Production function, 95
Propositions, 17, 20, 21, 22, 23, 27, 28, 30, 56, 143, 146–49, 182

Quetelet, Adolphe, 80

Raiffa, Howard, 164
Rand Corp., 104, 110, 116

Randomness, 18, 37, 41, 42, 49, 68, 91, 96, 108–9, 111, 114, 116–17, 134, 136, 180. *See also* Sample, random
Random numbers, 109–11, 114, 116
Reagan, Ronald W., 17, 22, 23, 29
Regression, simple, 79, 80, 81, 88–89, 90–91, 97; multiple, 79, 91, 93, 96–97
Reichenbach, Hans, 41
Relative frequency. *See* Probabilities, relative frequency
Response in Kind, 178, 189
Returns to scale, constant, 95; decreasing, 95; increasing, 95, 96
Richards, Bradley L., 144, 148–49
Risk, 3, 5, 6, 10, 156–57, 162; accepting, 162–63; avoiding, 162–63; neutral, 162; premium, 159
Russell, Bertrand, 20

Sales, 79, 80, 93–96, 131–32, 136
SAM (surface-to-air missile), 27, 28, 183
Sample, random, 18, 35, 37, 42, 66–67, 90, 97, 108, 114–15, 117, 125, 129, 136, 138–39
Sample size, 45, 55, 56, 57, 59, 63, 66, 67, 68, 88, 97, 109, 125, 137, 143
Savage, Leonard, 180–82
Scali, John, 29
Services, 104, 106–7, 109, 110–12, 114–15, 117
Shafer, Glenn, 143–44, 145–46, 149, 181
SIMSCRIPT, 104, 116–17
Simulations, 103, 108, 110, 112, 114–17
Simulation language, 104, 116–17
Slemon, Air Marshall C. Roy, 12, 17, 19, 21, 26
Smokler, Howard E., 21
Sorensen, Theodore, 29, 30, 179–80, 184
Soviet Union, 3, 4, 5, 6, 8, 9, 11, 13, 17, 19, 20, 21, 27, 28, 29, 178, 180, 183, 185, 189
Squires, Henry, 18
Standard deviation, 55, 57, 59, 60, 61, 63, 70, 89, 129–31
Standard error, 89, 90, 96
Statistical independence, 41, 43, 46

Statistically significant, 36, 38, 64, 67
Statistics, 80, 82, 97, 104, 110, 116, 178, 189
Stocks, 155, 157–62, 174
Strategic nuclear war (SNW), 5, 8, 9, 11, 13, 177–78, 181–82, 186, 189, 195
"Student." *See* Gossett, William Sealy
Subjects, 64, 67, 70
Subsystems, 155
Supply, 106–9, 112, 114–15
Support functions, 143, 145, 149, 177, 181–82, 189
System budget, 155, 173
System objectives, 156, 166, 169–70, 174
System performance measures, 155, 165–66, 170, 173. *See also* PFN
Systems, 38, 93, 104, 116, 155, 166, 167–68, 171, 173

Table of correspondence, 109, 110, 114–15
Territory, 79, 94–95
Test of significance, 89, 91
Threats, 177–78, 185, 186, 187–88, 194. *See also* Bluffs
Tiao, George, 129
Trade-offs, 155, 164
Treatments, 36, 38, 44, 56, 64, 67–68, 70
Tversky, Amos, 143–44, 149
Type I error, 3, 4, 6, 10, 11, 13
Type II error, 3, 4, 6, 10

Uncertainty, 3, 4, 5, 130–31, 139, 156–58, 163, 165, 177, 180, 182

Union of Soviet Socialist Republics, 28, 29, 188–89
United States, 3, 4, 5, 6, 8, 9, 11, 12, 13, 18, 19, 20, 22, 26, 27, 28, 29, 55, 62, 64, 66, 93, 178–79, 185–87, 189, 194
Utility, 156, 158–61, 163–64
Utility function, 155, 157, 160, 162–65, 173–74, 177, 180–81; additive, 155, 164–65; multiattribute, 155, 163–65, 174; Neumann-Morgenstern, 165

Values, 62, 64, 66, 68, 70, 80, 82, 91, 97, 105–6, 114, 130, 134, 138, 147, 160, 164, 178, 182
Variables, random, 57, 70, 77, 79, 81, 82, 90–93, 96, 103–9, 110, 114, 116–18, 123, 134, 143, 146–47, 149, 153, 179, 182–83, 189, 195
Variance, 62, 63, 64, 66, 68, 130–31, 139
Variations, 56, 63, 67–68, 70, 97, 107
Venn, John, 41
Vertical weights, 155, 171. *See also* Horizontal score
Von Mises, Richard, 41

Waiting: customer, 103, 107, 114–15, 117; facility, 103, 107–8, 117; line, 103, 107–8; time, 108, 112, 114–15, 117
Wald, Abraham, 41
Walker, Helen M., 62

Zadeh, Lotfi A., 143, 147, 149

About the Author

GEORGE K. CHACKO, Professor of Systems Science at the University of Southern California since 1970, classroom-tested this book, his 39th, in the United States, Europe, and the Pacific for 20 years. A postgraduate fellow at the Indian Statistical Institute in Calcutta, he later invented a computer-based statistical forecasting method that won him a U.S. National Science Foundation award. He has applied statistics to various fields: to education, as Associate in Test Development in Mathematics, Educational Testing Service; to business and industry, as Manager of the Operations Research Department, Hughes Semiconductor Division, and as Senior Staff Scientist, TRW Systems. He was twice named to a senior Fulbright professorship in Taiwan where he was Taiwan National Science Council senior visiting research professor in 1988–89.